GLOBALIZATION, PHILANTHROPY, AND CIVIL SOCIETY

Toward a New Political Culture in the Twenty-First Century

NONPROFIT AND CIVIL SOCIETY STUDIES

An International Multidisciplinary Series

Series Editor: Helmut K. Anheier,
*London School of Economics and Political Science, London, United
Kingdom and University of California Los Angeles, Los Angeles, California*

CIVIL SOCIETY AND THE PROFESSIONS IN EASTERN EUROPE:
Social Change and Organizational Innovation in Poland
S. Wojciech Sokolowski

DILEMMAS OF THE WELFARE MIX:
The New Structure of Welfare in an Era of Privatization
Edited by Ugo Ascoli and Costanzo Ranci

GLOBALIZATION, PHILANTHROPY, AND CIVIL SOCIETY
Toward a New Political Culture in the Twenty-First Century
Edited by Soma Hewa and Darwin H. Stapleton

NEIGHBORHOOD SELF-MANAGEMENT:
Experiments in Civil Society
Hillel Schmid

PRIVATE FUNDS, PUBLIC PURPOSE:
Philanthropic Foundations in International Perspective
Edited by Helmut K. Anheier and Stefan Toepler

THE PRIVATE NONPROFIT SECTOR:
Measuring Its Impact on Society
Edited by Patrice Flynn and Virginia Hodgkinson

STRATEGY MIX FOR NONPROFIT ORGANISATIONS
Vehicles for Social and Labour Market Integration
Edited by Annette Zimmer and Christina Stecker

THE STUDY OF NONPROFIT ENTERPRISE
Theories and Approaches
Edited by Helmut K. Anheier and Avner Ben-Ner

THE VALUES OF VOLUNTEERING
Cross-Cultural Perspective
Edited by Paul Dekker and Loek Halman

WORKFORCE TRANSITIONS FROM THE PROFIT TO THE NONPROFIT SECTOR
Tobie S. Stein

A Continuation Order Plan is available for this series. A continuation order will bring delivery of each new volume immediately upon publication. Volumes are billed only upon actual shipment. For further information please contact the publisher.

GLOBALIZATION, PHILANTHROPY, AND CIVIL SOCIETY
Toward a New Political Culture in the Twenty-First Century

Edited by

Soma Hewa
Research in Philanthropy and Social Development
Chateauguay, Quebec, Canada

Darwin H. Stapleton
Rockefeller University
Sleepy Hollow, New York

 Springer

Library of Congress Cataloging-in-Publication Data

Springer Science + Business Media, Inc.
New York, Boston, Dordrecht, London, Moscow

ISBN 0-387-26148-6 (Hardbound)   Printed on acid-free paper.
ISBN 0-387-26150-8 (eBook)

Printed in the United States of America.   (BS/DH)

9 8 7 6 5 4 3 2 1

springeronline.com

Contributors

Helmut K. Anheier, School of Public Policy and Social Research, University of California, Los Angeles, CA, 90095

Victoria Lyon Bestor, North American Coordinating Council on Japanese Library Resources, Newton, MA, 02468

Kathy Brock, School of Policy Studies, Queen's University, Kingston, Ontario, Canada K7L 3N6

David Brook, Public Policy Forum in Ottawa, Ontario, K1P 5G4 Canada

Siobhan Daly, *Visions and Roles of Foundations in Europe*, Centre for Civil Society, London School of Economics, London WC2A 2AE

Janice Elliott, Public Policy Forum in Ottawa, Ontario, K1P 5G4 Canada

Peter Frumkin, Hauser Center for nonprofit Organizations, Harvard University, Cambridge, MA 02138

Raymond Grew, Department of History, University of Michigan, Ann Arbor, MI 48109

Gary R. Hess, Department of History, Bowling Green State University, Bowling Green, OH 43403

Soma Hewa, Research in Philanthropy and Social Development, Chateauguay, Quebec J6J 2B1 Canada

Michael D. Mehta, Department of Sociology, University of Saskatchewan, Saskatoon SK S7N 5A5 Canada

Balmurli Natrajan, Department of Anthropology, Iowa State University, Ames, IA, 50011

Lester M. Salamon, Institute for Policy Studies, Johns Hopkins University, Baltimore, MD 21218

Wolf Schäfer, Center for Global History, Department of History, Stony Brook University, Stony Brook, NY 11794

Darwin Stapleton, Rockefeller Archive Center, Rockefeller University, Sleepy Hollow, New York, 10591

ACKNOWLEDGMENTS

The extent to which civil society activities have reached a global scale became evident in the aftermath of the tsunami disaster in South and Southeast Asia in December 2004. As soon as the news broke out, civil society groups around the world went into high gear to organize relief operations for millions of distraught people in the region. The response proved that we are now living in a globalized world.

Although this volume is a result of an international conference titled "Globalization, Philanthropy, and Civil Society" held at the Rockefeller Archive Center in Sleepy Hollow, New York, more than a year before the disaster, the overwhelming response to this tragedy by the global community provides further context for several key questions discussed at this conference. In particular, one of the fundamental questions was what historical forces have brought humanity together in the latter part of the twentieth century. This disaster showed that neither international agreements nor the geopolitical interests of nation-states have the capacity to mobilize the global community to the same extent as human generosity. It is the shared values of humans across the globe that enables us to speak of a global civil society. The papers included in this volume are thus timely reflections on the sources and results of human generosity, and become in part a tribute to these profoundly human values that we often overlook in a rapidly moving and bustling world.

This volume is also a testimony to the long-standing commitment to scholarly research in an expanding field of philanthropy by the Rockefeller Archive Center. Without doubt, I have been very fortunate to be a beneficiary of this support for more than twelve years. The idea of a conference on globalization, philanthropy, and civil society was born in my mind during a visit to the center in the summer of 2001. Both Dr. Darwin H. Stapleton, the executive director, and Dr. Kenneth W. Rose, the assistant director, enthusiastically supported the idea, and the center provided the major funding for the conference. Without their steadfast support, this conference would not have been possible. From the very beginning of the planning stages of the conference to the completion of this volume, Dr. Stapleton was a source of invaluable guidance and advice. I am very grateful to him.

In numerous ways, Camilla Harris, an administrative assistant at the Rockefeller Archive Center, assisted me in organizing this conference. She was both meticulous and thoughtful in all aspects of the planning process. Without her help, many things could have gone wrong. During the conference, several members of the Archive Center staff, including Roseann Variano, Thomas Rosenbaum, and Susan Irving, helped in various ways to make the event successful. Following the conference, Norine Goodnough was responsible for coordinating the project by communicating with authors regarding various aspects of preparing the papers. Her careful attention to detail made the organization of this volume considerably easier. I want to express my deep appreciation to all of them.

I also want to thank Professor Harley Dickinson of the University of Saskatchewan for coming aboard right from the start of the organization of this conference, and for securing financial support from the government of Canada to enable several professors and graduate students from the university to attend the conference. Professor Bruce

Mazlish, of the Massachusetts Institute of Technology, provided a great deal of support in identifying several speakers and inviting them to participate in the conference. He was a gracious and able coleader of the conference itself. He also provided helpful suggestions on a number of organizational matters, both during the planning stage of the conference and preparing this volume. I very much appreciate his help.

Organizing a conference that brings together intellectuals from a diverse range of specialties raises its own challenges. However, we were fortunate to have had the commitment of a group of prominent scholars in the field of philanthropy, civil society activity, and globalization who have shown a keen interest in those subjects. Their contributions to this volume are deeply appreciated. At very short notice, Dr. Erwin Levold and Dr. Kenneth W. Rose, of the Rockefeller Archive Center, and Dr. George Smith, of the University of Saskatchewan, kindly agreed to chair sessions of the conference and to conduct discussions despite their busy schedules. I express my deep appreciation to all who made the conference an enjoyable as well as worthwhile event. I also want to thank Dr. Helmut Anheier, editor of the series in which this volume appears. His interest in the conference, and commitment to providing an opportunity for publication energized all of those involved in this project.

On a more personal note, both Darwin and I would like to take the opportunity to thank our wives, Elizabeth and Donna, who offered continuous encouragement to us, and took time to attend the conference. In particular, I would like to recognize Elizabeth's invaluable assistance during several stages of this project and preparing the text for publication. Finally, I want to thank our children, Leonard and Nelanthi Hewa, who cheerfully traveled to New York with us. They encouraged me, pestered me, and celebrated with me, but most of all, they put up with me.

Soma Hewa
Research in Philanthropy and Social Development
Montreal (Châteauguay), Quebec

*****

While fully affirming all of Dr. Hewa's remarks above, I want to extend our thanks to certain other supporters. The Rockefeller Archive Center was an appropriate venue for this conference because the records entrusted to it by its founding institutions, the Rockefeller Foundation, the Rockefeller Family, the Rockefeller University, and the Rockefeller Brothers Fund, are substantially global in nature. These founding institutions have been joined by others over the years, and all have been committed to promoting scholarship at the center, including a program of scholarly meetings.

Since the center's founding in 1974, the Governing Council of the Archive Center has provided the substantial financial support needed for a conference program, although other organizations often have been conference partners. In this case, the Sociology Department of the University of Saskatchewan, and its chair, Harley Dickinson, joined in conference planning and development, very appropriately because of the interest of its faculty and students in international nonprofit and nongovernmental organizations.

I want to echo Dr. Hewa's appreciation of Professor Bruce Mazlish's very timely and enthusiastic commitment to this conference. His vision, his vast scholarship, and his extensive knowledge of the terrain of the globalization field assured that the conference would be a success.

Every conference and meeting at the Rockefeller Archive Center is soundly based on the skills and professionalism of the center's staff. It is they who begin the planning months before the opening remarks, and who oversee the details until the last words are spoken. They deserve greater recognition than I can ever provide. At a late stage in this volume's preparation for the press, Jim Gullickson agreed to take on copyediting tasks and did so enthusiastically and efficiently.

Dr. Hewa has demonstrated on multiple occasions all the ingredients of an ideal conference organizer, among them a vision of what a group of scholars can be challenged to accomplish, a commitment to a diversity of views, and an expectation of excellence. It is a privilege to work with him.

Darwin H. Stapleton
Rockefeller Archive Center
Sleepy Hollow, New York

LIST OF FIGURES

FIGURE 5.1
International Giving as a Percentage of All Giving by Foundations 103

FIGURE 5.2
Percentage Distribution of International Grants by Dollar Amount 104

FIGURE 7.1
Civil Society Organization Workforce as a Percentage of Economically Active Population, by Country 145

FIGURE 7.2
Distribution of Civil Society Sector Workforce by Field and Type of Activity 146

FIGURE 7.3
Sources of Civil Society Organization Revenue, 34-Country Average 147

FIGURE 9.1
Common Typology of Globalization 178

FIGURE 9.2
Model for the Cultural Work Within Globalization 188

BLANK PAGE

LIST OF ABBREVIATIONS

AID	Agency for International Development
AIDS	Acquired Immune Deficiency Syndrome
A SEED	Action for Solidarity, Equality, Environment and Diversity
CDU	Christian Democratic Union
CFPI	Central Family Planning Institute
CGIAR	Consultative Group on International Agricultural Research
CJD	Creutzfeldt-Jakob disease (the human form of mad cow disease)
CSU	Christian Social Union
EFC	European Foundation Centre
EU	European Union
FFA	Ford Foundation Archives
FFAR	Ford Foundation Annual Report
FPCAR	Family Planning Communications and Action Research
FTE	Full-time Equivalent
GE	Genetically Engineered
HYV	High-Yielding Varieties
IADP	Intensive Agricultural District Program
IARI	Indian Agricultural Research Institute
IHB	International Health Board
IHJ	International House of Japan
INGOs	International Nongovernmental Organizations
IPR	Institute of Pacific Relations
IRRI	International Rice Research Institute
JCIE	Japan Center for International Exchange
JDR	John Davison Rockefeller
MIT-CIS	Massachusetts Institute of Technology's Center for International Studies
NATO	North Atlantic Treaty Organization
NGH	New Global History
NGOs	Nongovernmental Organizations
NIHAE	National Institute of Health Administration and Education
NPO	Nonprofit Organizations
OECD	Organization for Economic Cooperation and Development
RAC	Rockefeller Archive Center
RF	Rockefeller Foundation
SARS	Severe Acute Respiratory Syndrome
SSRC	Social Science Research Council

TCA	Technical Cooperation Administration
TRIPS	Trade-Related Aspects of Intellectual Property Rights
UN	United Nations
UNDP	United Nations Development Program
USDA	U.S. Department of Agriculture
WHO	World Health Organization
WTO	World Trade Organization

CONTENTS

INTRODUCTION

Structure and Process of Global Integration   **3**
Soma Hewa and Darwin H. Stapleton

HISTORY AND GLOBALIZATION:
DEFINITIONS AND CONCEPTUAL ISSUES

Chapter 1
Global History and Globalization   **15**
Raymond Grew

Chapter 2
How to Approach Global Present, Local Pasts, and Canon of the Globe   **33**
Wolf Schäfer

PHILANTHROPY AND GLOBALIZATION
DURING THE COLD WAR ERA

Chapter 3
The Role of American Philanthropic Foundations in
India's Road to Globalization During the Cold War Era   **51**
Gary R. Hess

Chapter 4
The Rockefeller Blueprint for Postwar U.S.–Japanese
Cultural Relations and the Evolution of Japan's Civil Sector   **73**
Victoria Lyon Bestor

PHILANTHROPIC FOUNDATIONS AND CIVIL SOCIETY
IN A GLOBALIZED WORLD

Chapter 5
American Foundations and Overseas Funding:
New Challenges in the Era of Globalization   **99**
Peter Frumkin

Chapter 6
Foundations in Europe:
Roles and Policy Scenarios in an Age of Globalization   117
   Helmut K. Anheier and Siobhan Daly

Chapter 7
Globalization and the Civil Society Sector   137
   Lester M. Salamon

Chapter 8
Globalization and the Third Sector:
The Canadian Experience   153
   Kathy Brock with David Brook and Janice Elliott

GLOBALIZATION OF CULTURE AND TECHNOLOGY

Chapter 9
Beyond Homogenization versus Heterogenization:
Difference and Culture in Globalization   177
   Balmurli Natrajan

Chapter 10
Risk, Reflexive Modernity, and the Unbinding of Politics:
Agricultural Biotechnology in a Globalized World   193
   Michael D. Mehta

   About the Authors   205

   Selected Bibliography   209

   Index   221

INTRODUCTION

STRUCTURE AND PROCESS
OF GLOBAL INTEGRATION

Soma Hewa and Darwin H. Stapleton

The best philanthropy, the help that does the most good and the least harm, the help that nourishes civilization at its very root, that most widely disseminates health, righteousness, and happiness, is not what is usually called charity.

–John D. Rockefeller
Random Reminiscences of Men and Events[1]

This volume is a result of a conference titled "Globalization, Philanthropy, and Civil Society" held at the Rockefeller Archive Center of the Rockefeller University in New York, June 5–6, 2003. Although there have been numerous conferences on globalization in recent years, this conference was unique in that it examined the contribution of philanthropy within a broader context of civil society activities vis-à-vis globalization. It takes the view that philanthropy is both a major force in twentieth century globalization but is at the same time one of the least understood. The organizers of the event were specifically interested in the *role* of philanthropy in past and present globalizations, and invited the participants to explore the scope and degree of the interrelationships between "globalization," "philanthropy," and "civil society." The papers included in this volume, based on archival and contemporary sources, demonstrate these relationships from both empirical and theoretical perspectives.

*****

Globalization is perhaps the most extensively discussed topic in contemporary academic literature and mass media. However, despite its wide usage, there is no precise definition of globalization. This is due, in part, to the multidimensional nature of globalizing forces that existed throughout history. From the beginning of humanity, people crossed borders, exchanged ideas, traded commodities, and established all forms of social relations. These basic forms of globalization grew rapidly with improved communication and transportation networks leading to a complex global integration in the twentieth century. For the purpose of this volume, and as it emerged during discussions at the conference, we define *globalization* in terms of a growing "sense of interconnectedness of humankind" around the globe. This definition acknowledges both the *continuity* of globalization and the *countless* human activities that constantly draw nations closer to one another. Thus, we have adopted the view that globalization is a decidedly historical process evolving toward the intersection of local and global communities, whereby local agencies and terms of reference effectively give way to a structure of relations and institutions that operate in a truly global context. In other words, a wide range of political, economic, and social institutions, ideas, and values cross over one another's borders, continually creating global communities.

A wide range of social and political changes, scientific achievements, and ambitions has shaped each historical period of globalization. For example, European colonial expansion in Asia, Africa, and the Americas between the fifteenth and early twentieth centuries initiated the most decisive political, social, and economic changes in modern history. The global integration of local communities during this period was unprecedented, and marked by protracted hostilities. Western political institutions, administrative apparatus, and value systems came into direct conflict with the Asian, African, and Amerindian patterns of governance and cultures. Missionaries, who sought to expand the influence of colonial regimes as part of their "civilizing" mission, legitimized the subjugation of indigenous cultures in order to establish Western values.

The conversion to Christianity offered social and economic opportunities such as access to Western education and medical services, which were denied to the larger society. Organized charities conducted by missionaries and churches were not always sensitive to the local customs, languages, and values. They often competed with existing social structures that provided care and welfare based on extended family, ethnicity, and religion. In many respects, globalization during this period was one-directional in that the "local" was either marginalized or replaced with more powerful and rapidly expanding global languages, cultures, institutions, and methods imported from Europe. The result was a consolidated global community ruled by the West. The anticolonial struggles in the early twentieth century not only revitalized the indigenous cultures, but also broadened the scope for alternative forms of globalization, which were more inclusive and transparent.[2] It was in this context that Western philanthropy in the early twentieth century ventured into many parts of the world.

*****

What makes modern philanthropy different from previous globalizing forces, and what are the underlying principles of philanthropy? To answer these questions we must examine briefly the philanthropic foundation as an exemplar of twentieth century philanthropy. Organized philanthropy was a product of the "Progressive Era" of the United States, a period characterized by "the transformation of America from a collection of individual communities to a mass society. The forces of urbanization, industrialization, commercialism and globalism that had all been gathering strength throughout the nineteenth century, reached during this generation a critical mass that changed not only the form but also the content of American culture and society."[3] Philanthropic foundations were institutional innovations of the early twentieth century resulting from the coming of age of an American civil society that had a long tradition of responding to societal needs through collective efforts. The underlying ethical principles that shaped the method of "scientific giving" or "whole-sale giving," as described by pioneer philanthropists, were the "promotion of human well-being throughout the world" by means of "science and scientific methods." Philanthropy became a practical solution to the problem of bringing the public interest in line with private economic interest. These ethical principles were fundamentally different from those of organized charities of previous generations. Unlike charities provided by missionaries and religious institutions, which were "mercy-giving" in that they aimed at alleviating individual suffering, organized philanthropy was aimed at improving the socioeconomic conditions of the community.[4] Appeals for grants were evaluated based on broad criteria, which included the ability to sustain long-term support within the communities themselves.[5] The ultimate goal of philanthropy was to eradicate poverty, illiteracy, and disease, and to uplift the community through programs known as "development" throughout the world.[6]

International development programs sponsored by philanthropic foundations played a catalytic role in disseminating modern Western science, medicine, and technology to societies in Asia and Africa, thereby connecting local communities with global society.[7] This process of integration, although considerably limited in its scope compared to that of information technology and trade in the current process of globalization, had a profound impact on the development of scientific medicine, public health, agriculture, and education in many parts of the world. Unlike organized charities that operated under the patronage of colonial regimes, philanthropy adopted a much more receptive attitude, enabling a broad segment of civil society to become actively involved in various international development programs. Although individual philanthropists themselves were motivated by their personal moral values, the unique aspect of twentieth century philanthropy was the way it brought together individuals of all walks of life—wealthy industrialists, public administrators, ministers, educators, doctors, and scientists—in developing programs, methods, and strategies deemed beneficial to each community. It was the programs and methods of philanthropic foundations (e.g., the International Health Board and the Rockefeller Foundation) that prepared the groundwork for the development of such major international institutions as the World Health Organization (WHO) and the United Nations Development Program (UNDP), which are at the forefront of the current process of globalization.[8]

Equally important, though often overlooked in the overwhelming emphasis on the dimension of human generosity, is the political influence exerted by these early philanthropic programs in shaping the nature of regional political alliances, placing a counterweight to other global political forces operating in the Cold War period.[9] Inspired by national and international concerns of the early twentieth century, philanthropic leaders responded with a global vision of promoting democratic values and civic responsibilities in societies where authoritarian regimes had resisted the development of civil society organizations and public debate.[10] Philanthropic leaders also recognized the importance of building social and cultural links among nations through transnational nongovernmental organizations (NGOs) to overcome the distrust, prejudice, and political conflicts, which had marked previous centuries of international relations. For example, the Institute of Pacific Relations (IPR) was one of the premier NGOs that functioned as an unofficial diplomatic channel at the international level to receive support from the Rockefeller Foundation during the early twentieth century.[11] By providing financial support and technical expertise to local communities, philanthropic foundations encouraged the formation of local civil society groups to strengthen democracy, human rights, and international cooperation. For example, following World War II, the

Rockefeller Foundation took a special interest in promoting independent nonprofit organizations in East Asia. Local civil society groups in Japan during the Cold War effectively restrained the nation's military ambitions as it became a major economic superpower. Japan's civil society groups and philanthropic foundations are now spearheading the campaign to promote peace and environmental protection in that region. This was one of the most important contributions of American philanthropic foundations to the modern world.[12] In this sense, both the scope and methods of philanthropy as a globalizing force in the twentieth century penetrated almost every aspect of life. It promoted not only science, medicine, and economic development, but also the basic ideals of democracy, human rights, and world peace.

In the current process of globalization, one of the most challenging tasks for the philanthropic foundations is to create a mechanism by which philanthropy, international organizations (such as the World Trade Organization, the International Monetary Fund, the World Bank and the WHO), and NGOs will be able to cooperate more effectively in responding to the broader socioeconomic implications of globalization. Currently, no single administrative body exists to coordinate the activities of these organizations. They often compete or view each other as adversaries, which leads to inefficiency and a waste of resources. Although civil society groups have long been involved in national and international governance, globalization has augmented this role owing to their effectiveness in mobilizing grassroots participation and their capacity to bring about desired social changes. By addressing democracy and human rights in the context of poverty and global trade, civil society groups help bring local issues and concerns to the center stage of globalization, demanding that policy makers pay attention to specific programs designed to alleviate poverty and improve health.[13] The United Nations Commission on Human Rights recently praised civil society groups around the world for drawing attention to the impact of globalization on human rights. It urged the international community to work with global civil society groups to develop a framework for trade based on the fundamental principles of human rights, so that economic globalization would not continue on its inherently asymmetrical course.[14]

However, sharp ideological differences continue to undermine constructive cooperation among international organizations, states, and civil society groups on most issues. Although international organizations are generally willing to work with major philanthropic foundations that have their own resources to initiate specific projects, they often distrust NGOs and avoid dealing with them when making major policy decisions.[15] In this context, philanthropic foundations can play a constructive role in bringing together these key stakeholders in globalization, as they have both the resources and experience working in various political and cultural settings around the world. More important, the reputation of philanthropic organizations as being transparent and inclusive may help them to cut through the distrust between international organizations and NGOs, and find some common ground in promoting international trade while upholding human rights, democracy, and environmental standards throughout the world.

*****

As stated at the outset, the purpose of this volume is to contribute to the understanding of the role of philanthropy and civil society groups in the context of globalization. The range of issues discussed is intended to be illustrative, rather than representative, of complex and diverse relationships among civil society groups, philanthropic foundations, international organizations, and nation-states that have emerged as key stakeholders of globalization. The ten chapters included in this volume are organized into four major sections, reflecting the historical and sociocultural dimensions of philanthropy, civil society, and globalization. While separate chapters reflect individual authors' expertise in the field, and can be read in any order, they are thematically interrelated based on theoretical and empirical reflections on the role of philanthropy in past and present globalizations. A brief overview of the main arguments discussed in each chapter is presented below.

History and Globalization:
Definitions and Conceptual Issues

Taking globalization as a historical continuum, the papers in this section offer a critical overview of various globalizing forces in history, and their implications for the development of theoretical and methodological perspectives on globalization. Raymond Grew and Wolf Schäfer have suggested in their contributions to this volume the need to identify "perspectives on global history," or "approaches to understanding most or all of human history." In this respect, globalization fosters philanthropy, civil associations, human rights, and communication networks around the world, providing perspectives on global history that began as "local past" and have emerged as "global present." It is these global perspectives of economic, political, social, and cultural integration that we describe as globalization.[16] From the perspective of global history, what we celebrate as "globality" is essentially an extension of certain local universalities to the whole world. For example, Schäfer argues that modern science, human rights, and environmental standards that originated in western Europe as local values and practices have now become universal. By comparing and contrasting critical issues and problems of globalization with those of key methodological perspectives in the emerging field of global history, Grew and Schäfer articulate a theoretical framework by which students of globalization can study significant historical changes across space and time.

Philanthropy and Globalization
During the Cold War Era

Reflecting on geopolitical interests and strategies that shaped early philanthropic programs during the Cold War period, the authors contributing to this section focus on the history of philanthropy. As a globalizing force in the early twentieth century, American foundations defined their role on the global stage with long-term objectives of strengthening democracy, civil society, and economic growth around the world. These pioneering works contributed to expanding the existing global frontiers of economic and political relations among nations. In their contributions to the volume, Gary Hess and Victoria Lyon Bestor explore the implications of these programs for contemporary international politics and their impetus to globalization. Both the Rockefeller and Ford Foundations sponsored programs in education, agriculture, and rural development in India that helped to modernize its agricultural practices, develop high-yielding varieties (HYV) of food grains, and, most important, prepare a new generation of scientists, public administrators, and health experts. These programs, described as "the struggle against communism in the developing world," not only prevented India from becoming an ally of the Soviet Union, but also helped that country to overcome its massive social and economic problems following years of colonial rule, argues Hess. Likewise, according to Bestor, building mutual trust and friendship were at the heart of the Rockefeller philanthropic programs in post–World War II Japan. The legacy of these programs persists to this day as the Japanese civil society groups and nonprofit organizations continue to foster the ideals of social responsibility and good corporate citizenship throughout the region.

Philanthropic Foundations and Civil Society
in a Globalized World

The papers in this section examine globalization from the contemporary perspective and recognize the expanded roles and responsibilities for philanthropic foundations and NGOs, which are at the forefront in delivering public goods, monitoring human rights, promoting democracy, and representing grassroots interests in international negotiations among states and multinational corporations. Reflecting on a broad scope of social and economic implications of globalization, Peter Frumkin and Lester Salamon draw attention, inter alia, to the burgeoning civil society organizations and philanthropic activities around the globe. Frumkin argues that there has been an upsurge of philanthropic activity by American foundations throughout the world. While many of these programs have been triggered by recent world events, global crises have always drawn the attention of philanthropic foundations.

Complementary to Frumkin's analysis of the global dimension of philanthropic activities, Salamon points out that diverse and distinct civil society groups have existed for centuries, and have been an important constituent of the public sphere that helped transform the authoritarian states in Eastern Europe and elsewhere in recent years.[17] As Salamon maintains, these civil society organizations, with their deeply held religious, cultural, and social roots, have served as a buffer between communities and states, and played a critical role in stimulating the collective consciousness and promoting human rights, accountability, and greater openness in the democratic process long before the onset of the current process of globalization.

It is to this particular theme that Helmut Anheier and Siobhan Daly address their contribution to this volume by concentrating on the rich "tapestry" of foundations in Europe. They argue that there is no philanthropic foundation model against which the structure and functions of such organizations in all cultures and societies can be evaluated. Even in more or less similar political environments, as in Europe, there are fundamental structural differences. The central argument is that not all foundations are equal. Yet, as Anheier and Daly point out, there is an increasing pressure on foundations, which exist in diverse sociocultural contexts, to act according to a uniform vision.

The contribution of Kathy Brock, David Brook, and Janice Elliott draws attention to the problem of the lack of resources for civil society organizations in the age of globalization. Taking the major economic restructuring of corporate Canada as a specific case, the authors illustrate how a large number of civil society groups and philanthropic foundations are competing for support from an increasingly shrinking donor pool. Thus, as Brock and her colleagues argue, policy makers must take a closer look at structural diversity and the access to resources by foundations and various civil society groups before formulating serious global strategies and policies that depend on the support of these organizations.

Globalization of Culture and Technology

The two chapters in this section examine a complex yet often overlooked aspect of globalization—namely, culture and technological transfer. In any historical period of global integration, one of the most complex and controversial aspects is the impact of global cultural forces on local cultures. The current process of economic globalization is a catalyst for social change. Although globalization has been able to bring communities together, the burgeoning cultural homogeneity has intensified a sense of cultural insecurity among nations.[18] Balmurli Natrajan, in his contribution to this volume, explores the inherent contradictions of globalization by reflecting on the cultural homogenization and heterogenization debate. He argues that globalization, like capitalism in general, requires cultural unevenness to sustain its own growth and proliferation.

This particular view of culture vis-à-vis globalization ideally fits with Michael Mehta's observations on the contribution of philanthropic foundations to the development of agricultural biotechnology in this volume. Describing modern industrial society as a "risk society" obsessed with the idea of continuing growth, Mehta argues that the Western world has "decontextualized risk" by promoting technological innovations. Taking the Rockefeller Foundation's program of the Green Revolution as a case study, Mehta suggests that the program succeeded around the world because it was able to adapt to local needs, practices, and customs of the people.

*****

Overall, the essays in this volume, whether critical, laudatory, or in-between, locate organized philanthropy among the most vital actors in the globalization process. As a civil society institution dedicated to promoting economic and social well-being, democracy, and global peace, the philanthropic foundation in the twentieth century is a model of open generosity anchored not in narcissism but in unassuming openness to others. Described by a plethora of terms such as "charity," "civil society activity," "development assistance," "nonprofit," "international relations," and so on, which refer merely to the *means*—convenient, trendy, or logical in time and place—receptive generosity manifests itself in the most rational form in organized philanthropy. The core values and practices of the twenty-first century are consistent with those of the underlying principles of organized philanthropy, and as the global community becomes increasingly open and interconnected, philanthropy will play a decisive role in shaping the new international order. These are complex issues, and no single conference or volume can address them fully to the satisfaction of everyone interested in philanthropy, civil society, and globalization—but if it raises more questions than it answers, that in itself justifies this project.

Endnotes

[1] John D. Rockefeller, *Random Reminiscences of Men and Events*, Sleepy Hollow Press and Rockefeller Archive Center, NY, 1984, p. 93.

[2] Soma Hewa, "The Protestant Personality and Higher Education: American Philanthropy Beyond the Progressive Era," *International Journal of Politics, Culture and Society*, vol. 12, 1998, pp. 135–63.

[3] Steven Wheatley, "Introduction," in Raymond B. Fosdick (ed.) *The Story of the Rockefeller Foundation*, Transaction Publishers, New Brunswick, NJ, 1989, pp. VII–XIX.

[4] Robert Payton, "Philanthropy in Action," in Robert Payton et al. (eds.) *Philanthropy Four Views*, Transaction Publishers, New Brunswick, NJ, 1988, pp. 1–10.

[5] Raymond B. Fosdick, *The Story of the Rockefeller Foundation*, Transaction Publishers, New Brunswick, NJ, 1989, pp. 22–3.

[6] Kathleen D. McCarthy, "From Government to Grassroots Reform: The Ford Foundation's Population Program in South Asia, 1959–1981," in Soma Hewa and Philo Hove (eds.) *Philanthropy and Cultural Context: Western Philanthropy in South, East and Southeast Asia in the 20th Century*, University Press of America, Lanham, MD, 1997, pp. 129–56.

[7] Emily S. Rosenberg, "Mission to the World: Philanthropy Abroad," in Lawrence J. Friedman and Mark D. McGarvie (eds.) *Charity, Philanthropy, and Civility in American History*, Cambridge University Press, Cambridge, UK, 2003, pp. 241–57.

[8] David P. Fidler, "The Globalization of Public Health: the First 100 Years of International Health Diplomacy," *Special Theme–Globalization, Bulletin of the World Health Organization*, vol. 79, 2001, pp. 842–9.

[9] Lawrence J. Friedman, "Philanthropy in America: Historicism and Its Discontents," in Lawrence J. Friedman and Mark D. McGarvie (eds.) *Charity, Philanthropy, and Civility in American History*, Cambridge University Press, Cambridge, UK, 2003, pp. 1–21.

[10] Rockefeller Archive Center, "The Charter (1910–1913)," in *Rockefeller Foundation Archives*, RAC, "Source Book for a History of the Rockefeller Foundation," RF History, vol. 7, p. 6.

[11] Lawrence T. Woods, "Letters in Support of the Institute of Pacific Relations: Defending a Nongovernmental Organization," *Pacific Affairs*, vol. 76 (winter), 2003–2004, pp. 611–621.

[12] Reiko Maekawa, "The Allied Occupation, the Cold War, and American Philanthropy: The Rockefeller Foundation in Post War Japan," in Soma Hewa and Philo Hove (eds.) *Philanthropy and Cultural Context: Western Philanthropy in South, East and Southeast Asia in the 20th Century*, University Press of America, Lanham, MD, 1997, pp. 115–28. Also see Akira Iriye, *The Globalizing of America, 1913–1945*, Cambridge University Press, Cambridge, UK, 1993.

[13] Kelley Lee and Anthony Zwi, "A Global Political Economy, Approach to Aids: Ideology, Interests and Implications," in Kelley Lee (ed.) *Health Impacts of Globalization*, Palgrave MacMillan, London, 2003, pp. 13–32.

[14] Chakravarthi Raghavan, "HRC Adopts Resolutions on Economic, Social and Cultural Rights," *TWN: Third World Network*, www.twnside.org.sg/2003.

[15] Médecins Sans Frontières, "Countries Must Save Lives Before Celebrating Success," www.doctorswithoutborders.org/pr/2003.

[16] Warren F. Ilchman, "Philanthropy and Civil Society in Asia," in Soma Hewa and Philo Hove (eds.) *Philanthropy and Cultural Context: Western Philanthropy in South, East*

and Southeast Asia in the 20th Century, University Press of America, Lanham, MD, 1997, pp. 279–93.

[17] Lester Salamon, S. Wojcsiech Sokolowski and Regina List, *Global Civil Society: An Overview*, Johns Hopkins University Press, Baltimore, MD, 2003, pp. 1–2.

[18] Jeremy Fox, *PostModern Encounters: Chomsky and Globalization*, Icon Books, Duxford, UK, 2000.

HISTORY AND GLOBALIZATION:
DEFINITIONS AND CONCEPTUAL ISSUES

Chapter 1

GLOBAL HISTORY AND GLOBALIZATION

Raymond Grew

All the commentators agree: "Globalization is the catch-word of the day."[1] It has become the single most important buzzword of the early twenty-first century";[2] used in the 1980s, the term had become by the 1990s[3] "an increasingly influential paradigm."[4] Such comments, although declaring globalization to be in vogue, also convey some uneasiness. After all, intellectual fashions are always dangerous, for they camouflage loose thinking. During this academic year in my own university, and I am sure it is fairly typical, there have been more than a hundred public lectures with global in their title, many of them on the expected topics of world trade or law and civil rights, but also on many others, ranging widely from a series of lectures titled "Crisis and Confrontation in Global Perspective" (emphasizing gender issues in "Religion, Security, and Violence") to very specific topics such as the account of a nineteenth-century explorer called "Scientific Travel and the Global Network of Knowledge" or a discussion of Armenian literature and globalization.

*****

Given such imaginative uncertainty as to what globalization means, we might begin by asking why so awkward a neologism has become so prominent. Two reasons stand out. The first reflects common awareness. We see daily evidence of global connections in news and pictures, in the goods made in one part of the world and sold in another, in organizations (corporate and nongovernmental) with a global reach, in migrants moving about the world, and in transnational campaigns in behalf of environmental, religious, and moral causes. Such evidence must be taken seriously in itself and may also reflect a widespread sense that individuals and whole societies are being pushed against their will by outside forces.

A second reason for the popularity of the term rests on a narrow meaning: increased capital flows and the removal of restrictions on trade that create a global market in response to the pressures that capitalism generates and many governments abet. To most Europeans, that is the core definition of *mondialization*, the one dictionaries give. In more general usage, the concept of globalization quickly enlarges to include the international agreements, policies, and technologies that facilitate this expansion.[5] Increasingly, globalization is also associated by many with threats to the environment, with a global division of labor that exploits poor regions, and with the erosion of national measures to protect workers or culture or food.

Both conceptions benefit from the suffix, for "-ization" is remarkably popular in writings about society, not for its beauty but for its implication of analytic depth. A suffix that by itself suggests process and implies direction has obvious appeal and, especially in the case of globalization, invites highly instrumental usage. By describing globalization as inevitable and resistance as counterproductive, exponents transform Adam Smith's unseen hand into destiny's bulldozer. That also makes globalization invaluable as a target that can unite in opposition otherwise disparate groups of environmentalists, critics of neoliberalism (or the International Monetary Fund or corporate interests or the foreign and trade policies of the United States), advocates of assistance to underdeveloped countries, and social activists of many sorts. The millions of people who demonstrated in Seattle, Porto Alegre, and Prague represented an extraordinary array collectively described in the press as the "anti-global" movement. The worldwide demonstrations on February 14, 2003, were organized in Florence by a group called the New Global, which was hailed as the "first global demonstration in history." That international opposition is, of course, in itself an important example of globalization.[6]

To some students of international relations, "globalists" are idealists who doubt the utility of force and image a single world community and culture. Futurists predict on the basis of developments they (fore)see in communication, technology, and transportation; the declining importance of the nation-state and the shrinking of the world; increased interdependence in politics and economics; and the growing importance of international organizations, leading to the routinization of international affairs.[7] On the other hand, an international panel of government officials considers that globalization brings—in addition to global cooperation (they cite the eradication of smallpox) and accelerating changes in communication and technology—porous frontiers, the drug trade, terrorism, and traffic in nuclear materials.[8] That conceptions of globalization are vague and politically charged hardly means that globalization is not occurring, but this does serve as a useful warning: the term has a magnetic attraction for hidden assumptions and covert purposes.[9] To talk about globalization without critical reflection is to think in terms of someone else's program and prejudices.

Similarly, the assumption that all this marks a new era deserves to be questioned precisely because it arises so automatically. There are reasons for skepticism. After all, Western culture has for more than two centuries interpreted itself in terms of historical change, and ideas recapitulated in the discourses of globalization are omnipresent in social thought, running through the texts of the eighteenth-century Scottish philosophers, Saint-Simon, Karl Marx, Emile Durkheim, Michael Polanyi, and Joseph Schumpeter, among many others.[10] Theories meant to explain and predict the process of change lie at the heart of the social sciences. In daily discourse as well, journalists and commentators regularly inscribe ordinary events by placing them within presupposed trends, and those trends in turn are taken as evidence of some underlying historical process. Thus, announcements that we have entered a new era are the common coin of importance in advertising as well as politics, even though most of those announced new eras have quickly passed or gone largely unnoticed. Even the most common statements intended to establish fundamental historic change are disconcertingly vague and general. There is no way to prove that the pace of change is ever faster in some measurable way (or even that nineteenth-century changes were not greater and more disruptive). Pronouncements about the decline of the state rely more on their futurist ring than present evidence.[11] Our overwhelming sense of living in a distinctive global era thus begs for some close analysis.

The fact that globalization has greater resonance than clarity says more about the way we think than about what we need to study. For that we must turn to others. Journalists and academics often make globalization a central term in writing on a variety of topics, and there is a smaller but still considerable literature by social scientists on the concept of globalization itself. It is these latter that I find wisest and most helpful. Without pretending that these authors all agree, I think some important themes recur within their different emphases and interpretations.[12] I will mention four that seem to me analytically fundamental: (1) Globalization must be analyzed not as some external force but as a sustained historical *process*. (2) Globalization is about much more than economics, including culture in all its forms (with popular culture most often cited), including value systems (from human rights to religion), institutions (governmental and nongovernmental), modes of communication, urbanization, and the movement of peoples. (3) Globalization incorporates multiple and even conflicting tendencies and is therefore not simply a unidirectional process. (4) Globalization consists of the intersection of the global and the local rather than a clash between them and results not in the defeat of one or the other but in the reconstitution of both.[13] These points seek to detach globalization from the more simplistic notions of modernization that social scientists have been battling for more than a generation, notions that continue to fester in nearly every cliché about globalization. For those who have thought about it the most, such as Helmut Anheier and Lester Salamon, globalization is a much more complex and varied process than common usage implies. That complexity is well represented in the other chapters in this volume, as well. Kathy Brock demonstrates the widespread awareness of, yet divergent reactions to, globalization with remarkable quotations from "civil society practitioners" around the world; and Michael Mehta opens up issues of the global risks inherent in the technological domination by certain multinational companies.

*****

Historical perspectives can contribute something to these discussions. The problem is not so much that writings on globalization often ignore history, but that they invent it. Starting from what they see as globalization today (sometimes shrewdly observed, sometimes merely based on a set of assumptions), they then (on the basis of another, albeit related, set of assumptions and prejudices) use selected examples to outline a historical pattern that leads to their view of the present and provides a trajectory predicting the future. With the past as incidental prelude, no wonder the predictions are more intensely debated than the interpretations of history on which they appear to rest. Not surprisingly, then, descriptions of where globalization is headed often reveal in remarkable detail the historical moment in which they were written.[14] It is worth remembering that the record of prognostication in the social sciences has been mixed at best, despite the enthusiasm for futures research a generation ago[15] and that "historical experience should caution us against making too rapid predictions."[16]

Everyone agrees that historical knowledge is a good thing, like vitamins or exercise, and that globalization is about change over time. More careful attention to history can at least provide the kind of ballast that feels like wisdom, an awareness that even dramatic change carries great continuity with it and that the most significant consequences are often unintended. Such historical awareness discourages hyperbole and resists the teleological temptations built into many views of globalization; tendencies inherited from ideas of modernization that proved powerful in the 1950s and 1960s (and have played their part in promoting globalization). History is, after all, the best laboratory of human behavior we have.

In addition, the application of historical knowledge can provide some focus through the use of historical analogies and thereby helpfully prompt critical thinking. With regard to philanthropy, for example, policy makers working in an era of globalization might consult modern research on missionaries. Their heroic determination to promulgate truth around the world fascinates historians and anthropologists because of the revealing evidence of how their efforts were affected by the invasive cultural baggage that missionaries brought with them. Weightless to them, it was heavy with European prejudices and customs that made their work more difficult and blinded them to the lessons about nature and humanity that indigenous peoples could teach.[17] But analogies like this can also mislead, and it takes careful work to make them more than suggestive. Methodologically, then, something more is needed.

Almost instinctively, historians look to chronology. One of the most obvious questions arising from talk of a global era is, when did the era begin? This seems a deceptively clear-cut and neutral question until conflicting answers roll in. Many see the end of the Cold War as the major demarcation of a new era, opening the world to an expansion of capitalist trade and American influence. Others favor the 1950s, pointing to new international organizations, agreements on trade, and global communication through television and popular culture, with Sputnik as the symbolic opening of a new vision of the world. Such claims immediately lead to others, however; that world trade and interconnection already marked the world of the 1920s, for example, or that the beginning of globalization lies in the 1890s, at the height of European imperialism, when world trade was a larger part of GNP than it would be a century later.[18] A broader historical view starts from the industrial revolution of the early nineteenth century, describing it as the first globalization; and European commentators commonly refer to our era as the second globalization.[19] If the expansion of capitalism, trade, and empire is the core of globalization, however, perhaps analysis should look to the sixteenth and seventeenth centuries. That perspective adds important dimensions by recalling the ideas and institutions, the state making, the banking, and the printing that emerge from the Renaissance. For each specific circumstance cited as the starting point of modern globalization, earlier precedents and parallels are quickly found.[20] These responses, frustrating to those for whom the newness of globalization is self-evident, easily prompt overreaction. Historical parallels should neither be dismissed as pedantic irritants from academics rooted in the past nor heralded as the arrows that puncture metatheories and inflated claims. Historical examples remain an indispensable path to understanding global processes, but their identification rests on much more.

*****

Beyond a valuable historical awareness, there is thus an opening for a specifically global history, a field of historical study directly concerned with all these issues; and many current intellectual trends come together in the growing interest in its possibilities.

Postmodernist currents subvert familiar "master narratives" of progress, liberal triumph, and Western dominance. The ethnocentrism unmasked in subaltern studies of imperialist policies has spurred a critical rejection of the parallel ethnocentrism underlying much of European and North American historical writing. Scores of scholars have returned to the old issue of Western supremacy in the world, dismissing the triumphalism that topic used to evoke in favor of new models of international economic and political relations. And for more than a generation, increasing numbers of historians have expressed impatience with the restricted vision that follows from accepting the nation as the boundary within which historical research is done. Finally, there is renewed interest in attending to the natural sciences as the basis for conceiving of global history. Concern for the environment has undoubtedly stimulated this tendency, but it goes much deeper, making use of work in geology, biology, and ecology to connect the physical world, sometimes with archaeology as a natural bridge, to the history of human society. All these trends were present at the Nineteenth International Congress of Historical Sciences held in Oslo in 2000, where "Perspectives on Global History" was the number one theme of the conference. Beyond their considerable interest, the papers offered there also stand as evidence for the lack of consensus as to just what global history is. Authors used the term *global history* interchangeably with *universal history, world history, Big History,* and *long-term history.*[21]

It seems to me that global history is usefully thought of as different from and perhaps less grand than any of those others. The fundamental argument for global history, I think, lies elsewhere than in the grand schemas it may stimulate, more matter-of-factly in the world around us than in the intellectual trends of current scholarship, consonant though they are. Contemporary experience has made us sensitive to something that historical analysis has tended to slight: the multiple and complex importance of global connections on perceptions and policies, on cultures and economic activity, on values and styles.[22] Like the history of gender, environmental history, labor history, and ethnic history, global history should prosper as a topical field to which historians had always given some attention but which gains fresh vigor from its obvious importance in contemporary life. "History," Lucien Febvre wrote more than fifty years ago, "is a way of organizing the past to keep it from weighing too heavily on the shoulders of men . . . for history does not present them with a collect of isolated facts. It organizes those facts. It explains them, and thus in order to explain them makes a series of them to which it by no means gives equal attention. Because whether or not we wish it so, it is as a function of present needs that history systematically gathers and then classifies in groups the facts of the past. It is as a function of the living that it interrogates the past."[23]

Nor do I think that explorations in global history need be put off by disagreements over when globalization began. Autonomous chronologies cannot resolve the question in any case, because the logic of periodization demands an explicit conception of the historical problem to be resolved and how it should be analyzed. Scholars who have comprehensive visions of global relationships and who are willing to consider all of history can discern very large patterns. These then lead to one sort of periodization (Wolf Schäfer's in this volume is a notable instance). More commonly, historians will fruitfully settle for a smaller scale, one sufficient to establish what philosophers have called the context of discovery, within which the questions that will direct research are posed.[24] As researchable problems are explored, analytically, empirically, and comparatively, they become the basis of periodizations appropriate to a specific problem.[25]

The study of global history in terms of selected historical problems can still be expected both to shed new light on current concerns and to raise fresh questions about many eras of the past. In doing that, global history will establish its place within the historical discipline, as a set of questions and interests initially uncircumscribed by predetermined chronology or geography, "because it is not proper for a discipline in the process of organizing or reorganizing itself to impose prophetic directions from outside. Let it develop its own experience."[26] The risk comes not from beginning with the present but when the present is accepted as the necessary outcome of the past, overlooking historical events and developments that pointed (and may still point) to alternative outcomes, and when the present is assumed to lie just around the corner from a predicted future.

Global historians will investigate particular aspects of a selected topic as these unfolded in the context of specific places and times. So open and uncharted a beginning is daunting nevertheless; and many historians, even some sympathetic to global history, will turn aside, declaring the challenge impossible. No one, it will be pointed out, can command all of history (although it should help to recall that on even the narrowest of topics no scholar can be certain of knowing everything that might be relevant). In fact, global historians have much research on which to build. There are huge literatures to be plumbed on such obviously related topics as the history of trade, migration, and technology; much to be gleaned from works in world history that deals with global connections and historical processes. There are pioneering theories of ancient empires[27] and significant models of state making and empire building. Economic history has long addressed issues central to global history not only in work on modern capitalism and the wealth of the West, but also on the economies of other parts of the world, including Africa, and in all eras.[28] Immanuel Wallerstein and his many followers have explored the connections of capital and empire since the sixteenth century in valuable detail. These works, along with dependency theories and postcolonial studies exemplify how essential a theoretical structure is for extensive in global history.

Much of this literature is preoccupied with issues of power, and global history can make a further contribution by posing questions that do not assume a vector of development from West to elsewhere or frame cultural relations solely in terms of dominance and resistance. Scholarship on the history of science and of technology, long understood primarily as a subfield of intellectual history requiring arcane knowledge, has come more and more to emphasize the interdependence of science and society; and they thus open new vistas on global history.[29] Environmental history is a newer and burgeoning field of study inclined to consider the world as a whole. Nor is it just historians who provide global history a learned base. Much of the work in political science on international relations seeks historical and global patterns. A great deal of structural and cultural anthropology has from its beginning been framed in terms close in many respects to those of global history. And many a historical sociologist has achieved an ambitiously global reach.[30] Global history should seek to contribute to theoretical understanding even while remaining loyal to history's empirical bent; be sensitive to postmodern methodological caveats yet participate in the theory building more often pioneered in the other social sciences. In short, global history may be a relatively young venture, but it hardly has to build from scratch.

*****

Let me suggest some practical ways in which historians can engage global history, using familiar tools and accessible techniques while meeting the established standards of the discipline. A field that sees itself as new has many advantages. The sense of freshness stimulates a willingness to cross conceptual boundaries patrolled by intellectual customs. In this fresh air of a new look, even painstaking detailed research is likely to connect to the larger issues that form a burgeoning field of study. It is here that theory becomes important and that the global historian can engage with some of the areas of the social sciences that are currently among their liveliest. By its very nature interdisciplinary, global history can benefit from the turn to history in anthropology and sociology. Not in itself a method, global history is free to apply the established methods used in all forms of historical study.

Seeing history globally, however, requires something more than reassembling established knowledge and the ideas of others. Global historians will want to strike out on their own, asking fresh questions and tackling problems newly conceived. That means learning to think both globally and historically and then wrestling with infinite chains of relationships across space and time. The first task, then, is to make this less overwhelming. Global histories need to engage concrete realities. Fortunately, many of the historian's familiar and conceptually simple procedures can encourage fresh (global historical) thinking while leading to focused research. Let the reader have in mind a topic that he or she wishes to think about in a global historical framework. The global historical aspects of that topic can be explored by pursuing four categories of questions. They necessarily overlap, and taken together they launch a thought experiment that constitutes a further step toward more refined questions and closer research:

I. What global circumstances and global experiences are relevant to the specific topic an investigator has chosen? Natural disasters and ecology provide endless instances of similar circumstances around the world, and William McNeill's *Plagues and Peoples*[31] is a model of what can be done with such an approach. Indeed, by starting with geography, environment, and basic human needs, Robert Clark[32] and Jared Diamond[33] have each constructed an interpretation of global history. Knowing the circumstances in which a given subject matter is likely to have been salient, the investigator begins by noting global occurrences of those conditions. Asking about common human experience invokes the perspective of social history (refreshing here as a contrast to the tendency in history on a grand scale to begin from the centers of power).[34] Ida Blom has shown how asking this question leads to the recognition of gender as an important subject for global history,[35] and Paula S. Fass has suggested the need to place the history of childhood with a framework of global history.[36] Analyzing common historical experiences also quickly leads to the use of historical comparison,[37] in much the same way that the literature on empires and imperialism or state making frequently does. Someone interested in the global history of philanthropy might concentrate on the needs arising from specific kinds of disasters or diseases, or might assess the relative effectiveness of different forms of philanthropic organization and procedures. These become cases for comparison, and different responses to similar experiences invite new questions by demanding an explanation of differences. Lester Salamon does that in this volume by presenting an interpretation of civil society as a response to insufficiencies of the state. As the comparisons build and patterns emerge, the global historian will ask whether responses to the experiences under study are a source of significant historical change across space and over time. There will then be analytical reasons for including some cases and excluding others; and there will be a set of questions to pursue, questions for which concrete evidence is needed even as they are connected to a larger, global historical framework. Defining the historical problem to be resolved will follow, and serious research can begin.

II. Does the topic involve diffusion, a process whereby ideas, technologies, institutions, religions, or customs spread over time from place to place, weaving new intersections of local and global? Diffusion, a classic issue in anthropology, is a creative process in which nothing moves unchanged from one context to another. In every society new influences, however partially adopted and however thoroughly altered, stimulate changes in behavior and strengthen and subvert established ways and institutions. These alterations then often circle back to affect the sources from which diffusion came. Such processes must of course be studied specifically.[38] Those concerned with philanthropy might want to trace the spread of the very idea of philanthropy itself, the purposes assigned it, and the institutions designed to carry it out. Because the functions of philanthropy vary in different eras and societies, scholars will be attentive to the way particular philanthropies change in different contexts, and policy makers will want to assess the institutional ability to adapt. The speed and ease of communication obviously facilitates diffusion for all the carriers of culture, as it has historically done for merchants, missionaries, and armies, for touring companies in the arts, for migrants and tourists. An important characteristic of modernity, the movement of peoples, which creates increased possibilities of escape from repression and poverty (or taxes), also facilitates diffusion. The study of such historical instances thus raises questions important to global history about the factors that encourage or inhibit diffusion and determine its pace, about the qualities that facilitate the spread of particular ideas, technologies, institutions, or customs, and about the circumstances in which diffusion does or does not lead to the lasting ties that make for significant global relationships. Once the historian determines the patterns of diffusion critical to the topic at hand, it becomes possible to select and compare the specific instances that require closer study while establishing the relevant global historical framework.

III. What global connections intersect with the topic under study? Such connections have been well studied in terms of trade and traders,[39] business corporations, religions, political alliances, and cultural ties. Global historians will note the spheres of activity in which these connections become institutionalized and whether these relationships expand or contract over time—a useful counterweight to those teleological assumptions so difficult to exorcise. Thus it becomes important to assess when and how transnational connections in one sphere stimulate parallel connections in other spheres, forming a growing web of connections. Those formed by institutions—banks, trading companies, corporations, museums, universities, and foundations—are the easiest to trace, and they leave the kind of archival evidence historians know well how to exploit. The global connections of philanthropies, too, are shaped by their ties to each other and to other institutions (exemplified by Gary R. Hess in his chapter on foundations in India), through agreements with governments (discussed by Peter Frumkin on American foundations overseas), and by social and personal ties (see the chapter by Victoria Lyon Bestor on the Rockefeller Foundation and Japan). The web of connections formed through communication are more difficult to assess; but they can be pursued in terms of patterns of travel and the available technologies of communication (with the Internet a favorite theme in comments on globalization)[40] and the historical role of certain languages as a lingua franca (Greek, Latin, Chinese, Arabic, French, and Chinook are all examples). Laws, treaties, and capital flows reflect and engender transnational economic and political ties. When the webs of global connections affecting the topic under study are extensive and dense, they give further focus to research and invite a periodization of their global history.

IV. How have cultural encounters affected the topic at hand? From a global perspective, no aspect of modernity—not even science and technology, industrialization and economic growth, imperialism and urbanization, or literacy and mass communication—is more important as an engine of change than historical interaction between cultures. With reference to the contemporary world, Arjun Appadurai argues that culture has become the "arena for conscious choice," and "the imagination has become a collective, social fact."[41] Current predictions that the world is becoming increasingly homogenized or that it is destined to be split by wars between civilizations both rest on the interpretations of cultural encounters. Historical analogy, however, suggests something more complex and far more malleable, as Balmurli Natrajan discusses in this volume. There are many other examples. The great world religions spread not only core beliefs, but also Hebrew, Latin, and Arabic around the world, yet everywhere adapted to local languages, laws, foods, and customs.[42] Fundamentalisms, so unbending on many of these matters, readily adapt to modern technology and to political and economic circumstance.[43] The dots and dashes of Morse code, with its bias toward the Latin alphabet, and the more neutral bytes of computer code helped make English understood around the world yet function effectively in other languages. Religion, language, and custom simultaneously build barriers and construct bridges between societies, retaining distinctiveness even while borrowing from each other.

There has been so much debate about "the culture concept" in the social sciences that it is necessary to say a little more about culture. I believe, with William H. Sewell Jr., that culture refers to both symbolic systems and social practice, that cultures contain contradictions and are constantly changing.[44] These points are critical; cultures are not monolithic, and encounters need not be clashes. Global historians will investigate cultural encounters in terms of specific behaviors and values, and any essentializing should not be that of the researcher but that of contesting participants in those cases where the intersection of cultures is perceived and resisted. Issues of identity are salient in cultural encounters because they are always being reshaped and challenged and because they tend to proclaim cultural continuity while simultaneously provoking isolation, conflict, and assimilation—as among the Chinese in Malaysia, the Jews in the Ottoman Empire, the Turks in Germany, the French in Quebec, and the North Africans in France. Anthropologists have long been fascinated by the individuals they label cultural brokers, figures who bear the special role of interceding between outsiders (often imperial agents; sometimes missionaries, entrepreneurs, or academics) and local society.[45] The complexity and pain of that role and of those cultural encounters has troubled and enriched the cultural life of every society. Those most deeply engaged in bridging cultures, like the Indonesians who wrote novels and poetry in Dutch or Egyptians and North Africans who wrote in French, often ended as tragic figures, forgotten by Europeans and condemned by native nationalists. Leaders of liberation movements melded knowledge of their conqueror's culture with their understanding of local needs and resentments. Philanthropies, too, are part of this process, bringing, whatever their explicit project, unrecognized cultural content that is always selectively received and always has unanticipated consequences. No wonder, then, that Helmut Anheier suggests in this volume that philanthropies emerge along "the fault lines" of society. Whatever the specific outcomes, cultural regeneration stimulated by contact with other cultures remains an unending process, forever redefining what is alien or natural and reconstructing culture. The social customs central to group identity may, when they are similar in distinct societies, lead to other forms of connection. Always reaching out and penetrating within, changing social customs can serve historical analysis as an indicator of relationships functioning in global context.[46] In considering any specific topic in the context of global history, the scholar will want to explore both its cultural components and the global links that continually reshape it.

Building a framework for the global history of any topic can thus begin quite simply by investigating the respects in which it has been part of a global experience, has spread and evolved through diffusion, has existed in a nexus of global connections, and has been affected by cultural contacts. The four paths to finding global processes allow that each may have its own momentum, its own ways of developing. Inviting essentially empirical findings, they only provide a beginning, a way to identify specific historical problems for further research and suggest hypotheses worth testing. Research on a selected aspect of global history and construction of an appropriate global historical framework go hand in hand.

*****

Much scholarship important for global history operates in terms of global systems, and the procedures are somewhat different when a researcher suspects that certain pressures and constraints are inherent in the way states, corporations, or other large institutions function on a global scale. The search in this case is for patterns of global relations and the (often hidden) rules and regularities that create an international system, usually seen as being rooted in paradigms of power. The investigation is likely to begin with the explicit policies of the entities being studied. The result of conscious decisions (although not necessarily ones made with full awareness of the system into which they fit or of their global implications), policies leave a record. They emerge in response to particular challenges, which in turn have their own histories and are most often formed through competition and imitation. Collectively, these policies tend to create global systems with characteristic preoccupations and rules, and these systems can become motors of globalization.

Of the various approaches to global history, studies of global systems are best known; for they have prominent predecessors in histories of international relations, military, diplomatic, and economic. Arnold Toynbee's *A Study of History* is a prominent example. Following others, he argued that through their many conflicts, Italy's Renaissance city-states established systems of alliances and of diplomatic rules. He then extended the point to a larger argument: This flexible system for weighing power among states spread across Europe as Europe's new nation-states were drawn into Italian conflicts, and that in turn formed the basis for the whole system of international relations that Europeans imposed upon the world. Political scientists and sociologists, as well as historians, have traced the evolution of that system through the writings of major thinkers and the power politics and wars of the last four centuries. Study of its global spread, from the seventeenth and eighteenth centuries to the present, and much work on contemporary globalization are in this tradition.[47] Further understanding emerges when state practices are connected on the one hand to domestic politics and interests and on the other to their global implications.[48]

The importance of transnational corporations so dominates discussions of globalization today that it need only be mentioned here. This, too, has a history that runs from the international banks of the Bardi, the Medici, and the Fuggers through the great trading companies of the seventeenth and eighteenth centuries, European investment in America, North American investment in South America, the rise of European and American corporations from mid-nineteenth century through the mid-twentieth century, and subsequently of American and Japanese corporations after World War II. International banking also came to operate in an unusually rule-bound global system. Reaching new prominence in the late nineteenth century,[49] it assumed a still more public role following World War I and became still more important and more institutionalized after World War II. Related international agreements on tariffs, copyright, and the movement of capital have operated similarly. Despite limited effectiveness in the late nineteenth century and failure during the Great Depression, such agreements have become increasingly powerful, detailed, and global from the 1940s to the present. In the minds of many, they now represent what is good or bad about globalization. Comparable agreements on human rights and welfare and associated developments in international law constitute a system that has grown from foundations in the late-nineteenth-century treaties specifying the responsibilities of the imperial powers and gaining institutional form at about the same time with the establishment of the international court of justice at The Hague. Expanded and made more formal by the League of Nations, such arrangements have come since the 1940s to touch on so many subjects and proved so internationally influential that some now speak of a global civil society.[50]

*****

Belief that globalization is all around us inspires the interest in global history, but global history must be more than the history of globalization. That also means, however, that the history of globalization must stand as a topic in its own right, with distinctive preoccupations and approaches that distinguish it from the sort of global history discussed above. Historical study of globalization requires identifying the factors that underlie the historical processes drawing the world together, including those that historically seemed to foreshadow globalization but were aborted, diverted, or incomplete. That search cannot be restricted to contemporary history (even the modest claim that the present is different requires analysis of many pasts to establish just where that difference lies). Here, global history and the history of globalization come together.

The history of globalization, however, differs from global history in a number of respects.[51] It emphasizes what Bruce Mazlish (during discussions at the conference) calls "the synergy and synchronicity" of the factors identified as leading to globalization and seen as a distinguishing characteristic of our era. Thus it focuses on recent history, even if making deeper forays into the past as they seem important to resolving historical problems that arise from the analysis of contemporary globalization. More fundamentally, histories of globalization are concerned with a large-scale historical *process* and with identifying the factors that foster—and inhibit—that process. Theory building is intrinsic to the history of globalization, to the topic itself, to the formulation of research, and to its goals. To achieve its purposes, the history of globalization needs to query the idea of globalization itself (problematizing it, in the current jargon). That is, rather than accept globalization as some kind of natural phenomenon already under way, the scholar must probe the concept's hidden content (ideological, symbolic, and instrumental) as it investigates the ways in which ideas of globalization evolved, the interests they serve, and the uses to which they are put. Common assertions about homogenization or the decline of the state need to be challenged and specified.[52]

Theoretical approaches to globalization, in which historical sociologists have been leaders, often define globalization, almost philosophically, in terms of the altered effects of space and time,[53] and historians have much to contribute on these points. Change over time is a comfortably familiar emphasis, analyzing processes of development a standard practice. There is a vocabulary ready to hand for explaining how a little trade leads to more, trading posts to entrepôts, and entrepôts to the panoply of commercial institutions; how border clashes lead to conquest; how ideas—religious, philosophical, or aesthetic— win converts but are altered by their success. But time really is of the essence for histories of globalization, and they will necessarily tackle the challenge of demonstrating what difference it makes to complex processes of change—especially those related to diffusion and cultural contact—if transformations occur over centuries or decades.

These theoretical discussions of globalization commonly give as much attention to the changing significance of space as to the pace of change. Indeed, descriptions of globalization as the shrinking of space and contraction of time have become something of a cliché.[54] Here, too, historians have reason to urge greater precision and some restraint. Instantaneous communication by telegraph, radio, and Internet does not always eliminate local difference and can even amplify misunderstanding. The ease of travel that makes the world smaller also widens horizons and makes the world that people experience larger and more confusing. Global experiences remain marked by geography; webs of connection, too, have an obvious geographical component. They may shift the boundaries of region, trade, ideology, and social interaction while creating new boundaries and reinforcing old ones.

Historians of globalization will, as historians always must, seek indicators of globalization that are concrete, specific, and historically grounded. As societies are increasingly aware of each other, as individual experiences of work and consumption become more comparable, as standards of efficiency, ethical behavior, and legal procedure are applied more universally, shaping policies and organizations, then a process of globalization is clearly under way. The topic starts from evidence and demands research. Historians turning to this new field can look forward to finding it as complex as any other.[55] Global historical processes, sometimes constraining and sometimes reinforcing each other, can induce both cooperation and contestation, generate imitation and resistance, and be experienced as discovery and as conquest and subjugation as well. These processes can move in contradictory directions toward integration and sharpened separation, and the process of globalization is unlikely ever to seem complete.

Scholars of both global history and of the history of globalization can be expected to construct a research agenda narrowed according to the requirements of feasibility and to be analytically focused. As a relatively fresh mode of historical thought, global history will develop in many directions. Along the way, the perspective it offers can help us keep from being bedazzled by American power and can serve, as the serious contemplation of history always has, as a counterweight to hubris. There are also promising possibilities for deeper understanding of how societies function and how change takes place, and that is one of the exciting intellectual opportunities of our time.

Endnotes

[1] A.G. Hopkins (ed.), *Globalization in World History*, Pimlico, London, 2002, p.1.

[2] Ludger Kühnhardt, "Implications of Globalization for the Raison d'être of European Integration," www.arena.u10.no/events/papers/Kuhnhardt.pdf, 2003.

[3] Malcolm Waters, *Globalization*, 2nd ed. Routledge, London, 2001, pp. 1–2.

[4] Mike Featherstone and Scott Lash, "Globalization, Modernity and the Spatialization of Social Theory: An Introduction," in Mike Featherstone, Scott Lash, and Roland Robertson (eds.) *Global Modernities*, Sage, London, 1995.

[5] There are many skeptics, however; see Paul Q. Hirst and Grahame Thompson, *Globalization in Question: The International Economy and the Possibilities of Governance*, 2nd ed. Polity Press, Malden, MA, 1999.

[6] *La Republica*, February 15, 2003; Jackie Smith and Hank Johnston (eds.), *Globalization and Resistance: Transnational Dimensions of Social Movements*, Rowman and Littlefield, Lanham, MD, 2002. In commenting on the popularity of this opposition, Sidney Tarrow notes that its participants are not capable of changing the frame of discussion because they come from such independent spheres; see "Making Social Science Work across Time and Space: A Critical Reflection on Robert Putman's Making Democracy Work," *American Political Science Review*, 90, 1996, pp. 243–44. Gary Teeple, *Globalization and the Decline of Social Reform*, Garamond Press, Toronto, 1995.

[7] Ray Maghroori and Bennett Ramberg (eds.), *Globalism versus Realism: International Relations' Third Debate*, Westview Press, Boulder, CO, 1982. But contrast the different perspective in B. Ramesh Babu (ed.), *Changing Political/Ideological Context and Afro-Asia*, South Asian Publishers, New Delhi, 1996.

[8] *Our Global Neighbourhood: The Report of the Commission on Global Governance*, Oxford, UK, 1995.

[9] The mutual denunciations are remarkably strident. See Gregg Easterbrook, "Who's Afraid of Globalization," *Wall Street Journal*, April 14, 2000, who in a few paragraphs describes antiglobal protests as a "contradictory and self-defeating" opposition to rising incomes, increased literacy, and the erosion of dictatorships.

[10] Dave Renton (ed.), *Marx on Globalisation*, Lawrence and Wishart, London, UK, 2001.

[11] Joseph E. Stiglitz and Pierre-Alain Muet, *Governance, Equity, and Global Markets: the Annual Bank Conference on Development Economics, Europe*, Oxford University Press, NY, 2001.

[12] Roland Robertson has been particularly influential in developing this understanding. He has essays in many of the works already cited. Also see Roland Robertson, *Globalization: Social Theory and Global Culture*, Theory, Culture and Society Series, Sage, Newbury Park, CA., 1992; Tony Spybey, *Globalization and World Society*, Polity Press, Cambridge, UK, 1996.

[13] Robertson's argument is especially congenial to anthropologists, see Christopher Demazière (ed.), *Du local au global: Les initiatives locales pour le developpement économique en Europe et en Amérique*, l' Harmattan, Paris, 1996.

[14] See Charles W. Kegley Jr. and Eugene R. Wittkopf (eds.), *The Global Agenda: Issues and Perspectives*, Random House, NY, 1988.

[15] For a reminder, consult Jib Fowles (ed.), *Handbook of Futures Research*, Greenwood Press, Westport, CT, 1978. Ironically, there is a chapter on "the global diffusion of futures research."

[16] Orvar Löfgren, "Technologies of Togetherness: Flows, Mobility, and the Nation-State," in Dan Kalb, et al. (ed.) *The Ends of Globalization: Bringing Society Back In*, Rowman and Littlefield, Lanham, MD, 2000.

[17] Peter van der Veer (ed.), *Conversion to Modernities: The Globalization of Christianity*, Routledge, London, UK, 1996.

[18] Scott Lash and John Urry, *The End of Organized Capitalism*, University of Wisconsin Press, Madison, 1987.

[19] Similarly, reviewing the vast transformations in the nineteenth century and in particular the social effect on labor of economic and technological change, Michael Hanagan identifies two periods of globalization, 1850 to 1914 and 1950 to the present. See his essay "States and Capital: Globalizations Past and Present," in Kalb (ed.) *The Ends of Globalization: Bringing Society Back In*, Rowman and Littlefield, Lanham, MD, 2000.

[20] The essays of Jonathan Friedman, *Cultural Identity and Global Process*, Sage, London, UK, 1994.

[21] "Perspectives on Global History," paper presented at the Nineteenth International Congress of Historical Sciences, Oslo, 2000, available at: www.arena.ulo.no/papers.

[22] Arjun Appadurai, *Modernity at Large: Cultural Dimensions of Globalization*, University of Minnesota Press, Minneapolis, 1996. And see the essays in Mike Featherstone (ed.), *Global Culture: Nationalism, Globalization and Modernity* , Sage, London, 1990; Stuart Hall, David Held, and Tony McGrew, *Modernity and Its Futures* Polity Press, Cambridge, UK, 1992.

[23] Lucien Febvre, "Vers une autre histoire," in *Combats pour l'histoire*, Armand Colin, Paris, 1953.

[24] Hans Reichenbach, *Elements of Symbolic Logic*, Macmillan, NY, 1947.

[25] Even periodizations that take into account all of human history or reach much farther back in time are derived from the overall argument. Hopkins proposes a periodization

that runs through archaic, proto-, modern, and postcolonial globalizations; see Hopkins (ed.), *Globalization in World History*. Also see Wolf Schäfer, "The New Global History: Toward a Narrative for Pangaea Two," *Erwägen Wissen Ethik* 14, 2003, pp. 75–133. Starting with the fifteenth century, Robertson finds six stages; Robertson, *Globalization: Social Theory and Global Culture*.

[26] Febvre, "Vers une autre histoire," p. 438.

[27] Karl August Wittfogel, *Oriental Despotism: A Comparative Study of Total Power*, Yale University Press, New Haven, CT, 1957; S. N. Eisenstadt, *The Political Systems of Empires*, Free Press of Glencoe, London, 1963; Karl Polanyi, Conrad A. Arensberg, and Harry W. Pearson, (eds.) *Trade and Market in the Early Empires*, Free Press, Glencoe, IL, 1957.

[28] Philip D. Curtin, *Cross-Cultural Trade in World History*, Studies in Comparative World History, Cambridge University Press, NY, 1984; Karl Polanyi, *The Great Transformation*, Beacon Press, Boston, 1957; Sharon Zukin and Paul DiMaggio, *Structures of Capital: The Social Organization of the Economy*, Cambridge University Press, NY, 1990.

[29] For an unusually comprehensive vision of global history and the scientific history of the globe, see Wolf Schäfer's essay, "The New Global History,"and the rich array of comments that follow.

[30] Two examples: Christopher Chase-Dunn, *Global Formation: Structures of the World-Economy*, Basil Blackwell, Cambridge, UK,1989; Jack. A. Goldstone, *Revolution and Rebellion in the Early Modern World*, University of California Press, Berkeley, 1991.

[31] William H. McNeill, *Plagues and Peoples*, Anchor Books, NY, 1976.

[32] Robert P. Clark, *The Global Imperative: An Interpretive History of the Spread of Mankind*, in Bruce Mazlish, Carol Gluck, and Raymond Grew (eds.) Global History Series, Westview Press, Boulder, CO, 1997.

[33] Jared Diamond, *Guns, Germs, and Steel: The Fates of Human Societies*, Norton, NY, 1997.

[34] Haines Brown suggests thinking of interrelationships through common experiences rather than merely commercial connections. Interestingly, the point comes up in his comment on Eric Martin's "Global History vs. World History," an essay stimulated by Bruce Mazlish's writings, available at: www.hartford-hwp.com/archives/10/022.html.

[35] Ida Blom, Gender as an Analytical Tool in Global History," (paper presented at the Nineteenth International Congress of Historical Sciences, Oslo, 2000).

[36] Paula S. Fass, "Children and Globalization," *Journal of Social History*, vol. 36, 2003.

[37] The employment of comparison is discussed by Raymond Grew, "The Case for Comparing Histories," in Aram Yengoyan (ed.) *Modes of Comparison* (forthcoming).

[38] Two topics that have many produced studies of global diffusion are migration, see Wang Gungwu (ed.), *Global History and Migrations*, Global History Series, Westview Press, Boulder, CO, 1997; Raymond Grew (ed.), *Food in Global History*, Global History Series, Westview Press, Boulder, CO, 1999), and the bibliographies in each.

[39] Curtin, *Cross-Cultural Trade in World History*.

[40] Manuel Castells is a prolific and influential interpreter of the impact of modern communication whose views are provocatively summarized in Johan Muller, Nicole Cloete, and Shireen Badat (eds.) *Challenges of Globalization: South African Debates with Manuel Castells*, Maskew Miller Longman, Cape Town, 2001.

[41] Appadurai, *Modernity at Large*.

[42] A major theme of world history, the spread of religion has proved a complexly difficult subject for the modern era, but see van der Veer, *Conversion to Modernities.*

[43] Many have made this point; my comments are in "Seeking the Cultural Context of Fundamentalisms," in Martin Marty (ed.) *Religion, Ethnicity, and Self-Identity: Nations in Transition,* New England University Press, Hanover, NH, 1997, 19–34.

[44] William H. Sewell, Jr. "The Concepts(s) of Culture," in Lynn Hunt and Victoria E. Bonnell (eds.) *Beyond the Cultural Turn,* University of California Press, Berkeley, CA, 1999.

[45] In his useful summary of theories of globalization, Malcolm Waters can envision a globalized world that would have "a single society and culture occupying the planet" but thinks considerable diversity more likely; see Waters, *Globalization.*

[46] Anthony D. King (ed.), *Culture, Globalization and the World-System: Contemporary Conditions for the Representation of Identity,* University of Minnesota Press, Minneapolis, 1997; Jean-Pierre Warnier, *La mondialisation de la culture,* La Découverte, Paris, 2003.

[47] George Modelski, *Long Cycles in World Politics,* University of Washington Press, Seattle, WA, 1987; Peter J. Taylor, *The Way the Modern World Works: World Hegemony to World Impasse,* Wiley, NY, 1996.

[48] An excellent example is the work of Michael Geyer and Charles Bright, in "Global Violence and Nationalizing Wars in Eurasia and American: The Politics of War in Mid-nineteenth Century," *Comparative Studies in Society and History,* vol. 38: 4, 1996, pp. 617–57; "World History in a Global Age," *American Historical Review,* vol. 100: 4, 1995, pp. 1034–60.

[49] The classic account is Herbert Feis, *Europe, the World's Banker, 1870–1914,* Harvard University Press, Cambridge, MA., 1964. See Stiglitz and Muet, *Governance, Equity, and Global Markets,* for a current discussion.

[50] Note the lively discussions in W. Hutton and A. Giddens, *Global Capitalism,* New Press, NY, 2000.

[51] Nomenclature has proved confusing. Bruce Mazlish, who has been a leader in the drive to establish a new field of history cognizant of the globalizing changes of our time, initially adopted the label *global history,* to distinguish this approach from the well-established literature on world history. See Bruce Mazlish and Ralph Buultjens (eds.) *Conceptualizing Global History,* Global History Series, Westview Press, Boulder, CO, 1993, and his "Comparing Global History to World History," *Journal of Interdisciplinary* Studies, vol. 28, 1998, pp. 385–95. Subsequently, he has come to call the initiative New Global History, both to make the distinction sharper and to emphasize what I have called the history of globalization.

[52] Note Michael Burawoy's alternative, "repositioning of the state," Michael Burawoy et al, (eds.) *Global Ethnography: Forces, Connections, and Imaginations in a Postmodern World,* University of California Press, Berkeley, CA, 2000; Saskia Sassen, who has extensively studied cities and globalization warns that the interaction between globalization and the state is not a zero-sum game in "The State and the New Geography of Power," in Dan Kalb (ed.) *The Ends of Globalization: Bringing Society Back In.* Rowman and Littlefield, Lanham, MD, 2000.

[53] They are prominent in the essays in M. Featherstone, S. Lash and R. Robertson (eds.) *Global Modernities,* Sage, London, 1995.

[54] In Brenner's hands, global space becomes a means for thinking beyond the state; Neil Brenner, "Beyond State-centrism? Space, Territoriality, and Geographical Scale in Globalization Studies," *Theory and Society,* vol. 28, 1999, pp. 39–78. Wiarda finds regional and local development the important trend, see Howard J. Wiarda (ed.), *Non-Western Theories of Development: Regional Norms versus Global Trends,* Harcourt-Brace, Orlando, 1999). Geographers, however, can also be skeptical of globalization claims; Kevin R. Cox (ed.), *Spaces of Globalization: Reasserting the Power of the Local,* Guilford Press, NY, 1997.

[55] S. N. Eisenstadt, *Comparative Civilizations and Multiple Modernities: A Collections of Essays,* 2 volumes, Brill, Leiden, 2003.

Chapter 2

HOW TO APPROACH GLOBAL PRESENT, LOCAL PASTS, AND CANON OF THE GLOBE

Wolf Schäfer

To gain entrance into global history you have to satisfy a three-headed monster. Global present, local pasts, and canon of the globe are the names of its heads. If you cannot please all three, one head, if not all, will attack you. How to gratify the Cerberus of global history is unknown; you have to get past it and return to tell about it. What follows is but a rough profile of the three guardian heads and a road map to the lair of the monster.

*****

Gauging the global present is as important and necessary as it is hazardous. An autopsy would be best for this task, but one would be hard to perform on an entity that is still very much alive and ferocious. This difficulty is compounded by the uncertainty principle of contemporary history. To paraphrase Lewis Carroll, the more you analyze the present the "uncertainer and uncertainer" it becomes. Yet shielding contemporary global history from historical investigation would be risky, too.

With regard to the origin of our inspirations, there is no difference between historians and other social scientists. We are getting our hints from the present. Historical reconstructions follow cognitive threads that run from the present into the past. This temporality surfaces when one reads older works and recognizes the imprint of a past present. In contemporary historiography, however, the heuristic presentism of the historical study is usually obscured since most historical narratives turn hindsight into foresight and tell history the other way around, from a past beginning to a later end. Yet global historians are in a position to reveal this narrative trick. We are more inspired by the global present than by a particular past.

Approaching the past from the present affords long-range perspectives. Global historians can save the study of the global present from social-scientific myopia. Reviewing the local pasts in the light of the global present and connecting the global present to diverse local pasts will prevent the shortsighted presentism that permeates so much of social science. How to connect the present to its different pasts is, of course, a matter of historical research and debate. However, at the core of the New Global History

(NGH) is the understanding that all of us are now more affected by our contemporaries than by our ancestors.[1]

Global historians have to answer this question: "What is globalization, and how does it differ from past economic and political expansions under European colonial rule in the eighteenth and nineteenth centuries?"[2] The links between contemporary global change and the history of Western hegemony have to be explained without erasing the "inconvenient" features of the past or constructing a "convenient" past. We have to deal with the suspicion that "globalism" is nothing but the highest stage of imperialism.[3] Fruitful historical thinking about these questions can begin with Western capitalism, imperialism, and colonialism but has to go beyond the postcolonial discontent. We have to test the assumption that globalization differs only in scale from previous European expansions and push for a genealogy of the global present that does not recoil from the skeletons in the closets of local pasts. However, let me ask the main questions of this chapter: namely, how old is the global present? Does it have a *significant* local past? What is it all about?

The global present of this three-headed monster is roughly fifty years old; the beast has a noteworthy European pedigree and is encompassing the globalization of human affairs and human domination of the planet. Some fifty years ago, the birth of the global present coincided with the notion that Europe had reached the end of its historical significance. The impression of a decisive European breakdown was widespread after World War II, yet it was a global historian *avant le lettre*, Geoffrey Barraclough (1908–1984), who articulated not only the "end" of European history and civilization[4] but also the advent of *a new age*. In 1955, this British medievalist and universal historian heralded the global present as the twin novelty of *global politics* and a singular *global civilization*.

> Every age needs its own view of history; and to-day we need a new view of the European past, adapted to the new perspectives in which the old Europe stands in a new age of global politics and global civilisation.[5]

A few years later, in 1962, Barraclough's thinking about the new age had reached another crucial insight with the observation that it required a *new type of history*. The name Barraclough used for this new history was "universal history," but what he described was in fact the New Global History that is now developing.

> The reasons why the history most needed today is universal history lie all around us. They are a reflection of the unification of the world by science and technology and by the revolutionary advance of mass communications, a consequence of the familiar fact that we can no longer isolate ourselves from events in any quarter of the globe. Taiwan and Indo-China today are as near, and what happens there as relevant for us, as Greece or Portugal a century ago. Furthermore, the processes of industrial society, which originated in western Europe and North America, are now world-wide, their impact universal.[6]

Barraclough's inaugural understanding of the global present contained a number of keen perceptions; let me note six. First, Barraclough recognized that the globe had moved into the center of history after the "end" of European history. Second, he noticed that history had begun to operate on "a global plane, which only a universal point of view can elucidate." Third, he acknowledged that the "Europacentric" and nationalistic historical approaches had to be replaced by a historiography with "a global perspective." Fourth, he saw that the "political environment of today is world-wide" and hostile to "iron curtains." Fifth, he knew that the time for a truly global history had come because "our global age knows neither geographical nor cultural frontiers." Sixth, he urged us to keep "pace with our fast-moving world" or the "revolutionary shift in historical perspective" will "atrophy into a parade of fascinating but sterile knowledge."[7] The fact that many world historians,[8] and probably all global historians, are still subscribing to that list (without necessarily knowing its provenance) indicates that dating the beginning of the global present in the mid-1950s cannot be too far off. Even the name for our era—the global age—was already in use around that time.

In the second half of the twentieth century, multiple processes of globalization have constituted *globality* as the historical benchmark of the global present.[9] Globality extends locally achieved universalities to the whole earth and all of its peoples. It appeared hand in hand with the quantum leap from local pasts into the global present. The universal claims of modern science and enlightened philosophy—equal human rights and ubiquitous laws of nature—originated as local pronouncements in western Europe during the Protoglobal Age (1450–1950). Although Eurocentrism is politically incorrect, we must handle the fact that the DNA of the global present bears distinctive and important traits prominently from western Europe. Thus, a synopsis of the rise and fall of Europe's metageography is necessary to locate our time in relation to global history's most consequential local past.

*****

In a class on the global history of transportation and communication, a student wrote, "It was once said that all roads lead to Rome, but now we can fairly say that all roads lead to other roads!" The teacher was pleased and scribbled in the margin, "This is the essence of globalization: the networks grow longer and eventually span the whole globe."

The professor's lecture on Roman road building had, of course, shown that many, but not "all," roads led to Rome. But never mind; the student had grasped the spatial nature of globalization and given the old saying a synaptic turn. Synaptic globalization levels the Romes in the sky that attract the traveler for loftier reasons than good games, famous sights, and smooth paving. For some time Athens was such a fabled place, an imagined heaven for truth-seeking travelers.[10] Cities like Rome and Athens were real cities as well as metageographic places. They existed inside and outside Ptolemy's *Geography*; they had spatial and mental coordinates. The same holds true for Europe. It used to be a dull and poor part of the world, and yet it came to occupy a prominent space in the mind as well as large portions of the globe; indeed, so much so that external and internal critiques of Europe's spatial and mental expansions in the past have become the rule today.

However, in the fifth century BC, Europe was a dubious name and fuzzy part of the earth.[11] Herodotus even questioned the wisdom of naming individual components of the geobody, "since the earth is all one," but he also reported that Europe's physical extension was greater than Asia's and Libya's combined.[12] After Herodotus, Europe's size shrank as geographical knowledge grew, and five centuries later, the geographer Strabo considered Europe the smallest part of the ancient tripartite landmass. At that time, the Roman Empire still flourished, and nobody could imagine that the backwoods of northern Europe would ever inspire the human mind.

Around 1000, the Middle East and China were highly urbanized while Rome, once a city of 450,000, had fallen to 35,000 inhabitants. Córdoba, however, the center of Islamic Spain, had grown to half a million and Baghdad, with almost one million people, was standing tall as the largest city in the world. Its "House of Wisdom" (Dar al-Hikma) had begun in the ninth century to collect, translate, and synthesize the legacy of the advanced "foreign sciences," notably Greek, Persian, Indian, and Roman political, medical, and scientific treatises. A few centuries later, Europe was to reap a momentous benefit from this world heritage conservation, yet at the cusp of the first Christian millennium, northern Europe was an underdeveloped region with a very low chance of achieving global dominance in either civilization or culture.

Around 1450, Europe had put itself on the map with a potent mixture of new universities, free cities, three-field agriculture, heavy-duty plows, stirrups, horse collars and shoes, flour, saw and hammer mills, printing presses, magnetic compasses, cannons, caravels and galleons. Still, it was not apparent at the time of Prince Henry of Portugal and Johannes Gutenberg that the next five hundred years would amount to the "Rise of the West."[13] Even so, the great European attraction to water-and wind-powered machines, which provided access to nonmuscular energy, was already notable. In addition, the geographic lust of Western Christendom, whose members began to call themselves Europeans in the fifteenth century,[14] had not only been stirred by the Crusades and the fabulous travelogues of Marco Polo and John Mandeville but also by the later conquest of the Azores and the Canary Islands, the exploration of Africa's bulge, and the discovery of the North Atlantic triangle of navigation.

Yet around 1950, Europe was in ruins, literally and metaphorically. About this, I should like to speak from experience. Born during World War II and raised in the rubble of Frankfurt am Main, I can attest to the broken identities of my generation. We were ashamed to be Germans and, until much later, could not imagine Europe as an economic, political, or cultural community. For us, Europe was a continental place-name and a much-divided region. It was hard to overlook the ruins or to recognize the "European civilization" in the patchwork of different states, pacts, languages, cultures, cuisines, landscapes, histories, traditions, prejudices, policies, economies, ideologies, and the like. Moreover, the people who did talk about Europe in world-historical terms, the West German politicians of the Christian Democratic Union (CDU) and the Bavarian Christian Social Union (CSU) had distinctly medieval preferences. Europe was a word with six letters for us but the sacred Christian Occident for them. We thought about history after a temporal ground zero,[15] searched for an alternative modernity, and dreamed about history from below;[16] they proceeded to make postwar history as believers in the *Abendland* (Occident). Robert Schuman, Charles de Gaulle, Konrad Adenauer,[17] and Helmut Kohl— Catholic leaders with the "back to the future" advantage of a genuinely premodern perspective—bridged the continent's gaps and built the European Union.

Let me complement my point of view with another, less personal flashback. Around 1950, the "long" nineteenth century was over. It had started in London on May 1, 1851, with the opening of the Crystal Palace exhibition during the first world fair and ended on August 6 and 9, 1945, with "Little Boy" and "Fat Man" exploding over the cities of Hiroshima and Nagasaki. The world had followed the trajectory of this period via electrical telegraphs, radio broadcasts, moving pictures, and roving world fairs. In nearly one hundred years, Europe had gained enormously and then lost hugely. What she gained and lost both in her self-perception and in the eyes of the world was her metageographic fame. The "greatest achievement of organized science in history," as the White House had called Little Boy,[18] concluded the European phase of Western hegemony. Ten years later, Barraclough declared "the end of European history." The future Beatles were listening to American rock-and-roll records (brought to Liverpool by merchant seamen) when Barraclough explained what he meant by *end*.

> It does not mean, of course, that European history will come to a full
> stop; it means rather that it will cease to have historical significance.[19]

Indeed, European history did not stop after 1945 but became provincial once again. A small consequence of this ending without stopping was the effect that it had on the discourse of world history. The standard reference to the *European Civilization* faded and the *Western Civilization* of the American undergraduate course blossomed. Thus the prophecy of the decline of *the West*, which a liberal translation of Oswald Spengler's *Untergang des Abendlandes* had suggested, came true, but on the war-ravaged side of the Atlantic only.[20] Given the humanistic bent of the Old World, it may not be surprising that the rise and fall of western Europe found its most eloquent expression in the words of two philosophers: William Whewell and Max Horkheimer.

In November 1851, after the doors of the first Great Exhibition had closed, Whewell explained the European ascent to civilizational eminence in a lecture before the Society for the Encouragement of Arts, Manufactures, and Commerce.[21] In comparing "our progress" in art and science with the "nearly stationary" civilization of the "Oriental nations," he described the industrial works of technoscience as a "gigantic" success.

> The great chemical manufactories, which have sprung up at Liverpool,
> at Newcastle, at Glasgow, owe their existence entirely to a profound
> and scientific knowledge of chemistry. These arts never could have
> existed if there had not been a science of chemistry; and that, an exact
> and philosophical science. . . . They employ, some of them, five or six
> large steam-engines; they shoot up the obelisks which convey away
> their smoke and fumes to the height of the highest steeples in the world;
> they occupy a population equal to that of a town, whose streets gather
> round the walls of the mighty workshop. Yet these processes are all
> derived from the chemical theories of the last and the present century;
> from the investigations carried on in the laboratories of Scheele and
> Kirwan, Berthollet and Lavoisier. So rapidly in this case has the tree of
> Art blossomed from the root of Science; upon so gigantic a scale have
> the truths of Science been embodied in the domain of Art.[22]

If Whewell's address, "On the General Bearing of the Great Exhibition," provided his Victorian audience with a glorifying picture of British capitalism and technoscience, then Horkheimer's *Critique of Instrumental Reason*[23] formulated a general condemnation of technoscientific progress in a capitalistic framework. The dean of critical theory articulated the contraposition to Whewell's affirmative philosophy and argued that promoting industrial technoscience "as the automatic champion of progress"[24] was the "ideology" that was begetting the "opposite of progress"—namely, the failure of civilization.

Human toil and research and invention is a response to the challenge of necessity. The pattern becomes absurd only when people make toil, research, and invention into idols. Such an ideology tends to supplant the humanistic foundation of the very civilization it seeks to glorify. While the concepts of complete fulfillment und unrestrained enjoyment fostered a hope that unshackled the forces of progress, the idolization of progress leads to the opposite of progress.[25]

Eclipse of Reason[26] as well as *Dialectic of Enlightenment*[27] spawned dark thoughts about the course of modern history. The fires of World War II and the mushroom cloud of the atomic bomb cast an enormous shadow that now fell on the achievements of industrial modernity. Horkheimer and his associates denounced the ruling civilizational progress as a sure path to universal "dehumanization."[28] Shared initially only by a small circle of German émigrés in the United States, these dark thoughts blossomed later in West Germany and elsewhere.

The theory that questioned "the powerful machinery of organized research" and pronounced that "the victory of civilization is too complete to be true"[29] found a resounding audience in the 1960s[30] and began to mesh, however awkwardly, with other European critiques of occidental reason. A tragic chorus of intellectuals reaching from Heidegger to Derrida, Foucault, and Lyotard threnodized that reason had forfeited its critical capacity when it fused with the powers to be (political, military, and industrial; mass culture; patriarchy, etc.). Transcending the embedment of reason, the mandarins went overboard and carried their postmortem of occidental reason beyond the local realm of Enlightenment reason to a hypercritique of all reason. Yet as problematic as a supposedly true verdict about all reason is in logical terms, it does make historical sense if one understands it as a desperate lamentation. As such, *Eclipse of Reason* was an elegy about Europe's loss of metageographic power.

Around the beginning of the twenty-first century, America became the country with the badge of "historical significance" for all to see. Even the provocation of 9/11 made that point, albeit perversely. The vagueness of the transition from *European* to *Western* civilization disappeared and it became clear that *Western* now meant *America*—that is, the United States of America.[31]

In the eyes of many in the United States and especially its neoconservative elite, *the West* is going stronger than ever. It has won the Cold War and dwarfs whatever tangible and metageographic strength Europe had once possessed. European history, to be sure, was not idle; it has made progress with the European Union and advanced an already highly developed region even further. Nevertheless, the center of historical gravity has vacated Europe for good. From the Scottish Highlands to the Ural Mountains, Europeans are now searching for ways to cope with the global predominance of the United States. The outlook on power from the American side is different. Americans—"From the redwood forest to the New York island" and "From the snow-capped mountains to the Gulf Stream waters"[32]—are debating how to best exercise the global leadership position that has befallen them after the unexpected death of the Soviet Union. Yet many people on both sides of the Atlantic view the future of the global present with trepidation. Considering the rising interest in opinionated books about the history of empires, one can bet on an emerging market for lessons from the past.[33]

Hoping that "past experiences can be used as guiding threads to formulate current policies of globalization to achieve a truly prosperous and democratic global community"[34] is, of course, commendable, although one could also be skeptical and think that the pragmatic value of local knowledge for other than cultural identity purposes is slim. The global experiences of local pasts have their limitations; new and incomparable developments can never be ruled out; revolutionary change has happened before and is possible now. Historians who worry about the fallacy of "presentism" may want to care also about the pitfalls of "pastism"—the erroneous assumption that nothing under the sun will ever be new. Global history's canon of the globe, our third guarding head, is a good example for an evolutionary leap that could be observed in due course but was not predictable from experience.

*****

The American historian of medieval technology Lynn White Jr. (1907–1987), loved to unravel historical change with a strong hypothesis; in 1956, he wrote, "The canon of the Occident has been displaced by the *canon of the globe*."[35] Unlike White's arguments about the heavy plough, the horse collar, or the stirrup,[36] his observation about the new standard of the globe has yet to be criticized. In fact, I think it would be difficult to find a better and more positive expression for the historical transformation that has marked the global present. What undergirds the present period also connects the recent NGH approach with the earlier discoveries of White and Barraclough. The geobody of the globe joins us from below. The globe provides global history with a material as well as a cognitive paradigm and allows us to focus on the two principal thrusts of global power today: the worldwide domination of people and matter.

In 2003, the United States of America used its political and military muscle against the opposition of the United Nations and such loyal Cold War allies as France and Germany. The unapologetic use of American firepower created political shock waves, which are presently accumulating on the surface of global history. It seems safe to predict that global power politics will receive a lot of attention in the coming years. A myriad of articles, papers, books, and conferences is bound to explore America and the world at the dawn of a global empire administered from Washington, D.C. Nothing is wrong with that focus; on the contrary, power politics always was, and still is, much too important to be left to the professionals: politicians, generals, diplomats, policy wonks, journalists, international relations experts, and historians of choice. Yet the task to put the global present in perspective should not fall only on presidential scholars and historians of war, politics, and diplomacy, but on all kinds of historians: social, cultural, environmental, local, regional, world and global, as well as those of economics, gender, science, technology, and medicine.

An important service that global history can render derives from its intrinsic partiality to the canon of the globe. Working by the rules of globality, global historians can analyze the use and abuse of global power in political as well as natural terms. Although one cannot vanquish the Cerberus of global history in a chapter, we can point the way to its den. Let me therefore chart the road ahead. First, we have to establish a reasonable orientation for our map. To some degree, we have done that already by backgrounding the global present with its significant local past. Second, we have to make sure that our approach can handle the trends of fashion. The rising foam and thunder from contemporary politics must not overpower the less obvious motions below the historical surface. Third, we have to georeference our map for the age of "global politics and global civilization." This means that we have to bring our mapping into agreement with the whole planet. Nation-states and other local parts of the globe cannot determine the focus of global history. Fourth, we have to research the two planetary projects of the Global Age, the American empire and the human domination of nature.

Orienting the Map

When Barraclough observed that "the Europe of our history books. . . . is dead and beyond resurrection,"[37] the struggle between the Soviet Union and the United States was making global history, and nobody knew what the result would be. If the Soviet Union had stormed from success to success after sending the first Sputnik into Earth orbit in October 1957, neither the European Union (EU) nor the North Atlantic Treaty Organization (NATO) would have blossomed the way that they did. However, knowing the outcome of the Cold War, global history's first great battle, one can say that it has left the verdict about the comparative end of European history and civilization intact. The reprovincialization of Europe is the datum that allows us to orient the present in relation to the local past that mattered most.

The collapse of the Soviet Empire released a number of states in Eastern Europe with Western-oriented civil societies to join both NATO and the European Union. The EU is poised to expand from fifteen to twenty-five members in May 2004 and perhaps even adopt its first constitution later. Supposing that this impressive growth will happen as planned, cause only marginal stress, and prove to be largely beneficial, the expanding and consolidating Europe will nevertheless continue to play a secondary role. Turning into a superpower in political or military terms is not likely. Fifty years of chipping away at all aspects of Eurocentrism have taken care of Europe's metageographic influence. Yet what is more important is that the concurrent buildup of American military power has left Europe and the rest of the world far behind. Thus, the geopolitical situation of contemporary global history can be summarized in three short sentences: Europe had been the leading continent on all counts during the long nineteenth century. North America will be the continent with global power during the long twentieth century. Asia may assume leadership of the world after 2050, but not before.

To test the premise that large chunks of the global civilizational DNA germinated in western Europe requires inspecting the local past of protoglobal European history. We must explain the historical change from modernization to globalization and universality to globality to clarify the genesis of global history. What are the differences between globalization and modernization on the one hand and globality and universality on the other? How did the local civilization of western Europe ease the way to globality? How has globality transformed the superparadigm of modernity? How are the processes of globalization turning the universal claims of modern science and philosophy into globally distributed realities? Answering these questions should go a long way toward grasping the global present and its influential European past.

Checking the Trends

After some decades of blissful neglect, the American-led war against Saddam Hussein's Iraq has asserted with a vengeance that power politics and international relations are important fields of study. Correcting the recent overemphasis on grassroots, micro-, and identity politics by taking into account that history has obstinate political and military dimensions can only improve the charting of the global present. However, the academic world is as immune against trends of fashion as most subscribers to investor newsletters are. If technology stocks are the rage, the majority will go for them. In the 1990s, for example, globalization became the catchphrase in the media and the halls of learning. Initially, the view of it was overly positive, yet it swung within a decade from naive embrace to wary opposition. Now we have to worry that the pendulum of trends could swing too far to the side of traditional power politics.

The shift from Clinton-era multilateralism to Bush-era unilateralism, the "global war" on terrorism since 9/11, the military strategy of "preclusive preponderance," and the heady prospect of a global empire under the American flag are a potent set of attractions. It would be surprising if these things would not call extra attention to political history and international relations, which had been somewhat staid for a generation or two. The New Global History, however, would lose its complex focus if it would cater for the foreign policy market only. As much as a corrective upswing in the direction of political history is welcome, it should not narrow our range. Merely aiming at the political waves on the historical surface would create a Global History Lite and leave the underground tectonics of global history in the dark.

Georeferencing the Age

White wrote in 1956 that humankind had entered "a time of general shift more fundamental than any since agriculture and herding displaced food-gathering and hunting as the habit of human existence."[38] He, Barraclough, and other perceptive authors, notably Eric Fischer[39] and Oskar Halecki,[40] felt compelled by the expanding geographical horizon of history to modify the labeling of the ages.

> It has been suggested that a "Mediterranean age" was followed by a "European age," which is now being succeeded by an "Atlantic age." It is not necessary to discuss those appellations now. They seem to me to be better than the old ones—although the term "Atlantic age" begs a lot of questions: if we consider that to-day Russia and America face each other across the Bering Straits as England and Germany once faced each other across the Straits of Dover.[41]

Barraclough, looking beyond the familiar Atlantic, saw a "Pacific age" in the making and "the transition from 'modern' to 'post-modern' history."[42] Of course, "post-modern" has had its own rise and fall in the meantime and came to stand for a great deal more than Barraclough and other early users of this transitional tag—Arnold Toynbee and Peter Drucker, for example—had imagined. However, Barraclough's ocean age was moving in the right direction. The fact that we are still grappling with the periodization of global history[43] simply underlines that epochal transitions tend to be both lengthy and messy, with the declining and rising ages overlapping while coexisting.

The foregoing names for the ages emphasized specific parts of the globe: the Mediterranean Sea, the European continent, and the Atlantic and Pacific oceans. The historians who were playing with these names in the 1950s communicated historical significance with geographical terms. They referenced parts of the earth to signify where the center of historical action was at a given time. The whole planet did not count in the beginning, only parts of it, and what mattered was not derived from geography but from history, itself an intricate mixture of preconceived and researched notions. Greece, Rome and Christendom, as well as the United Kingdom, the Soviet Union, and the United States, to take a somewhat biased sample, changed places in terms of metageographic clout: when their worldly power rose, the imagined center of world affairs shifted to them, and when it waned, the center moved away and crowned another place. The entire globe never became the center of gravity for all human affairs before the global present and outside Newtonian physics.

From Barraclough's informal use of "our global age"[44] to Martin Albrow's[45] elevation of the words *global* and *age* into a full-blown theory of "The Global Age," the globe itself has been propelled into the center. As the adjective "global" is not georeferencing one part of the earth but the whole planet, the entire globe is imbuing our age with historical significance and global historians with a planetary focus. Scanning the Global Age for the footprints of a *global politics* and *global civilization*, we find two muscular actors: the United States and humankind. The United States can be seen as building a political empire spanning all nations and humankind as erecting an empire of civilization over all aspects of nature. Now that humankind is dominating the planet and its ecosystems, more and more members of the human species feel moved to canonize the globe.

Researching the Projects

Investigating the twin-empire proposition is not something global historians are undertaking alone; this research is interdisciplinary and involves the social and natural sciences as well as the humanities. Global historians nevertheless have something to offer that most other social scientists have lost or traded in for a higher degree of scientificity, and that is the ability to picture "the whole." Having learned to work with the concept of historical ages—holistic superconstructions, no doubt—we can see the global present as a complex unity that includes local cultures, an expanding political empire, and an unlimited technoscientific civilization.

The global political empire in the making could hardly be more controversial; it agitates everybody inside and outside the United States. The postulate itself is highly contentious. It is good to know how bygone empires functioned, but the past does not predict the mode of operation of an empire in the twenty-first century. The future of global political power is unclear. How does a hegemonic power operate in the context of a truly global world? Is a postconventional, democratic empire feasible? Does an empire with highly advanced, space-based means of command and control have to be territorial? Does it have to follow narrow national interests, or can it be embedded in a net of multinational agreements about fair trade, ecology, and nonproliferation of nuclear weapons? How well do global empire and imperial ignorance about local cultures go together? These are wide-open questions for global historians and their interdisciplinary friends.

The present historical situation of the United States requires a rethinking of empire. No other country looms larger in military, political, economic, technoscientific, or even cultural terms. It is manifest that the contemporary position of the United States is heavily inclined toward global leadership. Weapons of mass destruction, global terrorism, and neoconservative radicalism are incidental to that inclination. Either gently sliding in the direction of global empire or violently rushing ahead to fill that role, the United States is moving toward some kind of global captaincy. What kind of rule that will be remains to be seen. More often than not, however, the national and international discussion has acknowledged a rising American hegemony by merely debating alternative ways of its implementation and execution. The leaning of the United States toward global power, the worldwide scrutiny of American ambitions, and the options for empire now and then are eminently researchable topics. The comparable (or incomparable) historical record of pre- and protoglobal empires is easy to consult and contemporary sources abound.

*****

The human domination of nature, our own included, is the other grand historical project that is currently making rapid progress. Running parallel to the political venture but rarely recognized as a coherent global project, it too makes the front pages and editorials. The tone of the commentaries is sometimes triumphant,[46] sometimes ominous.[47] Over the years, readers have learned about acid rain, the ozone hole, Greenpeace actions, Windscale, Sellafield and Chernobyl, global warming, species loss, deforestation, Ian Wilmut's Dolly, gene-splicing, genetically modified plants, patents on man-made microorganisms, a green-glowing rabbit, molecular manufacturing, stem cells, Michael Crichton's nanothriller *Prey*, eco-mercenaries, the Kyoto Protocol, huge water-diversion projects in China, world summits on sustainable development, radio-collared horses, panthers, and porpoises, the bioengineering of immortal humans, and the like. This list is virtually endless because the project is practically unlimited and open-ended. Freeman Dyson recently suggested the next big step, a no-holds-barred "planetary genome sequencing project" that would "identify all the segments of the genomes of all the millions of species that live together on the planet."

> The goal would be to complete the sequencing of the biosphere within less than half a century, at a cost comparable with the cost of the human genome. This project would bring an enormous increase in understanding of the ecology of the planet, which could then be translated into practical measures to sustain and improve the environment while allowing continued rapid economic development. It could also lead to the stabilization of the atmosphere and the climate. Let this century be the century of cures for planetary as well as human diseases.[48]

We are now led to believe that the human species can successfully manage the earth, her cycles and ecosystems, and cure the globe and itself of all ailments, including death. Surely, this project needs global history research. Putting all of the pieces together should be among the first things to do. We want to know: Do these reports, headlines, setbacks, movements, and breakthroughs tell a million-and-one odd stories or one story in a million-and-one bits and pieces? Do they prepare us for the domination or the domestication of the planet?

A project this gigantic and yet obscure, furthered with private and public means, yet with no name, headquarters, government, or capital city, is difficult to observe, analyze, and discuss. But contemporary history will not wait for the future historian,[49] not in as hyperreflexive a time as ours. As for a name, I would call it the civilizational project.[50] Total control over animate and inanimate nature appears to be its objective and global technoscience its tool. The evolutionary steps of this megaproject demand a long historical perspective. The way in which molecular genetics and nuclear physics have opened up animate and inanimate matter, the Industrial Revolution incorporated new energy sources, the Neolithic Revolution pulled plants and animals into the human orbit, and the domination of fire domesticated the caves and started the culinary arts have all played a large part in the project to control nature. However, it is only now, as *Homo sapiens* is eyeing the complex mechanisms of the whole geobody, that we are turning to the canon of the globe to ask, is it a power-limiting supercode or just a weighty metaphor? Can it restrict the preeminent power of the United States? Will it limit the superpower of humankind? To answer these questions, you have to reach and overcome the Cerberus of global history on both the civilizational and political fronts.

Endnotes

[1] Wolf Schäfer "Global History and the Present Time," in Peter Lyth and Helmut Trischler (eds.) *Wiring Prometheus: Globalisation, History and Technology*, Aarhus University Press, Langelandsgade, DK, 2004, pp. 103–125

[2] Outline for the conference on "Globalization, Civil Society, and Philanthropy: Toward a New Political Culture in the Twenty-First Century." See the introduction to this volume: "Structure and Process of Global Integration," Soma Hewa and Darwin H. Stapleton.

[3] As has been argued by A. Sivanandan in *Race and Class*, a journal for black and Third World liberation, "If imperialism is the latest stage of capitalism, globalism is the latest stage of imperialism." Quoted after Farhang Rajaee, *Globalization on Trial: The Human Condition and the Information Civilization*, Kumarian Press, West Harford, CT, 2000, p. 32.

[4] "The End of European History" was the title of a public lecture delivered at Liverpool University, February 16, 1955; for "the end of European civilisation," see Geoffrey Barraclough, *History in a Changing World*, University of Oklahoma Press, Norman, 1956, P. 205.

[5] Ibid., p. 220.

[6] Geoffrey Barraclough, "Universal History," in H. P. R. Finberg (ed.) *Approaches to History*, University of Toronto Press, Toronto, 1962, p.83–109.

[7] Ibid., The quotes can be found on pp. 91, 92, 99, 99 n, and 100.

[8] A good case in point is the essay by Michael Geyer and Charles Bright, "World History in a Global Age," *American Historical Review*, vol. 100, no. 4, 1995, which concluded that "world history has just begun," p. 1060; the authors affirmed Barraclough's original statement that "we are in an era of world-history."

[9] See my NGH exposition of globality, globalization, periodization, world history, and methodology: "The New Global History: Toward a Narrative for Pangaea Two," *Erwägen Wissen Ethik*, 14, 2003, pp. 75–88; and "Making Progress with Global History," *Erwägen Wissen Ethik*, 2003, pp. 128–35.

[10] G. Büchmann, in *Geflügelte Worte*, Fischer Bücherei, Frankfurt am Main, 1957, p. 165, quoted Roman emperor Julianus Apostata (d.363), oratio VI: "Es dürfe nicht wundernehmen, dass wir zu der, gleich der Wahrheit, einen und einzigen Philosophie

auf den verschiedensten Wegen gelangen. Denn auch wenn einer nach Athen reisen wolle, so könne er dahin segeln oder gehen, und zwar könne er als Wanderer die Heerstrassen benutzen oder die Fusssteige und Richtwege und als Schiffer könne er die Küsten entlang fahren oder wie Nestor das Meer durchschneiden. Damals galt noch Athen als Ziel der Gebildeten; später wurde es Rom." [Regardless of the truth, it should not take miracles to reach the one and only one philosophy, because there may be various paths. For if one wants to travel to Athens (since at the time Athens was still the only destination of intellectuals, later it was Rome), then he should sail or walk. As a hiker he could use the military highway, or the footpath and shortcuts. As a sailor he could travel along the coasts or part the sea as Nestor did].

[11] See Herodotus, *The History* (trans.), David Greene, The University of Chicago Press, Chicago, 1988, p. 4.45: "No one knows whether it is surrounded by water, nor is it known whence came its name or who it was that put the name on it."

[12] Herodotus's *Libya* covered North Africa; *Asia* reached from Turkey to the Indus River.

[13] William H. McNeill, *The Rise of the West: A History of the Human Community*, The University of Chicago Press, Chicago, 1963.

[14] Denys Hay, *Europe: The Emergence of an Idea* (rev. ed.), Edinburgh University Press, Edinburgh, 1968.

[15] The loss of all historical context was captured in *die Stunde Null* (the hour zero), a phrase that was widely used to describe the first couple of years after the defeat of the Nazi Reich.

[16] See my earlier studies, (*Die Unvertraute Moderne: Historische Umrisse einer Anderen Natur- und Sozialgeschichte*. Fischer Wissenschaft, vol. 7356, Fischer Verlag, Frankfurt, 1985) of the historical outlines of an alternative natural and social history around 1840; namely, the possibilities of a "social and ecological technoscience" in Justus Liebig's agricultural chemistry and "collective theory formation from below" in the work of the tailor-philosopher Wilhelm Weitling and his comrades.

[17] In a review of Charles Williams's *Adenauer: The Father of the New Germany*, Gordon Craig wrote: "Williams has a fascinating passage in which he describes Adenauer studying the papal encyclicals *Rerum Novarum* and *Quadragesimo Anno*, which defined the attitude of the Roman Catholic Church toward the social and political questions of the day. Adenauer, he writes, was seeking a theoretical and authoritative underpinning for the practical policies that he intended to espouse in the future. It is clear also that, particularly during the years of Hitler's war, he spent a lot of time thinking about Germany's future, which he was the first to realize must be governed by different principles and policies than in the past." See *New York Review of Books*, vol. 48, no. 17, 2001, p. 20. Adenauer was mayor of Cologne from 1917 to 1933, when he was forced into retirement. In 1949, at age seventy-three, he became the first chancellor of West Germany.

[18] Richard Rhodes, *The Making of the Atomic Bomb*, Simon and Schuster, NY, 1986, p.735.

[19] Barraclough, *History in a Changing World*, p. 204.

[20] Introducing an abridged English edition of Spengler's *Untergang*, Helmut Werner wrote that "Spengler's prophecy that western Europe would lose its world hegemony has been fulfilled. Must Western culture also go under? Is a global culture, to take its

place, even remotely conceivable?" Oswald Spengler, *The Decline of the West*, Modern Library, NY, 1962, p. xiv.

[21] William Whewell et al., *Lectures on the Progress of Arts and Science, Resulting from the Great Exhibition in London, Delivered Before the Society for the Encouragement of Arts, Manufactures, and Commerce, at the Suggestion of H(is) R(Oyal) H(Ighness) Prince Albert, by Dr. Whewell et al*, A. S. Barnes, NY, 1856, pp. 3–25.

[22] Ibid., p. 22.

[23] The first German translation of Horkheimer's *Eclipse of Reason* (see note 24 below) was published in 1967 under the title *Zur Kritik der instrumentellen Vernunft*. As the "Frankfurt School" gained prominence in connection with the movements of 1968, the retranslation of this new German title into English as *Critique of Instrumental Reason* became the international catchphrase for the program of critical theory.

[24] Max Horkheimer, *Eclipse of Reason*, Continuum, NY, [1947] 1992, p. 59.

[25] Ibid., p. 153.

[26] *Eclipse of Reason* was the only book Horkheimer wrote and published in English, Oxford University Press, Oxford, UK, 1947. It was based on five lectures Horkheimer had delivered in Columbia University's Department of Philosophy in February and March of 1944.

[27] *Dialektik der Aufklärung* was completed in California in 1944 and published in Amsterdam in 1947. Horkheimer wrote that book together with Theodor W. Adorno in German; it was dedicated to Friedrich Pollock. Max Horkheimer and Theodore W. Adorno, Dialektik der Aufklarung: Philosophische Fragmente, Querido, Amsterdam, 1947.

[28] Wolf Schäfer, "Stranded at the Crossroads of Dehumanization: John Desmond Bernal and Max Horkheimer." in Seyla Benhabib, Wolfgang Bonss, and John McCole (eds.) *On Max Horkheimer: New Perspectives*, MIT Press, Cambridge, MA, 1993, pp. 153–83.

[29] Horkheimer, *Eclipse of Reason*, 1992, pp. 49, 100.

[30] Few German Jewish intellectuals returned to Germany after the war–Horkheimer, Adorno, and Pollock belonged to this group. The first offer to return to Frankfurt University had reached Horkheimer in 1946. In 1949, he accepted and resumed the professorial chair he had left in 1933. Horkheimer and his associates rebuilt the Institute for Social Research, which reopened in 1950 with Horkheimer at the helm. Horkheimer served as *Rektor* (president) of Frankfurt University from 1951 to 1953; never before in the history of the German university had a Jewish scholar been in that position.

[31] The term "U.S. civilization" might be appropriate, but has yet to surface and may never catch on.

[32] Woody Guthrie, "This Land Is Your Land," recorded during his last commercial session, New York, January 7, 1952.

[33] Two recent publications are significant in this respect: Niall Ferguson, *Empire: The Rise and Demise of the British World Order and the Lessons for Global Power*, Basic Books, NY, 2003, in which Ferguson promotes the British Empire as the historical model for an American empire, and Emmanuel Todd, *Après l'Empire*, Gallimard, Paris, 2002, whose thesis is the imminent "demise" of the American empire. Ferguson, who is British and currently teaching at New York University, wants the United States to move

from "informal" to "formal" empire; Todd, who is French and works at the Institut Nationale d'études Démographiques in Paris, predicts the rise of Europe and the corresponding fall of the U.S. empire. See also an interview with Todd, "Die Schwäche der Sieger: Amerika degeneriert, Europa ist die kommende Macht," in *Die Zeit*, Nr. 18, April 24, 2003, pp. 11.

[34] Quoted from the conference proposal "Globalization, Civil Society and Philanthropy," which is elaborated in the introduction to this volume.

[35] Lynn White's italics; see *Machina Ex Deo: Essays in the Dynamism of Western Culture*, MIT pres, Cambridge, MA, 1968, p. 12. The article "The Changing Canons of Our Culture" (1956), which contained this quote, was reprinted in this collection.

[36] See Lynn White, *Medieval Technology and Social Change*, Oxford University Press, UK, 1962, and Peter Perdue's critique of White's single-factor method, in "Does Technology Drive History?" found in Merritt R. Smith and Leo Marx (eds.) *The Dilemma of Technological Determinism*, MIT Press, Cambridge, MA, 1994, pp. 174–78.

[37] Barraclough, *History in a Changing World*, 1956, p. 217.

[38] Lynn White, *Machina Ex Deo*, 1968, p.11.

[39] Eric Fischer, *The Passing of the European Age: A Study of the Transfer of Western Civilization and Its Renewal in Other Continents*, Harvard University Press, Cambridge, MA, 1943.

[40] Oskar Halecki, *The Limits and Divisions of European History*, Sheed and Ward, London, 1950.

[41] Barraclough, *History in a Changing World*, 1956, p. 206.

[42] Ibid., p. 207.

[43] I have wrestled elsewhere with the problems of global periodization and an appropriate naming of the present age, for a detailed discussion, see Schäfer, "Stranded at the Crossroads of Dehumanization: John Desmond Bernal and Max Horkheimer," in Seyla Benhabib (ed.) *On Max Horkheimer: New Perspective*, MIT Press, Cambridge, MA, 1995, pp. 153–86; Schäfer, "Das 20. Jahrhundert hat gerade erst begonnen: Nach welchen Kriterien kann die Gegenwartsgeschichte periodisiert, kann eine Epoche konstruiert werden?" *DIE ZEIT*, 1996, October 25, P. 56; Schäfer, "The New Global History: Toward a Narrative for Pangaea Two," *Erwägen Wissen Ethik*, 2003, 14, no. 1, pp. 75–88; and Schäfer, "Making Progress with Global History," *Erwägen Wissen Ethik*, 2003, 14, no. 1, pp. 128–35.

[44] Barraclough, "Universal History,"1962, p. 99.

[45] Martin Albrow, *The Global Age: State and Society Beyond Modernity*, Stanford University Press, Stanford, CA, 1997.

[46] "Genetic Code of Human Life Is Cracked by Scientists" proclaimed a full-page headline of the *New York Times*, June 27, 2000, A1.

[47] See "Oceans in Peril," an editorial in the *New York Times*, May 27, 2003, A24. It asked for a new "oceans policy" based on a report in the journal *Nature* (which had found that "nine-tenths of the world's biggest and most economically important species of fish" had been wiped out by "mechanized fishing fleets" in the previous fifty years).

[48] See "Today's Visions of the Science of Tomorrow," *New York Times*, January 4, 2003, A11. The respondents had been asked to imagine that they had been nominated for White House science adviser.

[49] When we read, "There was no such thing as the Scientific Revolution, and this is a book about it" (S. Shapin, *Scientific Revolution*, University of Chicago Press, Chicago, 1998, p. 1), we are made aware of the timelag between a historical concept like the Scientific Revolution and Robert Boyle's experiments, for instance. However, when we research contemporary history, we must try to catch up with history running.

[50] My version of global history does not work with the conventional notion of civilization and culture. I am using *civilization* for the human transformations of first and second nature and *culture* for the symbologically mediated interactions with our own kind. See my essays "Global Civilization and Local Cultures: A Crude Look at the Whole," *International Sociology*, 16, no.3, September: 2001, pp. 301–19; and "The New Global History: Toward a Narrative for Pangaea Two."

PHILANTHROPY AND GLOBALIZATION DURING THE COLD WAR ERA

Chapter 3

THE ROLE OF AMERICAN PHILANTHROPIC FOUNDATIONS IN INDIA'S ROAD TO GLOBALIZATION DURING THE COLD WAR ERA

Gary R. Hess

In his inaugural address of January 20, 1949, President Harry S. Truman announced "a bold new program for making the benefits of our scientific advances and industrial progress available for the improvement and growth of underdeveloped areas."[1] What soon became known as the Point Four Program reflected an emerging consensus among the foreign policy elite that the United States needed to identify with and support the aspirations of the "emerging peoples." The Marshall Plan was demonstrating the capacity of the United States to rebuild war-torn Europe, strengthening democratic governments, and countering the influence of the Soviet Union. Asia now loomed as the critical area in the Cold War. As Truman spoke, the communists held the ascendancy in the Chinese civil war and their subsequent victory meant that the United States needed to demonstrate the capacity of Western liberal ideas and institutions to meet the political and economic problems of the newly independent nations—India, Pakistan, Ceylon, Burma, the Philippines—and to appeal to the nationalists fighting for independence in Indochina and Indonesia.

*****

The major foundations quickly joined in the struggle for Asia. The leadership of both the Rockefeller Foundation and the Ford Foundation believed that expanding their international missions was critical to the nation's interest. At Rockefeller, the board of trustees saw the foundation challenged by the "successful [communist] scheme for development," which necessitated supporting a "broader program of developing the resources, material and human, of the underdeveloped areas." At Ford, the Gaither Committee, which charted the foundation's future in its 1949 report, identified "the improvement of the standard of living and economic status of peoples throughout the world" as vital to alleviating conditions that fostered communism. Both foundations named leaders who had held prominent international positions in the Truman administration. Paul Hoffman became Ford's director (the title later being changed to

51

president) in November 1950, bringing to that position prestige earned in the private and public sectors as an efficient and imaginative executive. Hoffman had been president of the Studebaker Motor Corporation for thirteen years when President Truman in 1948 named him head of the Economic Cooperation Administration, which implemented the Marshall Plan. Once at Ford, Hoffman emphasized the foundation's commitment to "the relief of tensions in underdeveloped areas." In early 1952, Dean Rusk became Rockefeller's president after a decade of military and diplomatic experience, most recently as assistant secretary of state for Far Eastern affairs. Advising the foundation's trustees that political and economic developments in Asia, Africa, and Latin America would determine the world's fate in the latter half of the twentieth century, Rusk urged that the foundation "accept a responsibility for doing what it can to assist these countries to erect free societies, a task which is crucial to the purpose of the foundation itself."[2]

As they carried their new missions to Asia, the foundations were drawn principally to India, which, in the aftermath of the communist revolution in China, Americans regarded as the "essential democracy." India was seen as a critical test of the capacity of a democratic state to address the challenge of economic and social development. The performances of the Indian and Chinese economies, it was assumed, would affect the attitudes of peoples throughout the developing world toward communism and democracy. This sense of India's importance led Congress, at the urging of the Truman administration, to pass the Indian Emergency Assistance Act—which marked the first direct U.S. assistance to India.[3] Yet food aid was no substitute for development and India, despite its enormous problems, seemed a promising, as well as necessary, focus of assistance. Americans found that Prime Minister Jawaharlal Nehru's stature domestically and internationally, the political dominance of the Congress Party, an established civil administration, and a relatively advanced infrastructure gave India a degree of stability that was lacking in many newly independent countries. Moreover, the government of India was committed to a program of development, and Nehru and other Indian leaders recognized the necessity of Western assistance in their ambitious plans.

This congruence of American and Indian interests fostered India's continuing incorporation into the process of globalization. Newly independent India drew upon political and economic institutions and practices that had been introduced by the British and which oriented India to the West. The Indian elite, many of whom had been educated in England and who had led the nationalist movement, was committed to building a secular, liberal democracy and regarded close economic ties to the West as essential to the country's progress. As Americans approached India, they represented the tradition of "liberal developmentalism," which assumed that their political and economic development provided a model for other peoples and that the spread of their culture and political and economic institutions would benefit mankind. During World War I, Woodrow Wilson's "liberal internationalism" broadened this tradition into the vision of a new international order with the United States fostering an economically and politically interdependent world within a structure of democratic states and international institutions. Wilsonianism, as "liberal internationalism" is often called, thus identified American interests with a far-reaching transformation that would later be labeled globalization. Among the post–World War II American foreign policy elite, the collapse of international order in the 1930s demonstrated the need for a renewed liberal internationalism, and that commitment was reinforced by the imperatives of the Cold War. Thus, American foundations, as well as other institutions engaged in waging the struggle against communism in the developing world, were agents of liberal developmentalism and globalization.[4]

*****

Modernization theory addressed the question of how the United States could foster nonrevolutionary, pro-Western change in the developing world. True to the tradition of liberal developmentalism, early modernization thinking assumed that the American model could be easily transferred. The Massachusetts Institute of Technology's Center for International Studies (MIT-CIS), which was established in 1951 and generously supported by the Ford Foundation, was instrumental in the emergence of the field of developmental economics. Under the leadership of Max Millikan, who had earlier been the director of economic research at the Central Intelligence Agency, MIT-CIS emphasized "the application of basic social science research to problems of U.S. policy in the current world struggle" with "the ultimate aim of . . . the production of an alternative to Marxism."[5] Walt W. Rostow, who became MIT-CIS's most renowned economist, foresaw American-guided development as "a potentially constructive outlet for nationalism, a social solvent, a matrix for the development of new leadership, a means for generating . . . confidence in the democratic process" which would yield "in two or three decades . . . a preponderance of stable, effective, and democratic societies [that would] give the best promise of a favorable settlement of the cold war and peaceful, progressive environment." Rostow's influential *The Stages of Economic Growth: A Non-Communist Manifesto* (1960) offered a classic expression of the buoyant expectation that the Western experience provided a model to guide orderly change in the Third World. Rostow confidently asserted that the "tricks of growth are not all that difficult"—indeed, the "tricks" had already been perfected in the West.[6]

While sharing assumptions about their missions in the Cold War and representing the buoyant expectations of liberal developmentalism, the Rockefeller and Ford foundations at midcentury were very different institutions. The Rockefeller Foundation, established in 1913, was an established international philanthropy whose work in medical education, public health, and agricultural research had earned wide respect. It felt the turmoil of the postwar world directly, for the communist victory in China severed the foundation's considerable work in that country, including the Peking Union Medical College—perhaps its most renowned overseas enterprise. In contrast, the Ford Foundation was just emerging from modest local origins into the wealthiest and most ambitious American philanthropy. Its assets in 1951 were valued at $437 million, nearly four times that of Rockefeller. Hoffman's leadership embodied the Ford Foundation's wide-ranging mission; as one associate observed, "Hoffman was . . . just full of the idea that this was going to be the greatest thing in the world, that American philanthropy was finally going to be riding very high and be very important in American affairs."[7]

Reflecting on foundation programs, Francis X. Sutton of the Ford Foundation once remarked that "foundations are constantly scrutinizing the landscape to find directions in which they have a comparative advantage."[8] That described their entry into India. The question was not whether to support Indian development, but how the foundations could identify niches, where their efforts would be supportive, but not duplicative, of the work of the government of India, the Technical Cooperation Administration (TCA), which administered Point Four assistance, or international agencies. The interaction of each of the foundations with American and Indian officials was thus a political process, one that typically began with identification of a project of potential collaboration and continued with negotiation of the foundation's role.

The leadership of the Ford and Rockefeller foundations soon discovered that their interests and expertise could profitably build upon the extent to which Indian officials and scientists regarded the United States as a model of agricultural and rural development. Two American-led enterprises in India had demonstrated the adaptability of American ideas and practices. The Allahabad Agricultural Institute, founded by the missionary Sam Higginbottom in 1910, had long been recognized as a center of practical agricultural education and rural development; indeed, it had received generous personal support over the years from John D. Rockefeller Jr. A more recent undertaking was the Etawah Project, spearheaded by the American city planner, Albert Mayer. Strongly supported by Nehru and financed by the Uttar Pradesh state government, the Etawah Project brought together a small group of Americans and Indians in a program of rural development in north-central India. By the early 1950s, Mayer and his associates were widely credited with having increased agricultural production and facilitating economic and social reform.[9]

The movement of Ford and Rockefeller into India reflected their differing cultures. Nowhere was Hoffman's irrepressible optimism more evident than in his initiatives in India. Shortly after taking office, Hoffman asked Madame Vijayalakshmi Pandit, India's ambassador to the United States and Nehru's sister, if he might visit India to discuss Ford involvement in the country's development. His action built upon earlier foundation contacts with the State Department, which welcomed private programs as a means of demonstrating to Indians the widespread American interest in their country. In August 1951, Hoffman headed a mission that visited several Asian countries, but its focus was India. The Hoffman Mission's arrival in New Delhi was timely, for the government of India's Planning Commission had just completed the draft First Five Year Plan.[10] A major objective was a substantial increase in agricultural production, which, it was recognized, "could [not] have any chance of success unless the millions of small farmers in the country accepted its objectives, shared in its making, regarded it as their own and were prepared to make the sacrifices necessary for implementing it."[11]

Rural development became the focus of discussion between the Hoffman Mission and Indian officials. The Ford representatives were fascinated by the proposed Community Development Program. To Hoffman and his associates, nothing less than the future of Asia was at stake, for communists were exploiting the restlessness of the masses and the country's "desperate problems." The Etawah Project was demonstrating the potential of rural development, and Hoffman proclaimed that "there is no reason why all 500,000 of India's villages could not make a similar advance." A commitment to India's rural development, the Hoffman Mission believed, would enable that country to avoid China's fate. Hoffman wrote that had there been a comparable program in China ten years earlier, the result "would have been a China completely immunized against the appeal of the Communists. India, in my opinion, is today what China was in 1945."[12] Hoffman and his associates met with Nehru and other officials as well as leading private sector industrialists. At a dinner in New Delhi, Finance Minister C. D. Deshmukh reportedly stated that because of Hoffman's initiative and imaginative ideas, no other foreign mission "[had been] receive[ed] with any greater enthusiasm."[13] This collaboration between the foundation and the government of India was enthusiastically supported by Ambassador Chester Bowles, who became an ardent supporter of the Community Development Program.

Hoffman moved quickly. He appointed Douglas Ensminger as the Ford representative to India. A sociologist with experience in the extension service of the U.S. Department of Agriculture (USDA), Ensminger, at the time of his Ford appointment, headed the Extension, Education, and Training Division of the Office of Foreign Agricultural Relations, which was responsible for foreign extension programs under Point Four. Ensminger was in many ways a younger version of Hoffman. Combining the vision of a bold American role in transforming India with shrewd political instincts, Ensminger was destined to remain in India for nineteen years. By the time that Ensminger established the foundation's New Delhi office in January 1952, the board of trustees had approved grants totaling $3,725,000 over three years for the support for village development projects (as part of the government of India's Community Development Program, which was formally launched in October 1952) and the training of agricultural leaders at the Allahabad Agricultural Institute and other schools.[14]

As the Ford Foundation moved quickly into India, the Rockefeller Foundation cautiously explored means of broadening its role in the country. Beginning in 1920, Rockefeller had engaged in medical and public health work in India and in 1935 had established a permanent office in New Delhi.[15] Much of the prewar public health work was taken over by official agencies, but in the early 1950s, the foundation undertook a malaria control program in the state of Mysore and funded the Virus Research Center in Poona in cooperation with the Indian Council of Medical Research. During the early 1950s, the foundation's expenditures in India steadily increased, mostly in support of programs, research, and training in public health and medicine. In addition, the foundation funded some programs and research in the humanities and social sciences and two substantial grants on behalf of rural development: $150,000 for equipment to the Allahabad Agricultural Institute and $35,000 for the Rural Research and Action Center to the state of Uttar Pradesh.[16]

In late 1951, the Rockefeller Foundation sent a mission to Asia, but, as with the earlier Hoffman Mission, India was the focus. Headed by Warren Weaver, the director of the Division of Natural Sciences and Agriculture, the Rockefeller Mission included J. George Harrar, the deputy director for agriculture who had headed the renowned Mexican Agricultural Program (MAP), and Paul G. Mangelsdorf, a specialist in plant genetics and breeding with experience in the MAP.[17] The Weaver Mission quickly ruled out involvement in the Community Development Program, which it found was being led by "earnest and deeply sincere" men who were being thrust "into positions of tremendous responsibility for which they are unequipped, intellectually or in any other way." Skeptical of many aspects of the Five Year Plan, the Weaver Mission foresaw "a long future of slow improvement" rather than expecting India's problems to be "solved in some brisk Western tempo." It found two areas—research on improved varieties of food grains and reform of university-level agricultural education—in which the foundation's capabilities and experience seemed to coalesce with India's needs. They found that Indian scientists wanted to explore whether the MAP's success in developing improved varieties of food grains could be duplicated in their country.[18] The areas of potential collaboration identified in the Weaver Mission were explored further by a series of Rockefeller missions over the next four years.[19] After considerable discussion with Indian officials and with TCA functioning as a middleman, the Rockefeller Foundation in 1956 launched the Indian Agricultural Program (IAP), which focused on the development of the Indian Agricultural Research Institute (IARI) in New Delhi into the national center of graduate education and research on high-yielding varieties (HYV) of food grains.[20] The board of trustees already had approved a preliminary grant of $100,000 for the IAP, with the understanding that it might cost up to $350,000 annually.[21] This new mission of the Rockefeller Foundation in India paralleled its expanded role in other parts of Asia, including Japan, where similar Cold War objectives were applied in a different setting, an aspect of cultural expansion that is analyzed by Victoria Lyon Bestor in this volume.

By the time that the Rockefeller Foundation was launching the IAP, the Ford Foundation had been operating in India for nearly five years and expending far greater resources than Rockefeller was contemplating. As envisioned by the Hoffman Mission, Ford made a major commitment to the Community Development Program through grants totaling approximately $4.4 million between 1952 and 1955. It supported fifteen pilot extension projects, each covering about one hundred villages and fifty thousand people, and the training of village level workers at five extension training centers. The pilot projects were deemed sufficiently successful to be merged into a national extension service midway through the First Five Year Plan. The expansion of the Community Development Program necessitated more village-level workers (VLW) who were considered the key to success, so the number of training centers increased to thirty-four by 1955. Ford also broadened its commitment to the rural areas through the support, in the amount of some $1.5 million, of village industries. Beyond these initiatives centered in rural areas, the Ford Foundation also moved into the support of public administration. In conversations with Ensminger, Nehru spoke of the importance of well-trained government personnel in implementing development programs, and this led to two Ford-funded missions headed by Paul Appleby, the dean of the Maxwell School at Syracuse University. When Indian officials endorsed Appleby's recommendations, the Ford Foundation provided $350,000 toward the establishment of the Indian Institute of Public Administration. In 1955, the foundation also made a $2.3 million grant in support of secondary and higher education.[22] These substantial commitments and the breadth of the projects reflected Ford's success, which was largely a tribute to Ensminger's political skills, in winning the confidence of Nehru and other Indian leaders, who came to see the foundation as an important instrument of development. In Bowles' *Ambassador's Report*, published in 1954, the former ambassador praised the work of the foundation:

> Someday someone must give the American people a full report of the work of the Ford Foundation in India. The several million dollars in total Ford expenditures in the country do not tell one-tenth of the story. Under the leadership of Douglas Ensminger, the Ford staff in India became closely associated with the Planning Commission, which administers the Five Year Plan. Wherever there was a gap, they filled it, whether it agricultural, health education or administration. They took over, financed and administered the crucial village-level training schools. Their kind of straightforward service is in the finest traditions of our country.[23]

When Rockefeller's concentrated program was added to Ford's diverse efforts in community development, public administration, and education, the two foundations became the principal agents of private American support for Indian development. Both benefited from effective leadership. In 1957, Rockefeller appointed Ralph Cummings as director of IAP, and, like Ensminger, he quickly earned the respect of Indian colleagues. The forty-six-year-old Cummings, who held a doctorate in soil science, had taught at

Cornell University and North Carolina State University and had served most recently on an agricultural research mission in Peru. Cummings and Ensminger, who directed their foundations' programs in India until 1968 and 1971, respectively, were arguably the most influential Americans in India during the heyday of American involvement in the country's development, which stretched through the early 1970s.[24]

Ensminger and Cummings headed substantial missions. Ford's New Delhi office was its first overseas and, even as others were established, it remained by far the largest overseas office of any foundation. At its peak in 1966–1967, the Ford office in India was staffed by 72 American professionals and an administrative and technical corps of 177 Indian nationals, 63 other fulltime employees, plus 16 foreign employees of institutions being supported by the foundation. Although dwarfed by the Ford operation, the 13 Rockefeller Foundation personnel assigned to IAP made it by the mid-1960s second in size only to the foundation's agricultural program in Colombia.[25]

The foundations' expanded effort in India reflected their greater overseas ambitions as they defined their missions for the "development decade" of the 1960s—a Western-inspired term that saw the Cold War competition in the Third World at its critical stage. The foundations' leadership committed more resources and envisioned bolder initiatives in the Third World. With the approval of its board of trustees in 1962, the Ford Foundation updated the goals of the Gaither Report and emphasized the importance of expanded international programs in the 1960s; thus Ford's assistance for overseas development increased from about $15 million a year during the 1950s to approximately $50 million annually from 1963 to 1970. The same year that Ford outlined its new objectives, the Rockefeller board of trustees, in anticipation of the foundation's fiftieth anniversary in 1963, established a committee to chart guidelines for its future. The ensuing report proposed greater emphasis to projects in the developing countries, and the foundation restructured its programs to address five problems: world hunger, population pressures, university development in developing countries, equal opportunity, and cultural development.

*****

The foundations' most significant impact in India was their contribution to the Americanization of Indian agricultural and rural development. At IARI, Cummings built on the support of key officials and younger American-educated scientists who recognized the need for a radical transformation of agricultural education. Cummings proposed a broadly based curriculum with emphasis on problem solving, comprehensive examinations, and research, which marked a radical departure from the traditional Anglo-Indian system's emphasis on a standardized curriculum, rote learning, and external examinations. A system of merit replaced seniority as the principal criterion in selecting and promoting staff. Gaining unusually quick support from Indian agencies for funding and staffing, Cummings was able to open the IARI Post-Graduate School on October 1, 1958. The University Grants Commission, in a move unusual both in terms of policy and spontaneity, granted IARI university status. The Rockefeller Foundation appropriated $100,000 to improve the IARI library. Cummings was instrumental in the development of the school, serving as IARI acting dean in 1959–1960, and in agricultural education nationally, chairing the Agricultural Universities Commission.[26]

As the Rockefeller Foundation was launching the IAP, the Ford Foundation was undertaking its most ambitious rural development program. Poor crop yields in 1957–

1958, combined with evidence of accelerating population growth, led the Indian government officials to request Ford Foundation assistance in expanding food production. In early 1959, a twelve-person Ford Foundation team, representing various specializations, visited India and within three months completed *The Food Crisis Report*, which argued for the adoption of improved varieties of crops and technology as they became available and the establishment of a pilot Intensive Agricultural District Program (IADP)[27] In response to a request by the government of India for assistance in launching the IADP, a second Ford team recommended a "package of practices" pilot program, designed to provide educational, technical, and service assistance to achieve "adoption breakthrough." The pilot program was launched in 1960, with Ford providing financial assistance and a team of ten advisory consultants. It was an ambitious project, beginning with one district in each of seven states and reaching over a million farmers. In 1962, IADP was expanded to fifteen districts. By then it was reaching a total of 2.6 million farms, 7.6 million farmworkers, and a rural population of 23 million. IADP officers faced a formidable challenge of extending yield-increasing "packages" for crops, attracting farmers into the program, and getting supplies and credit available to participating farmers. This required coordinating individual village's needs with various agencies and working closely with VLW. While IADP had numerous problems, early studies showed that by 1966–1967 production of rice and wheat in IADP districts had increased significantly more than in non-IADP districts in the same states.[28]

The potential for the IADP was related to Rockefeller's HYV crop research, which in the late 1960s would be introduced into IADP districts. As had been planned, Rockefeller research initially concentrated on the maize program, but soon it expanded into millets, wheat, and rice, which were India's three leading food crops. Extensive experimentation led to promising HYV of maize, millets, and wheat, and Cummings lobbied the Ministry of Food and Agriculture to permit introduction of experimental varieties of those crops.[29]

Rice was, by far, the leading food crop—twice as many tons were produced as the millets and wheat combined. Its importance extended beyond India. Traditional production in most parts of Asia was expensive and inefficient; the overriding need was for higher-quality production at reduced cost. Meeting this challenge was seen as important geopolitically; as early as 1951, the economist John King, writing in *Foreign Affairs*, argued that improving rice production was instrumental to winning the Cold War in Asia. Beginning with the Weaver Mission, Rockefeller officials had recognized the imperative of a rice program. By the late 1950s, Ford Foundation officials had also become convinced of the need to address rice production. Harrar, after becoming Rockefeller's president in 1961, and F. F. Hill, vice president for international programs at Ford, were instrumental in building support within their respective foundations for the jointly sponsored International Rice Research Institute (IRRI) that was established at the University of the Philippines. In 1960, Robert Chandler, formerly of the MAP, who had been involved in planning Rockefeller's Asian rice program since 1954, became director of IRRI, and research involving scientists from six Asian countries went forward.[30] IRRI researchers harvested the first experimental crops in 1962. Two years later, Chandler reported that the "rice-breeding program . . . shows promise of developing within the next two years high-yielding, nitrogen-responding varieties . . . [that] are expected to have wide adaptability on well-managed soils throughout the rice-growing regions of the tropics and, if generally used, could increase greatly in the total production of rice."[31]

As promising HYV of rice was developed and greater progress was also made on HYV of wheat, Cummings drew upon the foundation's credibility to gain the support of the agriculture minister, Chidambaram Subramaniam, for introducing new varieties of those crops on an experimental basis. This came at a difficult time in Indo-American relations, for President Lyndon Johnson was conditioning official aid on India's willingness to give greater priority to agricultural production. Dependence on food imports thus became a sensitive political issue, as was any suggestion that Indian agricultural policy was being dictated by the United States. In 1965, India experienced its most severe drought of the twentieth century, resulting in a 20 percent decline in grain production and increasing the need for food imports under the PL-480 program. Johnson adopted a controversial "short-tether" allocation of food aid for the avowed purpose of pressuring India to adopt agricultural reforms. Collaboration with Rockefeller on the introduction of HYV grains clearly served India's needs, but political undercurrents, exacerbated by the short-tether policy, made it difficult for Subramaniam to take advantage of this advance. He encountered resistance from bureaucrats who feared that they would lose control of research and extension, leftists who charged that he was succumbing to American pressure, economists who warned that larger farmers would be the only beneficiaries of HYV of crops, and officials of the Planning Commission and Food and Agriculture Ministry who questioned the cost of importing the needed additional fertilizers. Yet spurred by the support of younger scientists, Subramanian convinced Prime Minister Lal Bahadur Shastri (and after his unexpected death in early 1966, his successor, Indira Gandhi) that the HYV semi-dwarf wheat and rice promised the most immediate means of gaining agricultural self-sufficiency and ending the dependence on food imports. That was a powerful, indeed almost irresistible, argument; as a result, the improved varieties of wheat and rice were introduced on a large scale.[32] The Green Revolution thus came to India, and, although not without problems, it did lead to the country's capacity to feed its people.

In 1951, Nehru famously remarked that "we produce more and more food, but we also produce more and more children. I wish we produced fewer children."[33] Nehru's comment underlined the relationship of development and population—a problem that by midcentury was attracting the concern of number of scholars and philanthropists, notably John D. Rockefeller 3rd, as well as private agencies. The foundations' role in the population field was more cautious than in agricultural policy, but they influenced the acceptance of population growth as a public policy issue and the development of research and contraceptive programs.

India symbolized the problem of overpopulation. Popular culture in the West, as well as scholarly works dating to the time of Malthus, had long portrayed India as a tradition-bound, chaotic, and overcrowded society. It was thus fitting that India would be at the center of the movement to study and address what was later described as "the population bomb."[34]

Indians had long been concerned about the ramifications of population growth. During the struggle for independence, Nehru and others, including a number of women's groups, advocated limiting population growth. Even before the famous visit of Margaret Sanger in 1935, birth control clinics had been established by a number of Indian physicians. After independence, population control became an even greater imperative, especially when the census of 1951 revealed that India's population had reached 360,000,000. Nehru was distressed by projections that the population would reach 520,000,000 by 1980. Under his leadership, India became the first state to adopt a policy of reducing population growth. While there was no strong cultural or religious tradition of opposition to birth control, some followers of Mohandas Gandhi were committed to his anticontraceptive teachings. The minister of health, Rajkumari Amrit Kaur, a Gandhian follower, used her influence to deflect early efforts at national family planning, stating that the government of India would not support artificial means of birth control. So there was little progress on family planning; besides the opposition of the Health Ministry, it also suffered from limited funding in the first two Five Year Plans and the lack of external support.

Despite increased international attention to population problems after World War II, official and private agencies approached the issue cautiously. The opposition of the Catholic Church to family planning and a general reluctance to deal with what was widely considered a matter of privacy limited public discussion, let alone funding. During the prewar period, small foundations, notably the Scripps Foundation and the Milbank Memorial Fund, had supported population research. The *Milbank Quarterly* became the most important source of population studies and Milbank also financed the establishment in 1936 of the Office of Population Research at Princeton University, with Frank Notestein becoming its director. The Rockefeller Foundation's early focus on public health research led it to support demographic and reproductive biology research, including grants to the Scripps Foundation and the Office of Population Research. Beginning in the late 1940s, its annual reports called attention to population issues, but in cautious and inoffensive language; for instance, the 1954 report talked of the "so-called population problem" and justified the support of demographic research because of its "important implications . . . about a large number of social needs" and its contribution to "consultation among different disciplines which seem to be working on different aspects of a larger problem—the ecological relation of man to his natural environment and the political and economic action he takes to improve his position."[35]

John D. Rockefeller 3rd, however, undertook initiatives to counter the prevailing reluctance to address the population issue directly. Long concerned with the problem of overpopulation, he sent a team of researchers to study public health and demography in six Asian countries (the Philippines, Indonesia, Japan, China, Korea, and Taiwan) in 1948. The ensuing report stressed the importance of systematic attention to the population issue, but it recommended "study rather than action in the years immediately ahead."[36] Still determined to force greater attention to the issue and spurred by Nehru's announcement of a family planning program, Rockefeller 3rd in 1952 organized a population conference at Williamsburg, Virginia, which devoted much attention to India's problems. Led by Notestein, who had been part of the Asian mission four years earlier, the Williamsburg conferees proposed the establishment of a separate foundation devoted solely to the population issue. At the same time, family planning groups around the world were becoming more active. Representatives of the family planning associations of eight countries met in Bombay in the summer of 1952 and established the International Planned Parent Federation.

In response to the call from the Williamsburg conference, Rockefeller established the Population Council in November 1952. Beginning with its founder's personal funding, the Population Council emphasized scientific research as a means of stimulating awareness of population issues and forcing assessment of policy options. It became the center of population work in the United States, supporting research and surveys, training demographers and biomedical scientists, and gradually moving into the design of family planning programs. Besides Rockefeller's personal support, the Population Council received the bulk of its funds from the Ford Foundation (approximately $300,000 per year) and, after 1958, the Rockefeller Foundation. Beginning in 1954, the Population Council supported demographic research in India through fellowships to Indian and American scholars.[37]

In New Delhi, Ensminger was frustrated by the reluctance of Ford Foundation officers in New York to provide direct support of population programs and the resistance of Ministry of Health to family planning. He did, however, play the role of a middleman in helping to arrange a Population Council mission to India in 1955. Amrit Kaur, who was under pressure to modify her opposition to birth control, asked Ensminger for assistance in bringing consultants who could advise her on developing a national policy. This led to a Population Council mission comprised of Notestein and Leona Baumgartner, a renowned public health physician who was commissioner of the New York City Department of Health, to study ways of addressing the population problem. Their recommendations, embodied in a report titled *Suggestions for a Practical Program of Family Planning and Child Care*, helped to persuade Amrit Kaur to support the establishment of a national Family Planning Board and the Demographic Training and Research Centre in Bombay, which was jointly funded by the Indian government and the Population Council. Ever since the Hoffman Mission of 1951, Nehru had talked about a major Ford Foundation role in family planning. In 1957, as resistance within his government lessened, Nehru formally requested Ford support, but, despite Ensminger's prodding, the foundation's board deferred action for two years.[38]

Then, in 1959, the Ford Foundation dramatically moved to the forefront of population work. The move was timely, for that same year the World Council of Churches endorsed birth control measures to counter the fear of a worldwide population explosion. Moreover, the Draper Committee, appointed by President Dwight D. Eisenhower to study U.S. overseas assistance programs, recommended the allocation of assistance funds for "practical" programs of "maternal and child welfare"—a euphemism for birth control. Public opinion polls showed a shift toward acceptance of a government role in family planning. The 1958 book *Population Growth and Economic Development in Low-Income Countries: A Case Study of India's Prospects,* by Ansley Coale and Edgar Hoover, presented a strong case for overpopulation as a principal burden to development and drew attention to India's problems in particular. Their argument was straightforward: investment in family planning would increase national income over time more than any other development expenditure.[39]

As the influential Coale and Hoover book underscored, India remained central to the growing international attention to family planning. In his February 1959 address to the Sixth International Conference on Planned Parenthood, which was held in New Delhi, Nehru spoke of the shortcomings of India's family planning efforts and the need for a greater commitment. Having decided in 1959 that it could no longer ignore the population issue, the Ford Foundation's board of trustees moved quickly. It expanded support of the Population Council with a $1.4 million grant and undertook programs overseas. In August 1959, the foundation finally moved into family planning in India with a grant of $330,000 to the Indian Ministry of Health as the first phase of a five-year commitment to the Family Planning Communications and Action Research (FPCAR) program. As the board of trustees committed the foundation to "breakthroughs on the problem of population control," administrative changes soon reflected new priorities, with the Population Program (later Population Office) established in 1963. The Rockefeller Foundation also assumed a greater role in the area; indeed, the fiftieth anniversary redefinition of its mission included among its five priority problems "the development of knowledge and experience to bring about the reduction of the growth rate of the world's population and its eventual stabilization." By that time, Ford, Rockefeller, and the Population Council were at the center of a steadily growing international population movement.[40]

The Ford Foundation influenced population work in India in a number of important ways. It supported FPCAR, which had the objective of motivating Indians to make greater use of the fifteen hundred government-operated family planning clinics that had been established during the previous decade. The strategy employed by FPCAR grew out of the collaboration between Dr. Moye Freymann of the Ford Foundation office in New Delhi and Lieutenant Colonel B. L. Raina, the head of family planning in the Ministry of Health. Ford supported FPCAR principally by bringing American consultants to India and funding fellowships for Indians to study public health in the United States. While Freymann was frequently frustrated by bureaucratic resistance to FPCAR's efforts to promote change, he was instrumental in FPCAR's most important regional success at the private Gandhigram Institute of Rural Health in southern India. Support from FPCAR enabled the institute (which later added "and Family Planning" to its name) to promote family planning in its district, leading to a significant birthrate decrease over the next decade. The Institute also became a center of studies on factors affecting acceptance of contraceptive practices.

Indian government officials, as well as representative of external private and official agencies, recognized the need for a more comprehensive program. Ensminger, Freymann, and public health consultants brought to India by Ford worked with the Planning Commission in formulating an expansion of family planning that involved sending thousands of educators, medical personnel, family welfare workers, contraceptive distributors, and others into the rural areas. The Third Five Year Plan (1961–1966) increased funding for family planning tenfold over that in the second plan. The IADP model was evident in the plan for nineteen intensive family planning districts.

To Ensminger, Ford's experience with the IADP gave it the opportunity to foster a breakthrough in family planning. In 1962, he requested $12 million to support an "integrated population program," which would focus on "strengthening the administrative foundation of the family planning program" and supporting "more fundamental knowledge of biological, demographic, and communications factors relating to human fertility." Besides support for the pilot project of nineteen intensive family planning districts, the "integrated population program" included funding two new institutions: the National Institute of Health Administration and Education (NIHAE), which was to coordinate the intensive district program and to provide in-service training as well as graduate work in health education and administration; and the Central Family Planning Institute (CFPI), which was to consolidate and coordinate a variety of family planning functions under different agencies. It took two years before the board of trustees, despite urgent pleas from Ensminger, finally acted on the request. And when it did so in June 1964, it reduced the allocation to $5 million, with $3 million designated for the intensive family planning districts. The reduced Ford commitment necessitated scaling back the intensive family planning district plan, which was also undermined by opposition from within the Ministry of Health. A part of the program went forward, but its potential was never tested.[41]

In the end, Ford's most important contribution to family planning was its support of reproductive research. The foundation brought to India Dr. Sheldon Segal, assistant medical director of the Population Council, and Dr. Anna L. Southam, a reproductive researcher on leave from the Columbia University School of Medicine; they led the development of reproductive research at the All-India Institute of Medical Sciences. In 1962 and 1963, Ford provided $1.7 million in grants to support research and training activities at ten Indian institutions. The largest grant supported the All-Institute of Medical Sciences for research on improved methods of reproductive biology and contraception. In the mid-1960s, Ford consultants enthusiastically promoted the intrauterine device (IUD), which had become an effective means of contraception in Taiwan and Korea but had not been widely adopted in India. With United Nations agencies and the Indian Medical Research Council also endorsing the IUD, S. Chandrasekhar, a renowned demographer whom Prime Minister Indira Gandhi placed in charge of health and family planning, endorsed an ambitious program to promote IUD contraception. The Ford Foundation contributed to a public relations campaign to promote family planning and a program to spread the use of contraceptive devices. Whatever the shortcomings of its efforts, the Ford Foundation had played a significant role in India's emergence as a major center of contraceptive research and in the wider adoption of contraceptive devices by the 1970s.[42]

Reflecting on Ensminger's vision for a major Ford impact on birth control policy, it is evident in retrospect that it was frustrated by his inability to gain support from New York during what turned out to be a relatively brief period of opportunity for a Ford Foundation initiative. Moving into this area in India on a large scale in 1959, the foundation and other private agencies were building on the greater public acceptance of such work, but soon that political change would lead to far larger government programs. The U.S. government, through the Agency for International Development (AID), began population work in 1966 and became India's dominant donor agency. During that interlude, Ensminger's ambitious plans were subject to close scrutiny by Ford officials in New York, which in itself was indicative of increased resistance to his visions of a seemingly boundless role for the foundation in India. So it took more than two years before the board of trustees acted on his "integrated population program" proposal and then reduced the funding by more than 50 percent. On the other side, Ensminger often moved too quickly for the Indians. For instance, he brought eighteen American population specialists to India, many having been recruited before their positions and the role of their Indian counterparts had been defined. Even Ensminger conceded that some consultants "simply floated around creating more problems than the rest of us could cope with."[43] Ensminger also tarnished the foundation's image among Indians by his overselling support for the integrated population program. Disagreements over family planning priorities led to a good deal of bitterness in the relations between foundation and government officers, leading to the government of India's termination of Ford consultants' contracts in 1971.[44]

*****

By the early 1970s, the foundations began scaling back their overseas programs. This reflected changes both in thinking about development and in institutional priorities. The optimism of the "development decade" faded, as political instability and economic stagnation in much of the Third World raised questions about the value of assistance programs and their underlying assumptions. A World Bank report of 1970 concluded that the prevailing development doctrines concealed the imbalance between the "one third of the world . . . pulling steadily ahead, leaving the remainder of mankind in relative poverty, in many cases to live without clean water, education, basic medical facilities or adequate housing."[45] Francis X. Sutton of the Ford Foundation observed that "there is growing doubt that we know what to do to bring about development. . . . We are less confident than we once were that the social sciences or tested practice offer ready means of dealing with [underdevelopment]."[46] Mahbub ul Haq's influential 1976 book, *The Poverty Curtain: Choices for the Third World*, criticized Western-led development for the priority given to GNP growth and the indifference to poverty; the director of the Policy Planning and Program Review Department of the World Bank, Haq called for an enlarged commitment to assistance that would be based on a dialogue between donors and recipients.[47] Thus, in the 1970s, priority in assistance programs changed—now the emphasis was meeting "basic human needs" of Third World peoples.

The reduced international role of the foundations also reflected pressures on their resources resulting from inflation and a decline in capital markets and their leaderships' decision to give greater emphasis given to compelling domestic problems. At the Rockefeller Foundation, Dr. John H. Knowles, who succeeded Harrar as president in 1972, spearheaded a reduction of international commitments and a reorientation of remaining overseas programs to focus on social issues.[48] This shift in priorities coincided with the leadership's conclusion in 1972 that IAP had had achieved its objectives and should be terminated, after nearly twenty years and the expenditure of $8 million. Prior to leaving office, Harrar stated that programs should be ended "when our investment in money and manpower, etc. have been justified by demonstrable accomplishment"; in sum, he wanted Rockefeller to leave India as "winners."[49] While the Ford Foundation did not terminate its India programs, it did reduce them, a step dramatized by the resignation of Ensminger in 1971. The departure of Ensminger, whose bold and wide-ranging ventures had long put him frequently at odds with the New York office, signaled a move toward a reduced role in India.[50]

Assessments of the foundations' efforts in India need to take into consideration the context of Indian political culture. Change, no matter how rational to its advocates and no matter how widely supported by Indians as well as Americans, inevitably upset interest groups and bureaucratic order. Besides the previously noted resistance to family planning, the foundations' leaders were frequently frustrated in their interactions with Indians. The Rockefeller Foundation, for instance, had prolonged and at points rather heated exchanges with Indian officials over the award of research grants and fellowships, with the foundation's determination to evaluate Indian applicants as part of international competition conflicting with the government of India's claim to better understanding of the country's needs. At Ford, Ensminger had similar disagreements; he was frustrated by the Indian practice of favoring grants for senior personnel, as a "reward for service and not in preference for more significant service."[51] Disagreements plagued many programs. Rockefeller's development of the IARI quickly found Cummings at odds with education officials who resisted the school's elevation to preeminence among agricultural universities. Struggles over admissions standards led to Cummings' resignation as acting dean in November 1960.[52]

In the implementation of Ford's diverse operations, Ensminger was discouraged by the increasingly formal and bureaucratic nature of interactions with the Indian government, especially after Nehru's death in 1964. The foundation's commitment to village development, culminating in the IADP, put it at odds with some Gandhian followers who resisted government programs in favor of voluntary ones in the rural areas.

The implementation of IADP was hindered at various levels by an administrative structure and system that was geared to stability rather than change, a tendency on the part of Indian officials to minimize the importance of increased production during years of good crops, and unevenness in the training of workers and in the level community commitments. Another high priority initiative—the implementation of the public administration program—was undermined by entrenched interests, leading Ensminger to withdraw support, which he reinstituted only after reforms assuring satisfactory standards were put in place. Likewise, a major foundation commitment to urban development in Calcutta suffered from political changes in the state of West Bengal, difficulties of coordination with Indian agencies, and the customary disagreements over qualifications of personnel for grants and staff positions.[53]

These problems not withstanding, the foundations contributed to India's transformation. As anticipated in their preliminary missions to India in the early 1950s, the foundations' most enduring work was in agricultural development broadly defined. The Green Revolution, which emerged from the spread of the Rockefeller agricultural research programs from Latin America to Asia and augmented by funding from Ford, quickly triggered both extravagant expectations and sharp criticism.[54] To early proponents, the Green Revolution promised to eliminate the chronic malnutrition and hunger in the Third World.[55] On the other side, critics argued that the Green Revolution was driven by American interests, perpetuated dependence, and benefited large landholders. HYV research, it was charged, diverted attention from drought and pest-resistant varieties of crops, while the HYV were dependent upon fertilizers that benefited American multinational corporations and caused environmental damage. Some argued that the Green Revolution was disrupting traditional social relationships in ways that could spur political unrest and possibly a mass revolutionary movement. In fact, the "elitism" of the Green Revolution became part of the rationale for the 1970s development emphasis on "basic human needs."[56] Over time, the early problems of HYV crops have been addressed, and studies of the "second generation" and "third generation" of the Green Revolution suggest that, at least in large parts of India, farmers have accepted changes and have been incorporated into the new agricultural system. While Indian agricultural policy has been justly criticized for many shortcomings, the Green Revolution has been the major factor in India's self-sufficiency in food supply—a vital step in the nation's development that once seemed unattainable.[57]

Besides the scientific breakthrough of the Green Revolution, the foundations were important in other ways in changing Indian agriculture. In collaboration with official agencies and land-grant universities, the Rockefeller Foundation contributed to the Americanization of agricultural education and research.[58] The IADP, as the culmination of the Ford commitment to community development, has been credited with achieving the substance of its objectives. As a "package program" of development, as contrasted with earlier essentially extension and education programs, the IADP endeavored to encourage change by reducing the risks for peasants in embracing change, including adoption of HYV grains. Comparative analysis of IADP and non-IADP districts demonstrated considerable success in achieving the principal objective of increased production. IADP provided the model for a more comprehensive program initiated by the Indian government.[59]

For all of the frustrations in the population area, Ford, as noted, contributed to significant long-term developments. Even after Ensminger's departure, the foundation, playing a notably lower-key role and with fewer resources at its disposal, worked with private Indian agencies, including the Family Planning Foundation, to support social science research, to bring consultants to India, and to foster wider acceptance of family planning.[60] Could Jawaharlal Nehru, Paul Hoffman, Doug Ensminger, and Ralph Cummings see India today, they would find the inevitable mixed mosaic. Depending on the criteria applied to measure economic and social change, one can find reasons for favorable or unfavorable assessments. It is a country of both enormous progress, much of it envisioned by those men fifty years ago, and distressing problems, mostly old and seemingly intractable ones. Whatever the shortcomings of its development, India has continued to move down the road of globalization.[61] Outside agencies, including the Rockefeller and Ford foundations, helped along the way; but in the end, change in India has been on its own terms.

Endnotes

[1] *Public Papers of the Presidents: Harry S. Truman*, 8 vols. Office of the Federal Registrar, Washington, 1961–1966, vol. 5, pp. 112–16.

[2] Waldemar A. Nielsen, *The Big Foundations, Twentieth Century Fund Study*, Columbia University Press, NY, 1972, pp. 47–66, 78–82; Francis X. Sutton, "The Ford Foundation: The Early Years," *Daedalus*, vol. 116, 1987, pp. 45–53.

[3] Dennis Kux, *India and the United States, 1941–1991: Estranged Democracies*, National Defense University Press, Washington, DC, 1992, pp. 68–90; Andrew J. Rotter, *Comrades at Odds: The United States and India, 1947–1964*, University of North Carolina Press, Chapel Hill 2000, pp. 188–219, 249–80; Robert J. McMahon, *Cold War on the Periphery: The United States, India, and Pakistan*, Columbia University Press, NY, 1994, pp. 11–79; Gary R. Hess, "American Perspectives on India," in A. P. Rana (ed.) *Four Decades of Indo-U.S. Relations: A Commemorative Retrospective*, Har-Anand, New Delhi, 1994, pp. 170–4; Dennis Merrill, *Bread and the Ballot: The United States and India's Economic Development, 1947–1963*, University of North Carolina Press, Chapel Hill, 1990, pp. 60–80.

[4] Emily Rosenberg, *Spreading the American Dream, Cultural and Economic Expansion, 1890–1945*, Hill and Wang, NY, 1982, introduced the concept of "liberal developmentalism" as a guiding ideology, which she divides into five points: "(1) belief that other nations could and should replicate America's own development experience; (2) faith in private enterprise; (3) support for free or open access for trade and investment; (4) promotion of free flow of information and culture; (5) growing acceptance of government activity to protect private enterprise and to stimulate American participation in international economic and cultural exchange" (p. 7). Wilsonianism has a vast literature, including, among its more important works, N. Gordon Levin, *Woodrow Wilson and World Politics: America's Response to War and Revolution*, Oxford University Press, NY, 1968; Arthur M. Link, *Woodrow Wilson: Revolution, War, and Peace*, Harlan Davidson, Arlington Heights, IL, 1979. Recent discussions of Wilsonianism's origins and influence include Tony Smith, *America's Mission: The United States and the Worldwide Struggle for Democracy in the Twentieth Century*, Princeton University Press, Princeton, NJ, 1994, pp. 60–109, 311–45 et passim, and Walter Russell Mead, *Special Providence, American Foreign Policy and How It Changed the World*, Knopf, NY, 2001, pp. 132–73.

[5] George Rosen, *Western Economists and Eastern Societies: Agents of Change in South Asia, 1950–1970*, Johns Hopkins University Press, Baltimore, MD, 1985, pp. 27–38.

[6] Michael E. Latham, *Modernization as Ideology: American Social Science and National-Building in the Kennedy Era*, University of North Carolina Press, Chapel Hill, 1999, pp. 53–7; Max F. Millikan and Walt W. Rostow, *A Proposal: Key to an Effective Foreign Policy*, Harper and Bros, NY, 1957, pp. 109–13 et passim; Walt W. Rostow, *The Stages of Economic Growth: A Non-Communist Manifesto*, Cambridge University Press, Cambridge, UK, 1960, p. 166 passim. Robert Packenham has summarized the underlying assumptions of development thought as "(1) change and development are easy . . . (2) all good things [political stability, economic growth, social reform] go together . . . (3) radicalism and revolution are bad . . . (4) distributing power is more important than accumulating power." See Robert Packenham, *Liberal America and The Third World: Political Ideas in Foreign Aid and Social Science*, Princeton University Press, Princeton, NJ, 1973, pp. 15–22 passim.

[7] Sutton, "Ford Foundation: The Early Years," pp. 63–71; Alan R. Raucher, *Paul G. Hoffman: Architect of Foreign Aid*, University Press of Kentucky, Lexington, 1985, pp. 80–3; Rosen, *Western Economists and Eastern Societies*, pp. 5–8.

[8] Sutton quoted in John Caldwell and Pat Caldwell, *Limiting Population Growth and the Ford Foundation Contribution*, Pinter Publishers, London, 1986, p. 32.

[9] Gary R. Hess, *Sam Higginbottom of Allahabad: Pioneer of Point Four to India*, University Press of Virginia, Charlottesville, 1967; Albert Mayer and associates in collaboration with McKim Marriott and Richard Park, *Pilot Project India: The Story of Rural Development at Etawah, Uttar Pradesh*, University of California Press, Berkeley, 1958; Alice Thorner, "Nehru, Mayer, and the Origins of Community Projects," *Economic and Political Weekly* (Bombay), January 24, 1981, pp. 117–20; Rosen, *Western Economists and Eastern Societies*, pp. 48–52.

[10] Rosen, *Western Economists and Eastern Societies*, pp. 8–11.

[11] Government of India, Planning Commission, *First Five Year Plan*, cited in V. L. Goswami, "The Work of the Ford Foundation in India," *International Labour Review*, 70, 1954 (September-October), p. 324.

[12] Rosen, *Western Economists and Eastern Societies*, pp. 8–11; Ensminger Oral History, Files A1 and C1, Ford Foundation Archives (*FFA*), New York City.

[13] Eugene S. Staples, *Forty Years, A Learning Curve: The Ford Foundation Programs in India, 1952–1992*, Ford Foundation, NY, 1992, p. 4.

[14] Ibid., pp. 4–11; Howard B. Shaffer, *Chester Bowles: New Dealer in the Cold War*, Harvard University Press, Cambridge, MA, 1993, pp. 63–79; Rosen, *Western Economists and Eastern Societies*, pp. 8–14; Chester Bowles, *Ambassador's Report*, Harper and Bros, NY, 1954, pp. 195–214. Initially, Ensminger was the Ford representative in both India and Pakistan, but a year later the foundation, at Ensminger's request, established a separate office in Pakistan. *Ford Foundation Annual Report 1952*, Ford Foundation, NY, 1953 (annual reports, hereafter as *FFAR*), pp. 16–9.

[15] Because of the warfare in China, the Far Eastern Regional Office was moved from Shanghai from 1942 to 1946. The India Office was moved to Bangalore in 1949 and, later that year, after the establishment of the Chinese People's Republic, was again

combined with the Far Eastern Regional Office. In 1953, the regional headquarters was reestablished in New Delhi.

[16] Historical Notes on Rockefeller Foundation Medical and Public Health Work in India, ca. 1953. Rockefeller Archive Center, Rockefeller Foundation (hereafter *RAC-RF*), 6.7, i, Box 6, Folder 35; *Rockefeller Foundation Annual Report 1951* (hereafter *RFAR*), pp. 33, 151–3, 360–1, 494; *RFAR 1952*, pp. 62–3, 82–3, 103–04, 185–6, 257; *RFAR 1953*, pp. 75–6, 280–1, 294–6, 464–6; *RFAR 1954*, pp. 211–2, 412–4; *RFAR 1955*, pp. 30–43, 322–3; Darwin H. Stapleton, "Technology and Malaria Control, 1930–1960: The Career of Rockefeller Foundation Engineer Frederick W. Knipe," *Parassitologia* 42, 2000, pp. 59–68.

[17] E. C. Stakman, Richard Bradfield, and Paul G. Mangelsdorf, *Campaigns Against Hunger,* Harvard University Press, Cambridge, MA, 1966, pp. 22–3; 235–40.

[18] Notes on Indian Agriculture, April 11, 1952, *RAC-RF* 1.2, Box 1, Folder 4; India Conference, March 26, 1952, *RAC-RF* 1.2, Box 1, Folder 4; Deborah Fitzgerald, "Exporting American Agriculture: The Rockefeller Foundation in Mexico, 1943–1953," in Marcos Cueto (ed.) *Missionaries of Science: The Rockefeller Foundation and Latin America,* Indiana University Press, Bloomington, 1994, pp. 72–96; Joseph Cotter, "The Rockefeller Foundation's Mexican Agricultural Project: A Cross-Cultural Encounter, 1943–1949" in Cueto, *Missionaries of Science,* pp. 97–125; Stakman et al., *Campaigns Against Hunger,* pp. 19–234.

[19] Excerpts from Harrar Diary, October 6, 1953 and January 21, 1955, *RAC-RF* 1.2, 464, Box 1, Folder 3; Memorandum of Conversation, Oct. 10, 1953, *RAC-RF* 1.2 464, Box 1, Folder 3; Parker to Weaver, October 19, 1954, *RAC-RF* 1.2 464, Box 1, Folder 3; Parker to Harrar, November 18, 1954, *RAC-RF* 1.2 464, Box 1, Folder 3; Parker to Harrar, January 24, 1955, *RAC-RF* 1.2 464, Box 1, Folder 3; pp. 235–42; Arthur A. Goldsmith, "The Rockefeller Foundation Indian Stakman et al, *Campaigns Against Hunger,* pp. 235–42, Arthur A. Goldsmith, "The Rockefeller Foundation Indian Agricultural Program: Why It Worked, in Soma Hewa and Philo Hove (eds.) *Philanthropy and Cultural Context; Western Philanthropy in South, East, and Southeast Asia in the 20th Century,* University Press of America, Lanham, MD, 1997, pp. 89–92.

[20] Chandler Diary, April 1, 1955, and September 22–30, 1955, *RAC-RF* 1.2 464, Box 1, Folder 3; Harrar Diary, May 24, 1955, *RAC-RF* 1.2 464, Box 1, Folder 3; Thapar to Bradfield, July 15 and September 2, 1955, *RAC-RF* 1.2 464, Box 1, Folder 3; Stakman et al, *Campaigns Against Hunger,* pp. 236, 286; Robert S. Anderson, "Origins of the International Rice Research Institute," *Minerva* 29, 1991, pp. 72–9; Thapar to Weaver, October 5, 1955, *RAC-RF* 1.2 464, Box 1, Folder 3; Bradfield to Harrar, October 19, 1955, *RAC-RF* 1.2 464, Box 1, Folder 3; Harrar to Bradfield, Nov. 1, 1955, *RAC-RF* 1.2 464, Box 1, Folder 3; Harrar to Thapar, January 5, 1956, *RAC-RF* 1.2 464, Box 1, Folder 3; Stakman et al, *Campaigns Against Hunger,* pp. 242–86; Anderson, "Origins of IRRI," pp. 67–83.

[21] RF Board Minutes, April 4, 1956, *RAC-RF* 1.2 464, Box 1, Folder 3; *RFAR 1956,* pp. 32–5, 181–2, 407–10; *RFAR 1957,* pp. 53–4, 346–7.

[22] *FFAR 1952,* pp. 59–63; *FFAR 1953,* pp. 25–34, 779–93; *FFAR 1954,* pp. 58–67, 77–91; *FFAR 1955,* pp. 72–5, 85–6, 235–62; Goswami, "Work of Ford Foundation," pp. 323–31; Ensminger Oral History, *FFA* B6 pp. 1–18.

[23] Bowles, *Ambassador's Report*, p. 340.

[24] Goldsmith, "Rockefeller Foundation IAP," p. 92; Leonard A. Gordon, "Wealth Equals Wisdom? The Rockefeller and Ford Foundations in India," *Annals of the American Academy of Political and Social Science* 554, 1997, pp. 104–16.

[25] Staples, *Forty Years*, p. 6; Oscar Harkavy, *Curbing Population Growth: An Insider's Perspective on the Population Movement*, Plenum Press, NY, 1995, pp. 130–1; *RFAR 1963*, pp. 81–5; besides the IAP staff, six other Rockefeller Foundation were assigned to India on medical and public health projects in 1963.

[26] Goldsmith, "Rockefeller Foundation IAP," pp. 96–7.

[27] IADP was later renamed the Intensive Agricultural Development Program.

[28] Carl C. Malone and Sherman E. Johnson, "The Intensive Agricultural Development Program in India," *Agricultural Economics Research* 23, 1971, pp. 25–35.

[29] Stakman et al, *Campaigns Against Hunger*, pp. 235–54.

[30] IRRA was formally established in 1962. Ibid., pp. 285–9; Anderson, "Origins of the International Rice Research Institute (IRRI)," pp. 61–89; Kenneth Thompson, "The Green Revolution: Leadership and Partnership in Agriculture," *Review of Politics* 34, 1972, pp. 180–5.

[31] Chandler report, cited in Stakman et al, *Campaigns Against Hunger*, pp. 294–5.

[32] Uma Lele and Arthur A. Goldsmith, "The Development of a National Research Capacity: India's Experience with the Rockefeller Foundation and Its Significance for Africa," *Economic Development and Cultural Change* 37, 1988, pp. 325–7; Robert L. Paarlberg, *Food Aid and Foreign Policy: India, the Soviet Union and the United States*, Cornell University Press, Ithaca, NY, 1985, pp. 143–69.

[33] Cited in Caldwell and Caldwell, *Limiting Population Growth*, p. 49.

[34] Rotter, *Comrades at Odds*, p. 1–24; Paul Ehrlich, *The Population Bomb*, Ballantine, NY, 1967.

[35] Caldwell and Caldwell, *Limiting Population Growth*, pp. 4–17; Harkavy, *Curbing Population Growth*, pp. 17–21; *RFAR 1954*, pp. 41–2.

[36] Marshall C. Balfour, Roger F. Evans, Frank W. Notestein, and Irene B. Taueber, *Public Health and Demography in the Far East*, Rockefeller Foundation, NY, 1950, p. 116 and passim.

[37] Phyllis T. Piotrow, *World Population Crisis: The United States Response*, Praeger, NY, 1973, pp. 12–5; Harkavy, *Curbing Population Growth*, pp. 23–37; Caldwell and Caldwell, *Limiting Population Growth*, pp. 20–9.

[38] [Elaine Moss] *The Population Council: A Chronicle of the First Twenty-Five Years*, Population Council, NY, 1973, p. 328; Judith Nagelberg, "Promoting Population Policy: The Activities of the Rockefeller Foundation, the Ford Foundation, and the Population Council" (Ph.D. dissertation), Columbia University, NY, 1985, pp. 22–44; Caldwell and Caldwell, *Limiting Population Growth*, pp. 37–47; Harkavy, *Curbing Population Growth*, pp. 20–7; Joseph C. Kiger, *Philanthropic Foundations in the Twentieth Century*, Greenwood Press, Westport, CT, 2000, pp. 24–31.

[39] Piotrow, *World Population Crisis*, pp. 24–5, 20–5, 36–42; Ansley J. Coale and Edgar M. Hoover, *Population Growth and Economic Development in Low Income Countries: A Case Study of India's Prospects*, Princeton University Press, Princeton, NJ, 1958.

[40] Harkavy, *Curbing Population Growth*, pp. 131–5; Nielsen, *Big Foundations*, pp. 66–8.

[41] Harkavy, *Curbing Population Growth*, pp. 133–43; Kathleen D. McCarthy, "From Government to Grassroots Reform: The Ford Foundation's Population Programs in South Asia, 1959–1981," in Hewa and Hove (eds.) *Philanthropy and Cultural Context*, pp. 134–9; Ensminger Oral History B-1, *FFA*.

[42] Richard Magat, *The Ford Foundation at Work: Philanthropic Choices, Methods, and Styles*, Plenum, NY, 1979, pp. 93–7; Harkavy, *Curbing Population Growth*, pp. 129–41, 153–5; McCarthy, "From Government to Grassroots Reform," pp. 133–7.

[43] Ensminger Oral History B-1, *FFA*; Harkavy, *Curbing Population Growth*, pp. 141–43

[44] McCarthy, "From Government to Grassroots Reform," pp. 134–9.

[45] Cited in Walt W. Rostow, *Eisenhower, Kennedy, and Foreign Aid*, University of Texas Press, Austin, 1985, pp. 80–2.

[46] Francis X. Sutton, "The Foundations and Governments of the Developing Countries," *Studies in Comparative International Development* 12, 1977, pp. 110–12.

[47] Mahbub ul Haq, *The Poverty Curtain: Choices for the Third World*, Columbia University Press, NY, 1976, pp. 1–87 passim.

[48] *FFAR 1970*, pp. 7–15; *RFAR 1974*, pp. 1–13; *RFAR 1975*, PP. 2–11; Nielsen, *Big Foundations*, pp. 69–70.

[49] Harrar cited in Goldsmith, "Rockefeller Foundation Indian Agricultural Program," p. 105.

[50] Ensminger Oral History A-25, pp. 1–32 and A-42, pp. 219–27, *FFA*; Harkavy, *Curbing Population Growth*, pp. 130–1.

[51] Gordon, "Wealth Equals Wisdom? pp. 1080–2; Ensminger Oral History A-30, p. 2, *FFA*.

[52] Goldsmith, "Rockefeller Foundation Indian Agricultural Program," pp. 94–5, 112 (n. 17).

[53] Ensminger Oral History, *FFA* : A-2, pp. 1–5, A-13, pp. 1–16; B-6, pp. 1–23; B-4, pp. 14–36; B-4 Attachments; Carl C. Malone and Sherman E. Johnson, "The Intensive Agricultural Development Program," *Agricultural Economics Research* 23, 1971, pp. 25–35.

[54] Thompson, "Green Revolution," pp. 174–89; Stakman et al, *Campaigns Against Hunger*, pp. 235–54, 285–99; Clifton R. Wharton Jr., "The Green Revolution: Cornucopia or Pandora's Box? *Foreign Affairs* 47, 1969, pp. 464–76.

[55] Lester R. Brown, *Seeds of Change: The Green Revolution and Development in the 1970s*, Praeger, NY, 1970.

[56] Keith Griffin, *Alternative Strategies for Economic Development*, Macmillan, London, 1989, pp. 147–53; Dinesh Abrol, "American Investment in Indian Agricultural Research," in Robert Crunden, Manoj Joshi, and R. V. R. Chandreskahar Rao (ed.) *New Perspectives on America and South Asia*, Chanakaya, New Delhi, 1984, pp. 161–89; Vernon W. Ruttan, "The Green Revolution: Seven Generalizations," *International Development Review* 19, 1977, pp. 16–23; Francine R. Frankel, *India's Green Revolution: Economic Gains and Political Costs*, Princeton University Press, Princeton, NJ, 1971.

[57] M. Bazlul Karim, comp., *The Green Revolution: An International Bibliography*, Greenwood, Westport, CT, 1986, pp. xiii–xxiv; Rita Sharma and Thomas Poleman, *The New Economics of India's Green Revolution; Income and Employment Diffusion in Uttar Pradesh*, Cornell University Press, Ithaca, NY, 1993, pp. 1–17, et passim;

Richard H. Day and Inderjit Singh, *Economic Development as an Adaptive Process: The Green Revolution in the Indian Punjab*, Cambridge University Press, Cambridge, UK, 1977, pp. 1–128 et passim; Eric Strahorn, "The Role of the Rockefeller Foundation in India's Green Revolution," (Ph.D. dissertation), University of Iowa, 1988; Sterling Wortman and Ralph W. Cummings Jr., *To Feed This World: The Challenge and the Strategy*, Johns Hopkins University Press, Baltimore, MD, 1978; Goldsmith, "Rockefeller Foundation Indian Agricultural Program," pp. 105–7.

[58] Lele and Goldsmith, "Development of National Agricultural Research Capacity," 37, pp. 305–43.

[59] D. K. Desai, "Intensive Agricultural District Programme: Analysis of Results," *Economic and Political Weekly* 4, 1969 (June 28), pp. A-30-A-90; Goswami, "Work of the Ford Foundation in India," pp. 323–31; Suleki C. Gupta, "Rapporteur's Report on Intensive Development Approach to Agricultural Development," *Indian Journal of Agricultural Economics* 21, 1966 (October-December), pp. 77–95; K. S. Krishnan and P. C. Mehtrota, "A Study of the Performance of High-Yielding Varieties of Wheat in Cultivators' Fields in the IADP Districts," *Agricultural Situation in India* 25, 1970 (October), pp. 713–9; Lele and Goldsmith, "Development of National Agricultural Research Capacity," pp. 25–35; Malone and Johnson, "Intensive Agricultural Development Program in India," pp. 25–35; John W. Mellor, Thomas F. Weaver, Uma Lele, and Sheldon R. Simon, *Developing Rural India: Plan and Practice*, Cornell University Press, Ithaca, NY, 1968, pp. 3–14; C. A. Robertson and R. K. Sharma, "Lessons from the Package Programme with Implications for the New Agricultural Strategy," *Indian Journal of Agricultural Economics* 21, 1966 (October-December), pp. 124–35; Rosen, *Western Economists and Eastern Societies*, pp. 227–41.

[60] McCarthy, "From Government to Grassroots Reforms," pp. 137–43; Kathleen D. McCarthy, "From Cold War to Cultural Development: The International Cultural Activities of the Ford Foundation 1950–1980," *Daedalus*, 1987, pp. 93–117. For an overview of the Ford programs in India, see *The Ford Foundation, 1952–2002: Celebrating 50 Years of Partnership*, 11 vols. Ford Foundation, New Delhi, 2002.

[61] Among the more recent works on Indian development and globalization are Gurcharan Das, *India Unbound: The Social and Economic Revolution from Independence to the Global Age*, Anchor Books, NY, 2000; Terence J. Byres (ed.), *The Indian Economy: Major Debates since Independence*, Oxford University Press, New Delhi, 1998; Jean Dreze and Amartya Sen, *India: Economic Development and Opportunity*, Oxford University Press, New Delhi, 1996; Vijay Joshi and I. M. D. Little, *India's Economic Reforms, 1991–2001*, Oxford University Press, New Delhi, 1996; John P. Lewis, *India's Political Economy: Governance and Reform*, Oxford University Press, New Delhi, 1995.

Chapter 4

THE ROCKEFELLER BLUEPRINT FOR POSTWAR U.S.–JAPANESE CULTURAL RELATIONS AND THE EVOLUTION OF JAPAN'S CIVIL SECTOR

Victoria Lyon Bestor

Much has been written about John Foster Dulles's role in negotiating the peace settlement with Japan and the long-term impact of those efforts on U.S.-Japanese relations and on the Cold War in Asia.[1] Less attention has been paid to the unusual role played by John D. Rockefeller 3rd (hereafter JDR 3rd) in the Dulles Mission. Likewise the extent to which JDR 3rd's eighty-page report to Ambassador Dulles may have offered a blueprint for postwar U.S.-Japanese cultural relations has not been fully examined. In particular, very little has been written with regard to the long-term influence that the initiatives and institutions outlined in that document may have had on U.S.-Japanese relations in the civil sector.[2]

*****

In January 1951, when JDR 3rd traveled to Japan as a member of the Dulles Peace Mission, he was charged with studying cultural relations and making recommendations to Dulles about ways to strengthen U.S.-Japanese bilateral relations in education, intellectual and cultural exchange, and scholarship. He was the only member of that mission who focused on issues other than political, and, in retrospect, the initiatives he proposed in that report, presented to Dulles on April 16, 1951, provide a remarkably accurate preview of Rockefeller philanthropic efforts in Japan in subsequent decades.

Building upon that written about the early postwar activities of JDR 3rd and about his affinity and advocacy for Japan,[3] this paper examines the long-term impact of these efforts and of the Rockefeller philosophy of social responsibility on U.S.-Japanese cultural relations and on the evolution of notions of civil society in postwar Japan.[4] This paper provides a brief outline of early Rockefeller interests in Japan, including JDR 3rd's first contacts with Japan; it reviews JDR 3rd's major Japan-related activities during his life; and it continues beyond his death to illustrate how the postwar initiatives supported by various Rockefeller philanthropies and the institutions they created have become leaders in Japan's civil sector. Through these institutions, JDR 3rd and his views of social responsibility have had a major impact on Japan's evolving notions of civil society and constitute an important part of his enduring legacy in Japan.

*****

In May 1950, John Foster Dulles, the leading foreign policy expert of the Republican Party, was asked by President Harry S. Truman and Secretary of State Dean Acheson to undertake the responsibility of negotiating a peace treaty with Japan that would bring the Allied Occupation to an end. World War II itself had been over nearly five years at the time, but the conclusion of a peace treaty had been held up by debates within the U.S. government over post-Occupation security within the region and because as yet no terms acceptable to the United States and other potential signatories, in particular the Soviet Union and China, could be found.[5] Finally in early 1950, as partisan criticism from the Republicans over the Truman administration's China policy intensified, the president saw the need for someone to help deflect that criticism. Dulles was considered the most suitable because of his international experience, "especially as a member of the Repatriations Commission at the Versailles Peace Conference and as an advisor at the San Francisco Conference that established the UN—and for his close relationship with Governor Thomas Dewey and the Republican leadership. He was also an acknowledged proponent of bipartisan foreign policy."[6]

For Truman and Acheson, the appointment of Dulles was as risky as it was logical, because Dulles was known for grandstanding through self-serving and sometimes partisan press leaks. He also brought with him strongly negative opinions about the Soviet Union and the threat of communism to world peace, and the conviction that the imposition of strong economic sanctions on the Japanese would be highly counterproductive.

Within a few weeks of his appointment, Dulles and his staff had prepared a memorandum to Acheson outlining the long-range objectives of the peace treaty. "The Japanese should be peaceful; should respect fundamental human rights; should be part of the free world; and should be friendly to the United States." The memo also noted the need for treating the Japanese as social equals of the West, addressing the racial problems inherent in what Dulles called the "Western sense of white superiority."[7]

Based on the preparatory trip he had made to Japan in June 1950, Dulles knew that nearly all the prominent Japanese leaders "suspected that the United States favored Japanese rearmament only for its own security interests." Aware that these suspicious were not without foundation, Dulles sought to put a different American foot forward. "He therefore requested John D. Rockefeller [3rd], who 'symbolized' cultural exchanges with Japan, to accompany him to Tokyo." Dulles "wanted it understood in Japan that we were not thinking entirely in military and economic terms but also hoped to strengthen long-range cultural relations between the United States and Japan." Dulles felt that a peace treaty would prove to be insufficient unless most of the people in both countries strongly supported it. As he explained to his staff on January 26, 1951, his goal in the negotiations with the Japanese was "a genuine meeting of the minds on all important issues."[8]

The official party arrived in Japan on January 25, 1951, and included both Mr. and Mrs. John D. Rockefeller 3rd along with Ambassador and Mrs. Dulles and a number of military and political advisers. The Rockefellers remained in Japan until February 22. The delegation had offices in the Diplomatic Section of SCAP in the Mitsui Bank Building and they met as a group each morning at 10 a.m. After the daily meeting, individual members followed their own agenda, meeting for events and often attending dinners or the theater in the evening. JDR was assigned a secretary, Miss Barry, and his schedule was packed with meetings. There were also a number of official events, including a duck-netting party as guest's of the emperor, which was hosted by the grand master of ceremonies of the Imperial Household Matsudaira; and teas with the emperor's brother, Prince Takamatsu. The Rockefellers met with leading representatives in the cultural sphere, including the literary and visual arts, education, religion, and the traditional Japanese arts in Tokyo and Kyoto, and JDR reacquainted himself with Japanese he had met on his first trip to Japan in 1929. In all, JDR 3rd was away from the family offices five weeks, and he returned to plunge immediately into the writing of his report.

*****

JDR 3rd's eighty-page report to Ambassador Dulles was presented approximately three months after his study had taken place. The basic objectives of the report were to examine relations between Japan and the United States in the cultural field in the broadest sense, as the report emphasized: "The term 'culture' is here used not in the narrow connotation of intellectual or aesthetic pursuits at the higher levels but rather in its broader sense as relating to the life of a people as a whole."

While changing American's opinions about their former enemy was certainly of great importance, it is equally obvious that influencing the Japanese to follow a Western democratic model through cultural diplomacy was the prime objective. A two-pronged strategy was recommended for Japan, with programs that would develop "contact through selective and direct channels with the group in the Japanese population that may be rather loosely designated as the intellectual leadership of the country" and a second "approach through use of the media of mass communications to the population of Japan as a whole." After the fall of China, and the then very recent outbreak of the Korean War in June 1950, the imperative of reaching and influencing the Japanese to prevent another domino from falling was of utmost importance. The strategy was not only timely given the then current world situation, but also in terms of the American domestic political climate (by then well into the second half of Truman's term), and it was extremely well calculated to appeal to Japanese interests and aesthetics.

The report particularly emphasized the need for new programs in the cultural field to be private in nature and at all cost separated from official government offices of either the United States or Japan. The report outlined three overall long-range objectives: "...to bring our peoples closer together in their appreciation and understanding of each other and their respective ways of life, to enrich our respective cultures through such interchange and to assist each other in solving mutual problems. To this end, ways should be found to allow each country to benefit from the experiences and accomplishment of the other, through a free and voluntary interchange of ideas and information."[9]

It should not be a surprise that many of the initiatives outlined in the document became important foci of Rockefeller philanthropy in the early postwar period. And indeed, while the report calls for private support of the efforts, it made it clear that that support should be broad-based and bilateral, which it was. However, the extent to which the document outlines what might be thought of as a blueprint for future Rockefeller initiatives in Japan during at least the next decade and a half is very striking. Major concrete examples include centers such as International House of Japan (planning launched in early 1952, opened in 1955), the Japan Society of New York, which JDR 3rd reinvigorated in the early 1950s, and the Asia Society, which he created in 1956. Support of students and scholars, much of which was funded through the Social Science Research

Council (SSRC) with support from the Rockefeller and Ford foundations, as well as programs such as Fulbright, will be discussed later in this paper.

*****

Dulles's inspiration to invite JDR 3rd to join the mission and to make recommendations on future aspects of U.S.-Japanese cultural relations was not merely a whim, nor was it simply a well-calculated strategy for involving a philanthropist in a series of major projects, Dulles was well aware of JDR 3rd's past experience with Japan. What he may not have been aware of was the extent to which JDR 3rd would personally invest in the initiatives and see them as an important avenue for making his mark in the world. By 1951, JDR 3rd's relationship with Japan dated back more than twenty years. His personal connection began in 1929 when he attended the Institute of Pacific Relations (IPR) Conference in Kyoto as part of a world tour following his graduation from Princeton. At the time, the IPR was just emerging as a major forum for internationalist discussions of world issues with a focus on the Pacific region, and it became an important counterpoint to the Eurocentric perspectives that still dominated world politics. The Kyoto IPR conference was the third conference since IPR's founding in 1925, and the first held in Japan.

By 1929, the IPR had already received significant Rockefeller funding, including annual gifts of $20,000 from John D. Rockefeller Jr. and gifts from the Laura Spelman Rockefeller Memorial, and IPR was beginning to receive considerable support from the Rockefeller Foundation. In Kyoto, JDR 3rd served as an assistant to members of the American delegation, functioning as a rapporteur. At the IPR conference, JDR 3rd met a number of senior Japanese participants including Takagi Yasaka, who would be important to him and to postwar U.S.-Japanese relations as a leader in American studies in Japan, and Tomohiko Ushiba, whose brother Nobuhiko was later ambassador to the United States and a major force in U.S.-Japanese bilateral relations.

The conference must have also been a fascinating glimpse for JDR 3rd into the growing political storm in Japan. Officially, the emperor was the host of the conference, and he sent his aide Baron Sakatani as his personal representative to welcome delegates. The Japanese delegation was headed by Yosuke Matsuoka, then chairman of the South Manchurian Railroad and later foreign minister. The delegation thus was caught between empire builders like Matsuoka and the group of internationalist statesmen like Takagi and Ushiba who were to reemerge following the war.

Even more than the taste of global politics that he gained in Japan, JDR 3rd was completely entranced by Japanese culture. His diaries are filled with observations on "the women's kimono, gardens, the cleanliness of the people and their cities; the kindness of the Japanese . . . We were treated in the same polite and friendly way wherever we went whether we were known or not. I hate to think of the contrast when we got back home again."[10]

The 1929 IPR Conference was also where JDR 3rd met Shigeharu Matsumoto, with whom he served as a rapporteur. Matsumoto was to become his lifelong friend and the head of the International House of Japan, one of JDR 3rd's major efforts in early postwar Japan. The relationship that grew between John and Shige, as they called one another, included close family ties. The importance of such close personal relationships was crucial to deepening Rockefeller contacts in many parts of the world, a factor that has been observed by a number of scholars who have studied the Rockefellers.[11] Japan was no exception, and indeed some of the connections John made on his first trip were critical to his postwar affinity for Japan.

The 1929 conference also came at an early stage in the Rockefeller Foundation's relationship with the Institute of Pacific Relations. John's participation in that conference, along with other "Rockefeller men" such as John McDonald, president of the Foreign Policy Association, helped to deepen the relationship—and undoubtedly the pockets— upon which the Institute of Pacific Relations would draw over the next two decades.

By the early 1950s, the Rockefeller Foundation alone had contributed nearly $2 million in over one hundred separate grants to the Institute for Pacific Relations.[12] The faith Rockefeller institutions placed in the IPR, however, was not to last beyond the early years of the postwar period. Following the war, just when the United States needed Asia-Pacific specialists the most, Senator Joseph McCarthy accused the IPR and individuals closely associated with it of being communist sympathizers, if not active party members.

This loss of trusted area expertise contributed significantly to the Rockefeller Foundation's later support for the development of academic area studies in American universities.[13] Area studies as an academic field came into their own in the climate of anticommunist passion, which guided the ways each of these fields constructed their intellectual agenda. The "agenda" of JDR 3rd's 1951 report to Ambassador Dulles set forth a paradigm of cultural exchange and cultural influence that involved the "translation" of key American concepts into Japanese contexts, set against a backdrop of "modernization theory."[14] The predominant view at the time was that there were universal steps along a "given" path of evolution to the "modern state." That view embodied a naive mechanical faith that if the United States showed the "way," the path would be self-evident. It was not so much a question of "translation" of American culture and ideas but of the "transmission" of those concepts to waiting and open minds.

A leading architect of Rockefeller policy on area studies was Charles Burton Fahs, then the head of the Rockefeller Foundation's division of humanities and social sciences, who was central to the development of Rockefeller's role in area studies in Japan. Fahs supported "a concept of area studies as a means of coordinating many different disciplines in the social sciences and the humanities toward the understanding of a single culture."[15] This aimed to generate "the type of understanding required for effective operation in international relations." This perspective was central to the Rockefeller Foundation's support for the development of American and Japanese studies as a means of putting cultural diplomacy to work in society and learning broadly from one another, about one another. In addition to Rockefeller, the fields were initially supported by Ford and other major foundations. Like American studies in Japan, Japanese studies in the United States is largely a postwar discipline. Prior to the war there existed only a very few venerable interdisciplinary language and culture departments, including those at Harvard and Columbia.

At the same time that the Rockefeller Foundation, the family, and other Rockefeller interests were reexamining their past relationship with the IPR and cautiously reevaluating ties with a range of organizations and individuals in the United States, old friends in Japan formerly connected with the IPR were quickly moving to the forefront of Rockefeller planning for Japan's future. Those Rockefeller efforts were strongly anticommunist in tone, in keeping with American foreign policy, and JDR 3rd's prewar Japanese contacts had principally come through the IPR. Yet former Japanese members of the IPR were not tarred with the same brush as their American counterparts.

There are a couple of important reasons for this. The history of communism—and in general of liberal and leftist movements in Japan—had been very different from its history in much of the rest of the world. As right-wing militarists tightened their hold on Japan's domestic and international activities in the 1920s and 1930s, left-wing groups were effectively suppressed through the promulgation and manipulation of the Peace Preservation Law of 1925 and its more stringent version, enacted in early 1941. As Japan's aggression in Asia intensified during the 1930s, participation in international organizations like the Institute of Pacific Relations was greatly restricted. The Japanese Council of the IPR struggled to keep dialogue open following the Japanese invasion of Manchuria in 1931, but increasingly its financial support in Japan was cut and its participation in international IPR conferences hampered. Finally, in 1935, the Japan Council of IPR was forced to merge with the Japanese League of Nations Association, and it ceased functioning until after the war.[16]

The suppression of communism in prewar Japan had been so thorough as essentially to prevent "contamination" of Japanese IPR members. The Japan Council's withdrawal from the IPR after the mid-1930s thus largely removed suspicion of communist influences within the IPR's international councils, effectively inoculating former Japanese members who were Rockefeller contacts in Japan from the taint, in the postwar era, of being suspected communists that haunted their American counterparts.

Nonetheless, many Japanese who had been in responsible positions in the fields of government, business, and the media during World War II were on the initial list of those to be purged from future leadership roles by the Occupation.[17] Ironically, having been isolated from presumed leftist international influences by Japanese militarists in the 1930s, they were now purged for their presumed associations with right-wing Japanese militarists. That list included Shigeharu Matsumoto, because he had been a journalist in China during part of the war. Fortunately for many Japanese, and for future Rockefeller plans in Japan, Occupation policies precipitated by the fall of China to the communists in 1949 and the onset of the Korean War in 1950 overwhelmingly emphasized the economic reinvigoration of Japan over the political reforms envisioned in the early years of the Occupation. Successful economic revitalization depended on the expertise of many former purgees who were quickly rehabilitated.

At the point when JDR 3rd returned to Japan as a member of the Dulles Peace Mission in early 1951, the "rehabilitation" of the purged was just beginning. During the following years, former members of the Japan Council of the IPR and their extended networks of peers became central to Rockefeller-supported institutions that have been pivotal to building postwar U.S.-Japanese relations. Among the de-purged were a number of former IPR members who became central to Rockefeller initiatives after the war; the closest of these to JDR 3rd was Shigeharu Matsumoto.

Matsumoto, related to the powerful Matsukata family on his mother's side, was the son of a largely self-made Meiji-era businessman. His father had insisted that he study both English and Chinese as a child. After the 1923 earthquake destroyed the law library at Tokyo Imperial University, where Matsumoto was studying, he went to the United States to continue his studies. At the recommendation of Takagi Yasaka, his lifelong mentor and IPR colleague, he went to study at Yale. At his father's urging, he made a point of developing a network of friendships with Chinese students while there. After his time in the United States, he spent two years in England, returning to Tokyo after the bank crisis in Japan that took place in the summer of 1927. Following his return, he married his cousin Hanako Matsukata, who had also been studying in London.[18]

"A typical product of Taisho Democracy and a member of that generation which imbibed democratic, international ideals in their youth, struggled unhappily through the years of resurgent Japanese imperialism in midlife, and survived World War II to work again for international order and world understanding" was the way he was described by his cousin Haru Matsukata Reischauer in her family biography, *Samurai and Silk*.[19] In those efforts, he called upon the ideas of his Yale mentor Charles Beard[20] and his network of prewar internationalist colleagues of liberal thinkers, university professors, and business leaders. Many of those were the same internationalists who had been part of the Japan Council of the IPR and whom JDR 3rd met in 1929. When John (as Matsumoto called him) returned to Japan in early 1951 as part of the Dulles Peace Mission, Shige (as JDR 3rd called him) who was still trying to determine his future plans, was ripe for resuming the friendship with Rockefeller begun in Kyoto in 1929.

According to Matsumoto's memoirs, the idea of International House of Japan (IHJ), which would serve as a center for scholars and opinion makers, emerged from his discussion with Rockefeller about possible cultural exchanges between the United States and Japan.[21] Certainly the blueprint for IHJ was outlined in Rockefeller's report to Ambassador Dulles; the project itself was launched with a planning committee in early 1952, and its opening in 1955 was presided over by John and Blanchette Rockefeller. IHJ became John and Shige's major lifelong collaboration, and one that they were both ripe to undertake at the time they met again in 1951.[22]

*****

At the end of World War II, JDR 3rd was already in his early forties, but he had yet to establish a firm and independent identity for himself. Dulles's inclusion of JDR 3rd in the delegation was not only a stroke of genius for the negotiations; it provided a life-changing opportunity for JRD 3rd himself. As a matter of style and demeanor, JDR 3rd was extraordinarily well suited to be respected and revered by the Japanese. In Japan, he was no longer the obscure oldest son, less ambitious and outspoken than his brash younger brothers, but was rather the assured *chōnan*, comfortable in the solid status of being the eldest son. In Japan, JDR 3rd finally came into his own as the quiet man with the towering presence, the scion of a fabulously wealthy American family, who was seen by the Japanese as a staunch defender of democracy and enemy of communism. His lack of overt political ambition and nonaggressive manner, which had previously made him rather an understated member of the famed family, appealed to the Japanese people, who were hungry for a gentler gesture of kindness and respect than that offered by General Douglas MacArthur. While many Japanese felt grateful to Rockefeller for his concern for the defeated country and its people, it is apparent that he believed that Japan could serve as an avenue through which he could establish his own identity as a worthwhile philanthropist and as an expert on Asian—especially Japanese—affairs.[23]

Rockefeller's task as a member of the Dulles Mission was to explore the possibilities of cultural exchanges between the United States and Japan within the context of the large exigencies of the peace settlement process. JDR 3rd had been strongly influenced by George Kennan, whose memos to Dulles he had read while preparing for the treaty delegation. In Kennan's April 1951 *Foreign Affairs* article, he stated that "the most important influence the United States can bring to bear upon internal developments in Russia will continue to be the influence of example: the influence of what it [the U.S.] is, and not only what it is to others but what it is to itself."[24] Rockefeller adopted Kennan's "influence of example" approach as he wrote his recommendation for Dulles.

To a great extent, Rockefeller's later activities in the Far East in the fields of cultural exchanges, agriculture, and population were extensions of some of his ideas and preoccupations expressed in his Dulles report. For example, the Intellectual Interchange Program at Columbia University established in 1952, reflects his emphasis on intellectual leadership. The program [25] subsequently brought to International House of Japan such leaders and intellectuals as Eleanor Roosevelt, Robert Oppenheimer, George Kennan, and David Reisman. In New York, the Japan Society, also revived by JDR 3rd in 1952,[26] and the Asia Society, founded in 1956,[27] also served as vehicles through which the high artistic achievements of Japan and other Asian countries were introduced to the American audience, in addition to helping to present the Intellectual Interchange Program to the public. Many of the bilateral and international cultural exchanges JDR 3rd envisioned in the Dulles report were implemented through these institutions.

While JDR 3rd's initial postwar involvement may have been shaped by his links to John Foster Dulles, clearly supporting the geopolitical aims of American foreign policy at that time, it is clear that to characterize early postwar Rockefeller interests as largely geopolitical is too narrow. The breadth of Rockefeller interests and the range of Japanese institutions supported demonstrate the cultural and social vision of the Rockefeller family. The programs thus supported suggest that the Rockefellers, in contrast to some assertions that Rockefeller philanthropy simply fostered American hegemony, were interested in creating a dialogue between Japanese and American culture and society, rather than simply exporting a Eurocentric vision of modern society.[28] International organizations, as well as larger Rockefeller networks in Japan, have interpreted and articulated Rockefeller philosophies of philanthropy and social responsibility through their own initiatives, and in doing so had and still have a major impact on the evolution of the nonprofit sector in Japan.

Although American cultural policy and Rockefeller's involvement in it could never be separated from politics in a larger context, his postwar activities in Japan centered on the "cultural sphere" in its broader and less politically charged sense; his efforts to promote intellectual and artistic exchanges seem most significant in retrospect. Yet JDR 3rd himself was not fully satisfied with the prospect of limiting his activities to purely aesthetic and intellectual concerns seemingly remote from realities of the world. He had a moment of reflection on his past activities as revealed in his 1953 memorandum entitled "Objective and Focus of My Asian Interest," in which he wrote: "To date my relationship [to Japan] has been mainly on the cultural side because of my assignment for Mr. Dulles. However, increasingly it becomes evident that it would be undesirable to have any one individual become too active in this area; hence I have been giving consideration to opportunities in the economic field having in mind particularly agriculture." His concern for the apparent weakness of the Japanese economy after the war led him to the idea of regional integration, or the strengthening of the working relationship between Japan and the countries of "Southern Asia."[29]

As an independent philanthropist as well as chairman of the Rockefeller Foundation, JDR 3rd became a tactful player in the international game played at the intersection of politics and philanthropy. American politicians who tried to strengthen the U.S.-Japanese alliance and the U.S. presence in Asia during the Cold War found Rockefeller useful in enhancing pro-American sentiments because of his financial resources and his popularity in this region. For JDR 3rd's part, he made the best use of his personal connections with the American foreign policy establishment and national leaders in Asia in order to fulfill his sense of mission as a planner and engineer of global affairs, including the population, food, and cultural communications, and in Japan his views on the subject of social responsibility also eventually found a ready audience.

*****

Even before World War II, Rockefeller philanthropy had had an influence on the formation of large-scale philanthropic institutions in Japan, as noted by Masayuki Deguchi, one of Japan's leading scholars of philanthropy.[30] The Mitsui Hō-on-kai, literally the Mitsui Association to Repay the Obligation (to the Nation), was founded in 1934. The Mitsui group's experience shortly prior to the founding of its huge zaibatsu-linked[31] philanthropic society distinctly resembled that of the Rockefellers in the years before the founding of the General Education Board in 1903, the Rockefeller Foundation in 1913, and other Rockefeller philanthropies. At the time the Mitsui Hō-on-kai was created, Japan was becoming increasingly militaristic, and the Mitsui group was heavily criticized for obliviously pursuing its private self-interests at a time of growing national crisis. Their alleged involvement in speculation on the U.S. dollar in anticipation of the imposition of the gold embargo led to the assassination of the head of Mitsui in 1932.[32]

The creation of the Mitsui Hō-on-kai was clearly an attempt to placate critics by aiding the national effort through support of public works and social welfare. During this period of ultranationalist fervor, Mitsui was not alone in creating large foundations that simultaneously refurbished corporate images and aided the national goal of building up Japan's industry and technological skills.

In recent years, as the role and evolution of civil society has been hotly discussed in Japan, much has been written about its origins. The possible roots of Japanese civil society have been traced variously to early Buddhist acts of benevolence,[33] to Japan's Confucian traditions,[34] to the theories of John Locke,[35] to Meiji-era popular rights movements,[36] and to Western models of philanthropy and concepts of social responsibility.[37] But as historian Andrew Barshay notes, "the history of civil society in Japan—that is, as a 'self-conscious' and 'self-aware' history—belongs to the postwar era."[38]

Japan's postwar discourse on civil society can be roughly divided into four periods:[39] (1) the period during the Occupation (1945–1952) when notions of civil society were tied closely to efforts to bring American-style participatory democracy to Japan, through 1955, when the Japanese economy "took off;" (2) the period of citizens' movements and popular protests during the 1960s and 1970s, when progressive intellectuals and liberal politicians gave voice to the need for minimum standards of well-being and when the effects of unbridled industrial growth produced mass protests against pollution; (3) the era of Japanese corporate philanthropy in the 1970s and 1980s when Japanese multinationals thrived and made charitable giving a strategy for success abroad and at home; and (4) the current post-bubble, post-Kobe earthquake (1995)[40] era, which began in the early 1990s, when Japan's continued economic decline has diminished prospects for all age groups—a period characterized by government ossification and its inability to reform from within. This has also been a time when natural and social disasters have starkly brought the shortcomings of the political establishment into focus, creating the opportunity, indeed the necessity, for Japanese citizens to redefine civic participation and voluntary action.

The Occupation Period and the Early 1950s

At the end of World War II, Japan lay in ruins, its industry and infrastructure destroyed by a series of Allied incendiary air strikes and the atomic bombs dropped on Hiroshima and Nagasaki. Initially, the U.S. Occupation of Japan, described by Roger Goodman as Japan's short-lived, eight-year experience of colonialism, undertook to completely remold Japan along an American democratic model.[41] The "Occupationaires" were a mixed collection of American career military officers and very idealistic young civilians. Together, they sought to radically change Japan through a process of "induced revolution" with a program of modernization and American-style democratization. Among the goals were to establish a responsible government in accordance with the freely expressed will of the people and strong civil institutions operating outside the sphere of government. Initial efforts included a new constitution, drafted in 1946, with a bill of rights that ostensibly guaranteed individual freedoms broader than those guaranteed by the American constitution, laying the groundwork for a fully participatory democracy ensuring individual rights and freedoms. Occupationaires saw a strong American-style democracy as challenging, discrediting, and replacing the ideologies that had brought Japan into the war. Western philanthropists like the Rockefellers also played important behind-the-scenes roles in the reinvigoration of cultural and civic organizations that have played major roles in the evolution of Japanese notions of the civil sector ever since.[42]

After the defeat of the Nationalist Chinese and the establishment of the People's Republic of China in 1949 and the outbreak of the Korean War in 1950, many of the reforms originally envisioned by the Occupation were quickly revised, reversed, or forgotten. New Occupation policy refocused on efforts to bring Japan firmly into the Western bloc as a client state and an ardent anticommunist ally. Emphasis on promoting civil society and broad individual freedoms declined. Democratic concepts of civil society and larger civic involvement were put aside in the midst of American paranoia about the communist threat.

Reinvigorating Japan's economy and making Japan "America's unsinkable aircraft carrier" in the Pacific became the central motivations of Occupation policy. The Japan that resulted was a market-led "developmental state" with the overarching objective of creating a strong industrial and economic sector at the expense, if necessary, of a broader range of personal liberties and social welfare. Accompanying these initiatives was a narrowing of political options that included the suppression of communist and leftist groups and the concentration of power in the hands of a group of conservative leaders who had been quickly "rehabilitated" by the Occupation to take over the reins of government.

However, the idea of civil society was not entirely lost as a political concept or ideal. Among Japanese intellectuals, the discourse on civil society continued as an important theme both in postmortem evaluations of the wartime experience and in discussions of how postwar democratic institutions in Japan could best evolve. After U.S. policy changed abruptly, notions of civil society and discussions of ways to promote it were largely restricted to intellectual circles. During much of this era, Japan's intellectuals were predominantly of the progressive or Marxist camp. Leading among them were Uchida Yoshihiko, Hirata Kiyoaki, and Maruyama Masao, whose works were widely translated in the West.[43] In Japan, the discourse was published widely in leftist monthly journals such as *Sekai* or *Shisō*. Social commentators like Sakamoto Yoshikazu, Hani

Goro, and Kuno Osamu believed in historical progress and were convinced that it was leading toward a socialist society in which the leading role would be played by the *shimin*, or citizens. From the end of World War II until the 1980s, the term *shimin shakai* was most commonly used in this progressive sense [44] to point toward an idealized socialist state in contrast to Japan's market-led enterprise state.

The 1960s and the Growth of Citizen Participation

The 1960 revision of the United States-Japan Security Treaty (AMPO)[45] became an important focus for citizens' action. Reacting to Prime Minister Kishi's high-handed ramming of the treaty through the Diet, opposition from Diet members and leading liberal and leftist intellectuals promoted the formation of a citizens' movement that mobilized major protests. Those efforts eventually led to the cancellation of President Eisenhower's proposed visit to Japan in June 1960 and eventually resulted in Prime Minister Kishi's downfall, although AMPO itself survived the crisis.

The aftermath of the 1960 AMPO riots further pushed discussions of civil society to the periphery. However the antitreaty riots also demonstrated the potential for citizens' action, which began to take hold as official policy more intensely emphasized market-led growth, industrial development, and expansion of the corporate sector at the expense of grassroots needs and initiatives. While national prosperity through the 1960s and 1970s increased enormously, little emphasis was placed on the individual, nor was attention given to the needs of urban neighborhoods or rural communities. As the wealth of Japanese corporations became more conspicuous, local interests began to demand spreading the wealth and creating accepted minimum standards of living. Again, Uchida was a key spokesman along with Hirata, who coined the term "enterprise state."[46] Another important leftist political theorist, Matsushita Keiichi, argued for a "civil minimum" of quality of life, access to resources, and public services.[47] His views were later influential on the progressive politician Minobe Ryokichi, who became governor of Tokyo in 1967, having been elected through a coalition of communist and socialist supporters. Governor Minobe strongly promoted "community consciousness" and "citizen participation" to make Tokyo a city truly "managed by the people themselves."[48]

Governor Minobe was also one of the first elected officials to take action on the environmental front. In 1970, he supported Diet legislation that passed fourteen environmental ordinances to curb pollution in the Tokyo area. Enforcement was not an easy task, for both industrial and labor interests' resisted full implementation of the initiatives. Minobe was in the forefront of the issues, but he had to rely heavily on the press and public opinion because he lacked the support of the conservative political-bureaucratic establishment.[49]

By the early 1970s, pollution had become a serious problem in many parts of Japan. During the 1950s, Japan was still struggling to recover from the war, and the prospect of industrial growth seemed to present future opportunities tantalizing enough to quell opposition despite the lack of much evident direct benefit to the average citizen. Two decades later, serious and widespread incidents of industrial pollution such as those in Tokyo, the mercury poisoning of fisheries stocks that became known as Minamata disease, and severe air pollution and endemic lung disorders in such industrial cities as Yokkaichi in Mie Prefecture led to local environmental awareness and activism throughout Japan. The opposition in the mid-1960s and early 1970s to environmental hazards produced by unbridled industrial growth began to create a groundswell of locally based citizens' movements, which came to be known as *shimin undo*.

Residents of rural areas affected by specific sources of industrial pollution joined with members of the urban middle classes whose consciousness had already been raised by urban pollution and Minobe's efforts to highlight such issues through the press. A broad range of middle-class professionals, doctors, scientists, lawyers, schoolchildren, teachers, and the media mobilized public interest and support both to aid the pollution victims in their long legal battles with polluters and to demand that preventive measures be taken to insure that industry behave more responsibly. The continued and intense focus of the media was particularly important in holding domestic Japanese attention on the problem and bringing the issue into the international spotlight.[50]

Other movements expanded simultaneously, including the antinuclear campaign, the anti–Vietnam war campaign, and a range of vigorous and diverse consumer protests, mostly made up of housewives. These movements focused broader attention on consumer needs, on food safety, on environmental hazards related more broadly to the general populace, and, most important, on the excesses of corporate Japan and its disregard of the consumer.

Contemporary citizens' movements and popular protests also stimulated interest in the history of the Freedom and People's Rights Movement (*Jiyū Minken Undō*) of the 1880s, including its challenges to the centralized authority of the Meiji state.[51] This contributed to an intellectual climate in which a popular version of civil society could be discovered in the past as well as in the present-day political, environmental, and consumer movements.

Pressure continued for implementation of social reforms, and by the late 1960s and early 1970s concrete plans were being made for the creation of a broad range of social programs. However, the so-called Oil Shock of 1973 severely jolted Japan (which was dependent on foreign sources for 98 percent of its energy needs) and derailed policies that were leading toward the creation of a Western European–style welfare state. Instead, what was created came to be known as the Japanese-style welfare society (*Nihongata shakai fukushi shakai*).[52] This offered far fewer entitlements than Western models and relied heavily on traditional Japanese support networks (although these traditional social elements were seen not as autonomous elements of civil society, but rather as subsidiaries of state policy).

By the 1970s, the economy recovered, and as prosperity spread throughout the Japanese populace and economic growth appeared unending, complacency seemed to settle over much of the Japanese middle class. During the 1970s and 1980s, the good life seemed within reach, and many Japanese concentrated their energies on better educating their children to get top jobs, investing in the booming real estate market and in savings, and in conspicuous consumption of luxury goods. Indeed, such an enormous percentage of Japanese thought of themselves as firmly middle class (roughly 85 percent) that they were called "the New Middle Mass."[53] While consumer action, civil militancy, and social involvement continued, for the most part they were concentrated in smaller, more factionalized or specialized movements.

The Era of Japanese Corporate Philanthropy

Throughout the late 1960s and early 1970s, Japanese corporate philanthropy grew dramatically. During that period, most Japanese corporate giving was domestic; it overwhelmingly supported projects aimed at facilitating continued economic growth, including Japanese rural development, improvement of medical care, student scholarships, and technical and scientific research funding. Government regulation of philanthropic activities ensured that most giving supported government projects and policies.

The formation of philanthropic organizations was based on the Meiji Civil Code of 1896. Article 34 of that code allowed for the creation of *kōeki hōjin* (public benefit corporations): "incorporated associations or foundations relating to worship, religion, charity, science, art, or otherwise related to public interest and not having for their object the acquisition of gain."[54] That statute allowed for the creation of juridical persons (*hōjin*), which are legal corporations granted permission by the government to operate for a specific purpose under the administrative oversight of a given ministry, regional governmental agency, or other governmental body. The creation of an *hōjin* requires a considerable endowment or annual revenue from dues or other sources, amounting to ¥300 million yen (approximately $3 million). In addition, very strict guidelines outline the focus of giving—for example, *gakko hōjin* (educational), *shukyo hōjin* (religious) *shakai fukushi hōjin,* (welfare), and *iryo hōjin* (medical), as well as *zaidan hōjin* (philanthropic foundations). Strict geographical restrictions are often applied, and approximately 75 percent of all Japanese *hōjin* have extremely local or regional spheres of activity.

By the 1970s, Japan's economic growth had become global, and Japanese corporate and government leaders began to see the need to improve Japan's image abroad.[55] Particularly in Asian countries that were increasingly becoming Japan's sources of raw materials, the sites of plants, pools of cheaper labor, and markets for Japan's industrial production, there was a need for Japan to try to overcome lingering memories of World War II. And in the West, there was the need to enhance Japan's profile as a world leader, to keep pace with its obvious economic strength, and to promote an image of Japan as more than simply an economic powerhouse.

Beginning in the early 1970s, Keidanren (the Federation of Economic Organizations), a major business organization, took the lead in coordinating Japanese corporate support for foreign institutions by working directly with institutions abroad for whom Keidanren agreed to act as the fund-raising agent. Over the years, Keidanren led fund-raising for Japanese studies centers at major North American and European universities, Japan wings at leading museums, and the presentation of Japanese culture abroad (e.g., cultural festivals, art exhibitions, and tours of performing artists).[56]

Japanese corporate philanthropy's move abroad coincided with the expansion of Japanese multinational corporations, following them into major new markets. Similar to the way that the government had provided the impetus and a template for earlier domestic corporate support, Keidanren pointed the way for new corporate philanthropies abroad. Following its lead, the late 1970s and 1980s witnessed an explosion in the number and range of internationally focused corporate-giving organizations.

At the same time, tensions between the United States and Japan over trade imbalances and market access continued to increase. Japan's growing international role, major corporate takeovers, conspicuous real estate investments, and dramatic gifts to leading American research universities increasingly became the subject of criticism in the United States.[57] Japan's U.S.-focused philanthropic activities led critics to question the goals and motivations of Japanese corporate giving, and some saw Japan's support as dangerous: buying American basic research and brainwashing the public.[58]

Throughout the period of mounting trade tensions, the Japanese government, Keidanren, the Japan Center for International Exchange (JCIE), the Japanese Chamber of Commerce, and Japan affinity groups (like the National Association of Japan-America Societies) worked consistently in the United States to promote positive dialogue on issues related to Japanese philanthropy and corporate citizenship. Keidanren, with JCIE, conducted study missions for Japanese corporate and foundation leaders to study corporate social responsibility in the United States. Those efforts led to the creation in Japan of the One Percent Club in 1989 to encourage corporations to commit at least 1 percent of profits to philanthropic purposes. The same year, the Council for Better Corporate Citizenship (CBCC) was founded by Keidanren to promote good corporate citizenship in the United States by Japanese affiliates. In connection with those efforts, in 1990 the Japanese Chamber of Commerce and Industry of New York published *Joining In! A Handbook for Better Corporate Citizenship in the United States,* a guide to grassroots volunteering in the United States.[59]

At the same time that Japanese philanthropy was skyrocketing abroad, an enormous range of philanthropic and quasi-philanthropic efforts in the arts, music, and culture were expanding in Japan. In contrast to earlier Japanese domestic philanthropy, which had been devoted largely to support the national infrastructure in the areas of scientific and technological advancement, health care, and education, philanthropic activity increasingly focused on the arts in the 1970s, 1980s, and early 1990s. There was an eclectic proliferation of museums of every kind, size, and focus; corporate-sponsored concert halls became engines of public relations; and organizations known as *mecenat* were established to funnel corporate support to the arts.[60] The burgeoning of this sector in Japan also led to the beginning of a professionalized corps of managers specializing in cultural and nonprofit organizations, many of whom were trained in or influenced by the professional norms of Western philanthropic organizations, with the Rockefeller and Ford foundations serving as major models.[61]

No sooner had this infrastructure been firmly put in place and the professionalization of the field of corporate philanthropy begun than the Japanese economic bubble burst, effectively gutting Japanese philanthropies in the early 1990s. Yet civil society in Japan would continue to become a more visible and active part of the cultural scene.

Civil Action After the Bubble Burst and the Ground Shook

The earthquake that hit Kobe on the morning of January 17, 1995, registered 7.2 magnitude on the Richter scale and has since come to be known as the Great Hanshin-Awaji Earthquake (Hanshin-Awaji Dai Shinsai). More than 6,000 lives were lost, 350,000 people were made homeless, and damage ran to many billions of dollars. Kobe, one of Japan's major international harbors, came to a standstill.

Initially, the Japanese government seemed frozen, unable to respond. Bureaucratic wrangling and turf wars prevented cooperation or even the coordination of basic information. Government relief efforts were paralyzed, while disputes among government agencies over jurisdiction prevented effective, coordinated crisis management.[62]

The quake generally awakened many Japanese to the inability of the government to act in the face of such an emergency and dramatically demonstrated the ability of a spontaneously formed coalition of local and regional voluntary, philanthropic, and religious groups. Accurate totals are unknown, but the number of individual volunteers is reliably estimated at more than 1.2 million in the first two months following the quake, reaching a total of possibly 2 million in following months.

Media attention focused on the volunteers from the beginning, no doubt encouraging even more participation. Donations from individuals and groups around the world streamed in to aid earthquake victims. Over the days and months that followed the quake and the marvelous outpouring of voluntary effort that followed, people began to imagine again (or anew) the potential of civil society in Japan. Barely six months after the earthquake, Kyodo Tsushin, one of Japan's major wire services, declared 1995 to be the "Beginning of Japan's Volunteer Era," or *borantia gannen* (Kyodo Tsushin, July 13, 1995).

Examples of the surge in volunteer activity that led to this declaration also include the huge numbers of volunteers who turned out to mop up following a major oil spill that threatened wildlife off the Japan Sea coastline of Fukui Prefecture in 1997 after a Russian tanker sank; and the outpouring of monetary and other support in the aftermath of a major quake in Taiwan that same year. Recognition of the considerable mobilizations of monetary and human capital required for these efforts produced a widespread realization that Japan lacked the necessary legal framework for the growth of civil society now conceived as this new form of voluntary relief activity. The accounts of volunteers aiding in these crises were followed closely in the media, and public discussion on the importance of civil society and the voluntary sector and the need for a stronger legal framework for that sector continued to grow.

Finally, the government spoke publicly of the need to draft legislation to aid the nonprofit sector. Nonprofit leaders and Diet members began to discuss legislation, which eventually produced the nonprofit organizations (NPO) Law, passed in March 1998. In Japan, where almost all legislation is drafted by bureaucrats, the submission and passage of a bill drafted jointly by ordinary citizens and Diet members set a new precedent.[63] The objective underlying the NPO bill was to confer legal status on NPOs that were too small to incorporate under the provisions of the old civil code. While the manner of bringing the legislation to the Diet was pathbreaking, the resulting law only created a patchwork solution that allowed NPOs to operate more easily within the preexisting legal framework, instead of amending the civil code fully. Disputes among Diet factions prevented the full implementations of the law as originally planned. The new law fell far short of redefining the provisions of 1896 civil code, but it did establish a range of newly defined activity eligible for corporate status, without conferring any special tax breaks, at that time.

*****

Japanese politicians, businessmen, and intellectuals who sought John D. Rockefeller 3rd's advice as well as his philanthropy after the war were far from being innocent and naive. In fact, some of them tried to use Rockefeller's prestige and influence in order to advance what they considered Japan's national interest or their own ambitions. They instinctively felt that closer U.S.-Japanese relations were crucial to Japan's survival in the postwar world. Their own survival in their respective careers, in turn, partly depended on their ability to perform as influential actors who could promote better bilateral relations. Maintaining close personal connections with such a prominent American as Rockefeller was certainly considered an important asset in advancing their future careers both inside and beyond the national border. Against the background of the Cold War, Japanese conservative politicians, in particular, emphasized alternately the helplessness of the defeated country and its new strategic importance as a super domino in Asia. Though what private philanthropy could do in terms of financial assistance was naturally limited, JDR 3rd was regarded as valuable in another respect. He was not only a spokesman for better U.S.-Japanese relations, but also one of a handful of Americans sympathetic to the Japanese situation and willing to enlighten American policy makers in regard to Japan's perspectives.

As John's circle of contacts and interests broadened and deepened, and as he and his Japanese friends and colleagues gained seniority, his stature continued to increase. He had many opportunities to discuss his philanthropic activities and views of America's evolving civil sector with Japanese leaders and in the media. Even though the Japanese media focused on Rockefeller as a celebrity and made their share of misinterpretations as to his motivations, the organizations with which he worked most closely paid careful attention to Rockefeller interests and followed JDR 3rd's speeches and published works. It was not only Rockefeller philanthropy and the individual philosophies of philanthropy and social responsibility of family members that made conscious impact on the Japanese; in fact, JDR 3rd and, later, David Rockefeller were influential on the Japanese not simply for what they actually said, but equally, for the importance of who they were.

As time passed, JDR 3rd increasingly saw public affairs and public service as key to the maintenance of the successful U.S. system of democracy, and he wanted to encourage the Japanese to follow that path. Behind the scenes, JDR 3rd's personal philosophy was absorbed and incorporated into the fundamental mission of organizations he helped establish. Such Japanese organizations took notice of JDR 3rd's *The Second American Revolution* (1973), the impact of which was likely greater in Japan than in the United States.

The influence of these organizations and programs in creating bilateral ties and evolving notions of civil society has been enormous. Of particular importance are the roles of a number of American institutions with a focus on U.S.-Japanese relations (or Asian issues more broadly) that were greatly influenced by the Rockefellers. These include the Japan Society in New York (reinvigorated by JDR 3rd after the war), which has existed since 1907 as a key crossroads of U.S.-Japanese dialogue in New York City; the Trilateral Commission (a major interest of David Rockefeller's), which has promoted dialogue among the United States, western Europe, and Japan at the level of top business and political leaders; the Asia Society, a creation of JDR 3rd's that addresses Asian issues broadly, including cultural exchange, the arts, and public education; and the Asian Cultural Council, which grew, after his death, out of the JDR 3rd Fund and has supported hundreds of Japanese artists and writers who have studied in the United States.

Added to these are key organizations in Japan: the International House of Japan, led until his death in 1989 by John's old friend Shigeharu Matsumoto; and the Japan Center for International Exchange (JCIE), founded in 1971 by Tadashi Yamamoto,[64] which has also served as the Japan secretariat of the Trilateral Commission. The Rockefeller vision of interdependent institutions in a civil society also shaped the development of these Japanese institutions. Over the years, they have expanded the scope of their activities from an initial focus on U.S.-Japanese relations to include support for the growing nongovernmental spheres of Japanese public life and the expanding Japanese involvement with other societies in East and Southeast Asia, as well as worldwide.

As Japan prospered, JDR 3rd was quick to encourage the institutions he founded to envision a Japanese nonprofit sector. In 1971, he spoke to Japanese leaders in Tokyo, saying that "perhaps the time has come for Japan to develop more alternatives for action, greater flexibility within the private sector for meeting the problems and opportunities of today—in particular, creating the conditions that would allow the institution of philanthropy to develop further." In that same speech, JDR cautioned that Japan was in danger of creating the impression of its "overpresence" by focusing too much on political and economic aspects of its international relations without greater consideration of cultural and interpersonal exchange.[65]

In that speech, JDR 3rd anticipated the image Japan was developing as an "economic animal" and simultaneously proposed one of the principal strategies Japan would choose in order to change that image—international philanthropy. It was not merely JDR 3rd's suggestion that philanthropy be used as a strategy by Japanese leaders; in fact, a number of Rockefeller-associated organizations soon took the lead in studying philanthropy in North America. Together, Keidanren (the Federation of Economic Organizations), the Japan Society in New York, the International House of Japan, and especially the Japan Center for International Exchange, became involved in efforts to study various aspects of philanthropy. With the guidance of close Rockefeller associate Datus Smith, JCIE established a program known as the International Philanthropy Project.[66] That project coordinated the first Japanese study mission on philanthropy to the United States and Canada in 1974. Datus Smith facilitated connections with North American foundations and nonprofit associations, and Yoichi Maeda, the executive director of International House of Japan, headed the Japanese mission. David Rockefeller topped the list of "leading figures in private foundations and corporations" with whom the group met.

Throughout the next several years, the International Philanthropy Project coordinated a number of conferences, study missions, and publications, each involving Rockefeller associates and Rockefeller and other funding. These included an international symposium held in 1976 on the impact of the Commission on Private Philanthropy and the Public Needs, known as the Filer Commission,[67] an international symposium in Japan on the role of philanthropy in advanced societies, and a seminar series on overseas philanthropy. JCIE's publication *International Philanthropy Project of the Japan Center for International Exchange (JCIE): A Case Study* (1991) summarizes JCIE's interest in the Filer Commission as follows: "The Japanese foundation and corporate officers and staff observing American philanthropy were interested in this active debate on the relevance and legitimacy of the voluntary sector in the United States. They were also impressed by the initiative JDR 3rd took in organizing research and study on private philanthropy in the changing social environment through the Commission on Private Philanthropy and Public Needs (Filer Commission)."

Working closely with JCIE has also been Keidanren, greatly influenced by David Rockefeller's close friend, the late Akio Morita (founder of Sony), and by other leaders close to David and/or the Trilateral Commission. From the 1970s through the mid-1990s, Keidanren promoted major efforts to expand Japanese corporate philanthropy, to encourage better corporate citizenship abroad, to increase expected levels of corporate giving, and to expand voluntary action in Japan. JCIE also served as secretariat of a number of so-called Wisemen's Groups that played major roles in evolving networks of business and public leaders and was often central to the convening of major conferences that involved U.S., Japanese, and other world leaders.

More recently, JCIE has been a leader in defining and professionalizing Japan's nonprofit sector,[68] and in 1997 it took a considerable role in organizing that community to support the new nonprofit corporation law (the NPO Law, 1998) through the Japanese

Diet. Given JCIE's close ties with established politicians and their intimate knowledge of the players and the process of Japanese politics, they were extremely well placed to work with Keidanren, nonprofit colleagues, and Diet members to pass that legislation. The legislation was groundbreaking less for the immediate impact of the law itself, than for the private sector initiative through which that law was passed. And JCIE's role, however important it was, was behind the scenes.

It would be easy to regard philanthropic initiatives such as these Rockefeller-inspired developments as simply an outward spread of American influence. Rather, they should be interpreted as a long-term collaboration that has evolved between a group of closely interrelated bilateral organizations and Rockefeller interests, a collaboration that has been intensely reflective in nature. Rockefeller ideas—those articulated by JDR 3rd in his 1951 report to Ambassador Dulles, in particular his views of a nonprofit sector, suggested in 1971; and those embodied in his commitment to truly two-way artistic and cultural exchange—have been central to the formation of key organizations that articulate and mediate bilateral relations as they have evolved during the postwar period. Once the Japanese economy took off, Rockefeller models guided Japan's growing international role and helped to define Japan's evolving nonprofit sector.

It is equally important to recognize that the longer-term success and impact of the institutions such as the Japan Society, the International House, and the Asia Society that were created or reinvigorated by the Rockefellers, as well as those like JCIE and others that have been major beneficiaries of Rockefeller philanthropy, depended as much on the perspectives and agenda of Japanese cultural leaders and intellectuals who had varying, if at time converging, views of the bilateral institutions that would restore Japan to a secure position in the postwar world order. These institutions and their changing mandates serve as a lens through which to examine the impact of Rockefeller philanthropy, and to observe how Rockefeller notions of social responsibility and the nonprofit sector continue to help define the evolution of those concepts in Japan in the twenty-first century.

In conclusion, this chapter endeavors to clarify the link between Rockefeller philanthropy during the early postwar period and the personal influence of JDR 3rd and his philosophy of social responsibility on the evolution of the concept of civil society in Japan. I argue that JDR 3rd's experience with the Dulles Peace Mission of 1951 played a crucial role in helping him to define his early postwar priorities and his future involvement with Japan. I also suggest that the interests developed and priorities outlined in his report to Ambassador Dulles provided a "blueprint" for Rockefeller philanthropy in Japan that molded U.S.-Japanese cultural relations and, more important, U.S.-Japanese cultural institutions that have come to play important roles in Japan's evolving civil sector.

As noted, I divide postwar discourse on civil society in Japan into four periods. The first two—the Occupation and the early 1950s, and the 1960s and the growth of consumer participation—were essentially those of institution building both for Japanese society and for the institutions founded, reinvigorated, and nurtured by Rockefeller philanthropic interests. During those earlier periods the impact of Rockefeller philanthropy was largely on infrastructure building and on promoting international intellectual and scholarly exchange, both of which established the foundations from which Rockefeller-supported institutions have come to play major roles in the two most recent periods of civil society expansion in Japan. It is particularly during the later periods—the era of corporate philanthropy, and the period after the bursting of Japan's bubble economy—that these institutions have become major leaders in defining and guiding Japan's civil sector. Many of those efforts in these latter two periods took place after JDR 3rd's death, yet they are equally part of his legacy in Japan.

Endnotes

[1] Notable among these are Louis Gerson's *John Foster Dulles*, Cooper Square, NY, 1967; Michael Schaller's *The American Occupation of Japan: The Origins of the Cold War in Asia*, Oxford University Press, NY, 1985; Frederick S. Dunn's *Peace-Making and the Settlement with Japan*, Princeton University Press, Princeton, NJ, 1963; and Michael Yoshisu's *Japan and the San Francisco Peace Settlement*, Columbia University Press, NY, 1983. Chihiro Hosoya's *San Furansisuko kowae no Michi* [The Road to San Francisco], n.p., Chuo Koronsha, 1984 is a notable work by a Japanese author. With the fiftieth anniversary of the signing of the Peace Settlement insight, no doubt many more studies are on the way.

[2] Research on the present project was begun officially in 1997. Recently the Japan Center for International Exchange (JCIE) has joined in by undertaking a study that is now looking at the impact of major philanthropies such as Rockefeller and Ford in these areas.

[3] A few important works that examine JDR 3rd's early activities related to postwar Japan include John Ensor Harr and Peter J. Johnson's *The Rockefeller Conscience: An American Family in Public and Private,* Charles Scribner's Sons, NY, 1991, and *The Rockefeller Century,* Charles Scribner's Sons, NY, 1988; as well as John Curtis Perry's article "Private Philanthropy and Foreign Affairs: The Case of John D. Rockefeller 3rd and Japan," *Asian Perspectives*, 8: 2, 1984, pp. 268–84; See also Shigeharu Matsumoto, (as compiled by Hiroko Kako) *Waga Kokoro no Jijoden* [The Autobiography of My Heart], International House of Japan, Tokyo, 1992.

[4] See Victoria Lyon Bestor and Reiko Maekawa, "The Philanthropic Roots of the Voluntary and Nonprofit Sector in Japan: The Rockefeller Legacy," in *The Voluntary and Nonprofit Sector in Japan: An Emerging Response to a Changing Society,* Stephen P. Osborne (ed.) Routledge, London, 2003, and Victoria Lyon Bestor, "Toward a Cultural Biography of Civil Society in Japan," in *Family and Social Policy in Japan: Anthropological Approaches,* Roger Goodman (ed.) Cambridge University Press, London, 2002. The present chapter utilizes and expands upon the arguments made in these two chapters with an explicit focus on the long term impact of JDR 3rd's role in the Dulles Peace Mission of 1951 upon subsequent Rockefeller philanthropy in Japan.

[5] Seigen Miyasato, "John Foster Dulles and the Peace Settlement with Japan," in *John Foster Dulles and the Diplomacy of the Cold War*, Richard H. Immerman (ed.) Princeton University Press, Princeton, NJ, 1990.

[6] Ibid., p.193.

[7] Foreign Relations of the United States, 1951, vol. 6: Asia and the Pacific, Washington, U.S. Government Printing Office, 1984, as quoted in Miyasato, "John Foster Dulles," pp. 195–6.

[8] Memorandum from Minutes of Dulles Mission Staff Meeting, January 26, 1951, *Foreign Relations*, 1951, 6: pp. 813–4. For Dulles's view on cultural relations, see Miyasato, "John Foster Dulles," p. 204.

[9] John D. Rockefeller, "United States-Japan Cultural Relations: Report to Ambassador Dulles," 1951, Rockefeller Archive Center [hereafter RAC], (files of JDR 3rd), R.G. 5, Series 1, Box 14, Dulles report folder.

[10] Perry, "Private philanthropy and Foreign Affairs."

[11] In addition to the many published accounts of the collaboration between Rockefeller family members and their associates, the 1998 ARNOVA conference included a panel focusing on Rockefeller support in Canada, South America, and the rural South, which discussed such personal networks.

[12] RAC, Rockefeller Foundation, R.G. 1.1, Series 200, Box 358, Folder 4251, "Institute of Pacific Relations. Grants to Member Councils," 10 September, 1951.

[13] A further discussion of area studies can be found in my unpublished paper presented at Doshisha University in June 1998.

[14] This was the then predominant view of modernization, a concept that changed over time on both sides of the Pacific until if finally went out of vogue. See essays by John Whitney Hall and Marius B. Jansen in Marius B. Jansen (ed.) *Changing Japanese Attitudes Toward Modernization*, Princeton University Press, Princeton, NJ, 1965.

[15] See references to Charles Burton Fahs's views as expressed in a memo on intercultural understanding, RAC, R.G. 3.2, Series 900, Box 31, Folder 165, memo dated January 1951.

[16] RAC, Rockefeller Foundation, 1.1, Series 200, I.P.R. files from 1935 to 1944.

[17] The Occupation forces known as SCAP (from Supreme Commander of Allied Powers) began the Occupation with a rigorous plan to purge all those who had lead Japan's military-industrial complex before and during World War II. However, following the takeover of China by the Communists in 1949 and the onset of the Korean War, Allied policy with regard to Japan shifted to a focus on economic reinvigoration that depended upon the skills, connections, and ties of many business leaders who had previously been on the list of those to be purged.

[18] Marriage between cousins was not uncommon in Japan at the time, especially among the more wealthy. Also, because Matsumoto was the son of a concubine, also a common practice among the aristocracy, he and Hanako shared only one grandparent.

[19] Haru Matsukata Reischauer, *Samurai and Silk*, Harvard University Press, Cambridge, MA, 1986.

[20] Charles Austin Beard (1874–1948) had important historical connections with Japan and with the Rockefeller Philanthropies. Before becoming a professor at Yale, he served as director of the New York Bureau of Municipal Research (BMR). In 1922, he went to Japan at the invitation of then mayor Goto Shimpei to conduct a study of Tokyo's municipal government, which was published in 1923 as *The Administration and Politics of Tokyo: A Survey and Opinions,* Macmillan, New York. The Tokyo Institute for Municipal Research, established in 1922, was modeled after the BMR in New York. Beard returned to Japan just after the great Kanto earthquake of 1923 and assisted with reconstruction as an adviser to the administration. I have not yet had the opportunity to study the papers of the Bureau of Municipal Reform in the RAC files of the Office of the Messrs. Rockefeller. Civil Interests Series 1899–1961.

[21] Matsumoto, *Waga Kokoro no Jijoden*, p.185.

[22] Ibid.

[23] See Bestor and Maekawa, "Philanthropic Roots," for a more detailed discussion.

[24] George F. Kennan, *American Diplomacy,* University of Chicago Press, Chicago, 1984, p. 153.

[25] The report on the first nine years of the Intellectual Interchange Program found in the files of the International House of Japan (IHJ) at the RAC states: "A few days after the formation of the Cultural Center Preparatory Committee in November, 1951, for the establishment of the International House of Japan, Mr. John D. Rockefeller 3rd had an initial talk with a small group on the idea of Intellectual Interchange. It originated from a suggestion from the Japanese side that it would be most helpful to invite one or two top level American intellectual leaders to Japan at the time of the coming into effect of the peace treaty, when the need for true understanding of American policy and thought was likely to be particularly acute." JDR 3rd Collection, R.G. 3, Sub-series 1-O.M.R., Asian Interests, Box 14B, Folder IHJ. 1954–61.

[26] Two days after being elected president of the Japan Society, JDR stated in a press release: "The Society's long range objective is to help bring the people of the United States and Japan closer together in their appreciation and understanding of each other and each other's way of life. It is our hope that a vigorous Japan Society can be of real benefit by functioning as a private, non-political organization interested in serving as a medium through which both our peoples can learn from the experiences and the accomplishments of the other." At the same meeting, John Foster Dulles was elected chairman of the board and JDR 3rd personally assumed chairmanship of the Executive Committee. JDR's associates Edgar Young and Donald McLean then "went to work on amending the certificate of incorporation and the bylaws of the Society to make its organizational structure smoother and sounder." E. O. Reischauer, *Japan Society, 1907–1982: 75 Years of Partnership across the Pacific,* Japan Society, Inc., NY, 1982, p. 50.

[27] "On June 28, 1956, the Asia Society was incorporated in the State of New York. Dr. Grayson Kirk of Columbia was named chairman and JDR was elected president, with Phillips Talbot and Ernest A. Gross as vice presidents, August Maffrey as treasury, and Edgar Young as secretary," Harr and Johnson, *The Rockefeller Conscience*, p. 101. Harr and Johnson further note that one of the first requests put to the new Asia Society came from the president of the IPR, who requested that the society take over some of the institute's functions. The Asia Society's charter had been expressly written to exclude political activities and limit its scope to social and cultural affairs. The IPR itself was soon to go out of existence.

[28] A recent example of this genre is Glenn Davis and John G. Roberts, *An Occupation Without Troops: Wall Street's Half-Century Domination of Japanese Politics,* Yenbooks, Tokyo. 1996.

[29] From John D. Rockefeller 3rd's 1953 memo "Objective and Focus of My Asian Interest," RAC, JDR 3rd papers, R.G. 3, Series 2.

[30] Masayuki Deguchi, "Not for Profit: A Brief History of Japanese Nonprofit Organizations," *Look Japan,* Tokyo, January 2000.

[31] Zaibatsu are described by Eleanor Hadley in the *Encyclopedia of Japan* (Kodansha, Tokyo, 1983), as "Industrial and financial combines of a conglomerate type that grew to great size and attained a dominant position in the Japanese economy between the Meiji period (1868–1912) and World War II. Although the holding companies of those combines were officially dissolved during the post–World War II Occupation period,

the new corporate groupings (*keiretsu*) that appeared after the war are often regarded as their direct successors and have become the subject of lively controversy."

[32] JCIE (Japan Center for International Exchange), 1989. See list of JCIE publications at www.jcie.org.jp/books. Also, a larger discussion of this topic is contained in my chapter "Toward a Cultural Biography of Civil Society in Japan" in Roger Goodman's book.

[33] Yoshinori Yamaoka, "History of the Nonprofit Sector in Japan," in T. Yamamoto (ed.) *The Nonprofit Sector in Japan*, University of Manchester Press, Manchester, UK, 1998.

[34] Mary Evelyn Tucker, "The Neo-Confucian Roots of Japanese Philanthropy," in Warren F. Ilchman, Stanley, N. Katz, and Edward L. Queen II (eds.) *Philanthropy in the World's Tradition*, University of Indiana Press, Bloomington, 1998.

[35] Masayuki Deguchi, "A Comparative View of Civil Society," *Washington-Japan Journal*: Spring 1999, pp. 11–20.

[36] Daikichi Irokawa, *Meiji Seijishi* [Meiji Political History], Tokyo University Press, Tokyo, 1964.

[37] Deguchi, "Comparative View of Civil Society;" Victoria Lyon Bestor "Reimaging Civil Society in Japan" in *Civil Society in Japan and the U.S.:* A Special Issue, *Washington-Japan Journal*, Spring 1999; Bestor, "Toward a Cultural Biography of Civil Society in Japan."

[38] Andrew Barshay, "Capitalism and Civil Society in Postwar Japan: Perspectives from Intellectual History," in Frank J. Schwartz and Susan J. Pharr (eds.) *The State of Civil Society in Japan*, Cambridge University Press, London, UK, 2003.

[39] Some other discussions of this history—for example, Deguchi's—divide this history into only three periods, omitting the period of corporate philanthropy. It is my contention that the period of corporate philanthropy was indeed an important and independent period, during which many Japanese executives became involved in voluntary efforts abroad.

[40] In addition to the Kobe quake, 1995 was also the year of the sarin gas attacks on the Tokyo Subway, and the outbreak of mad cow disease. The e-coli:0157 outbreak in the Kobe suburb of Sakai followed in 1996. All of these events rocked Japan.

[41] Goodman, *Family and Social Policy in Japan*.

[42] Victoria Lyon Bestor 1998 "Shimin Shakai to wa nani ka: Is Civil Society a Transnational Phenomenon or a Translational Dilemma in Japan?" unpublished paper presented at the Kansai Forum on United States-Japan Relations, Osaka American Center, Osaka.; Bestor, "Toward a Cultural Biography of Civil Society in Japan."

[43] Barshay, "Capitalism and Civil Society."

[44] Deguchi, "Comparative View of Civil Society."

[45] AMPO is an abbreviation of the Japanese name for the United States-Japan Security Treaty (Nichibei Anzen Hosho Juyaku). Taking the underlined portions of the treaty's name and following the Japanese linguistic convention, that when you combine a "ho" sound after another sound it often changes to either a "po" or a "bo" sound, thus it becomes "AMPO." It also always seems to be rendered in all capital letters.

[46] Barshay, "Capitalism and Civil Society."

[47] Keiichi Matsushita, "Present-Day Problems in Japanese Politics" *Journal of Social and Political Ideas in Japan*, (originally published in *Sekai*, January 1964), pp. 198–206.

[48] Crocker Snow, "Tokyo's Governor Minobe" *Japan Interpreter*, 8: 2, 1973, pp. 185–94.

[49] Ibid.

[50] Bradford L Simcock and Ellis S. Krauss, "'Citizens' Movements: The Growth and Impact of Environmental Protest in Japan," in Kurt Steiner, Ellis S. Krauss, and Scott Flanagan (eds.) *Political Opposition and Local Politics in Japan*, Princeton University Press, Princeton, NJ, 1980.

[51] Irokawa, *Meiji Seishish.*

[52] Goodman, *Family and Social Policy in Japan.*

[53] Yasusuke Murakami, "The Age of New Middle Mass Politics: The Case of Japan," *Journal of Japanese Studies*, 8: 1, 1982, pp. 29–72.

[54] Tadashi Yamamoto (ed.), *The Nonprofit Sector in Japan*, University of Manchester Press, Manchester, UK, 1998.

[55] John D Rockefeller 3rd, "The Challenge of the Quality of Life," speech delivered in Tokyo at International House of Japan, May 14, 1971, RAC, R.G. 5 (papers of JDR 3rd), Series 3, Box 95, Folder 776.

[56] Bestor, "Shimin Shakai to wa nani ka."

[57] Karel Van Wolferen, *The Enigma of Japanese Power: People and Politics in a Stateless Nation.* Knopf, New York. 1989.

[58] Stephanie Epstein, *The Buying of the American Mind*, Center for Public Integrity, Washington, DC, 1990.

[59] I believe that the volunteer experience first gained in the United States by many in the expatriate Japanese community later provided a possible template for voluntary action among corporate returnees, many of whom eventually found themselves unemployed or underemployed when Japan's economy contracted in the 1990s.

[60] The term *mecenat* (*mesena* in katakana), grew out of private Franco-Japanese dialogue exploring strategies for increasing support to the arts; the name was coined from the name of the Roman minister, Caius Maecenas, who protected the arts during the reign of Emperor Augustus.

[61] In 1997, the GAP Group (Kokusai Kodan Katsudo Kenkyukai) published the book *Kokusai Puroguramu Ofisa* (The International Program Officer) as a guide to the professionalization of the field. Since then, Katsuji Imata, a young, internationally oriented, U.S.-trained nonprofit administrator has coordinated a series of exchanges and internships between program officers from Japanese nonprofits and American counterpart organizations with funding from the Japan Foundation Center for Global Partnership.

[62] Robert Pekkanen, "Japan's New Politics: The Case of the NPO Law," *Journal of Japanese Studies*, 26:1, 2000, pp. 111–48.

[63] Ibid.

[64] I first interviewed Tadashi Yamamoto on this subject in early 1998. Since that time JCIE has launched a major research project examining the role of major philanthropies, including Rockefeller and Ford, in the development of Japan's civil sector, following the major theme of my own research.

[65] Rockefeller, "Challenge of the Quality of Life."

[66] RAC, Rockefeller Brothers Fund, Series 4–JCIE files, grants, various boxes, and folders.

[67] The Commission on Private Philanthropy and Public Need, known as the Filer Commission, was an initiative of JDR 3rd's that studied the importance of private philanthropy in the changing social environment of the United States. The JCIE, in

collaboration with other Rockefeller-related groups and individuals, organized the February 23, 1976 conference in Tokyo.

[68] The JCIE's Hideko Katsumata is a key member of the GAP Group (Kokusai Kodan Katsudo Kenkyukai) which has published a number of books on the subject.

PHILANTHROPIC FOUNDATIONS AND CIVIL SOCIETY IN A GLOBALIZED WORLD

AMERICAN FOUNDATIONS AND OVERSEAS FUNDING: NEW CHALLENGES IN THE ERA OF GLOBALIZATION

Peter Frumkin

American philanthropic foundations have long devoted their resources toward a wide range of human problems, often working on issues that neither government nor business sector have been able to fully address. As they have carried out their work, foundations have tried to overcome their comparatively modest resources by experimenting with a wide array of tools and techniques aimed at improving the effectiveness of their grantmaking.[1] Changes in the nature, size, and location of human problems over time have made this quest for effectiveness crucial. Never has this been more the case than in recent years. One of the most important challenges that American foundations have faced recently is the transformation of the playing field on which their grantmaking unfolds.

*****

For years, many foundations have concentrated on discrete geographical areas, often the cities or regions around them, with the intention of using philanthropic dollars in a concentrated way. Yet as the nature, scope, and source of many human problems have changed, so, too, has the direction of the gaze of foundations.[2] As many issues have taken on simultaneously local, regional, national and global dimensions, foundations have come to recognize that their grantmaking must be integrated into broader social systems, directed at problems that have porous borders, and related to trends that are playing out in countries around the world.[3]

The decision to focus giving on issues and problems outside the United States raises a number of interesting challenges for foundations. While some narrow aspects of the philanthropic transaction look the same when carried out domestically and internationally, other elements change in significant ways.[4] In particular, one area in which some serious rethinking may be required is that of the core rationales that guide giving, sometimes described as the theories of change or logic models.[5] Some of the more standard models of generating impact (the funding of basic research, policy advocacy, direct services, interorganizational collaborations, etc.) may prove difficult to implement in cultures that are substantially different, where the local nonprofit field is less developed, and where the tolerance of foreign government institutions for philanthropic interventions is lower. American foundations seeking to work overseas must be sensitive to these differences and begin to craft a new approach to grantmaking that takes into consideration the powerful changes wrought by globalization. After briefly sketching the evolution of American foundations abroad and the current dimensions of this work, this chapter suggests that new theories of change may well be needed if American foundations are to be successful in carrying out their missions across national borders.

*****

Over the past century, international grantmaking—defined here as giving by American foundations to causes outside the United States—has grown and evolved in four main stages, each of which correspond more or less fully to a specific phase of U.S. involvement in world affairs or a distinctive period of economic growth. The stages can be roughly defined as the beginning of the twentieth century to World War II, from World War II to the 1960s, from the 1960s to the end of the Cold War, and the post–Cold War period to the present. During these turbulent times, foundations have not always done the easy or obvious things and have at various times found themselves working with and against American foreign policy. Sometimes foundations have waited for opportunities to open up due to shifts in the international scene and then entered at carefully chosen points in time. At other times, foundations have taken a more activist role and sought to initiate change.

The first period started early in the twentieth century with the creation and initial grantmaking of some of most prominent foundations in American history, notably the Carnegie Corporation (1911), the Rockefeller Foundation (1913), the Kellogg Foundation (1930), and the Ford Foundation (1936). The emergence of these new, powerful and perpetual philanthropic institutions was a major step toward the institutionalization of American overseas giving.[6] With the exception of the years following the stock market crash, the United States experienced a sustained period of prosperity and took on a new role in world affairs. Through its involvement in the World War I and the ensuing efforts at European reconstruction, the United States shifted from an isolationist stance to a policy of broader engagement. Moreover, early signs of globalization were already becoming evident, as the period was marked by massive transatlantic flows of persons, goods and services, and capital.[7] The combination of these domestic and international factors provided an ideal context for the early development of international grantmaking. Along with a myriad of smaller-size foundations that emerged during the same period (e.g., Cameron Forbes Fund, New England Belgian Relief Fund, and Rosenwald Fund), philanthropic foundations focused at least initially on disaster relief and humanitarian aid. Cooperating with other governmental and relief agencies such as the Red Cross and the American Relief Administration, foundations tackled the pressing need for combating starvation and epidemics, especially in Eastern Europe and Soviet Russia.[8]

Following these successful relief efforts, the largest American foundations dedicated a substantial proportion of their resources to promoting international peace and understanding. Animated by the conviction that peace was advanced by the sharing of knowledge, the Carnegie Endowment for International Peace assisted in the rebuilding of devastated libraries in Belgium, France, Serbia, and Russia. It also encouraged international exchanges between university students and professors, and funded agencies such as the League of Nations, and the Institute of Pacific Relations.[9] The Rockefeller Foundation was also directly involved in the promotion of international understanding by subsidizing institutions such as the Council of Foreign Relations in New York, the Geneva Research Center, and the International Studies Conference in Paris. In addition, the Rockefeller Foundation extended its geographical focus even more broadly and funded education initiatives in Latin America and the Far East aimed at developing links between these regions and the United States.

The second period of American foundation activity abroad started with World War II and tracked the changes that were wrought by the war. In the aftermath of the conflict, many of the relief efforts and humanitarian assistance programs were taken over government and channeled through institutions like the United Nations Relief and Rehabilitation Administration, the Marshall Plan, and later the International Cooperation Administration. The U.S. government became the prime international funding source and overseas assistance was a potent tool of U.S. foreign policy. With the creation of this new geopolitical context, private philanthropic activity went through a period of change and adaptation. American foundations increased significantly in number, assets, resources, and overseas funding compared with the first period. In 1960, American foundations' assets were estimated at $11 billion with annual grants totaling $625 million. In 1957, about 8 percent of total grants were spent on overseas projects.[10] After a significant slowdown following the 1929 financial crisis, foundations resumed their efforts toward social and economic reconstruction in Europe, assistance to refugees in the Near East, and combating famine and infectious diseases in the Far East (particularly Korea and China) and Africa. For example, the Ford Foundation started its Overseas Development Program in 1951, which focused on promoting democratic principles in Asia and the Near East to consolidate world peace. The Carnegie philanthropies continued their earlier support of education through international grants and scholarships. As foundations grew in number and as the collective resources of the field expanded, the idea of using philanthropic funds to strengthen a new international agenda became more appealing and feasible. Foundation funds could both work on American social problems and look across borders at challenges—sometimes more acute and desperate—that were emerging in other parts of the world.

A third period in the evolution of American philanthropic activity abroad began with the end of European reconstruction efforts, grew through the elaboration of broader development issues, and culminated with the fall of communism. In the 1960s, the United States was in the midst of the Cold War and adopted a strongly interventionist stance in the global arena. The creation of the United States Agency for International Development in 1961 enabled the U.S. government to channel direct support to developing nations through long-term economic and social development programs. Helped by a long and sustained period of economic growth, American foundations followed the same trend by fostering overseas development based on American values and priorities. Foundations began focusing their efforts on attacking the root causes of poverty (lack of agricultural productivity, lack of technical skills, health problems, etc.) by promoting entrepreneurship, knowledge building, and democracy. The Ford and Rockefeller foundations broke new ground and initiated global successes in international crop research.[11] For example, the Ford Foundation allocated $10.5 million in 1960 to increase food production in India, a very large expenditure for philanthropy and a substantial amount within the local context. Another initiative of the Ford Foundation was aimed at helping the Indian government curb the demographic boom, one major cause of the country's poverty. Other foundations were taking similar action in other part of the world, including the Kellogg Foundation, which made grants to launch and enhance agricultural and health programs in Latin America. Continued Cold War concerns about peace, security, and American influence in the world also motivated foundations to support Asian, Near Eastern, and African study and research programs in American universities throughout the 1970s and 1980s. By 1990, 415 American foundations had cross-border activities, with total international grants adding up to $508 million.[12] While foundation grantmaking during this period unfolded in different places around the world and operated under widely divergent assumptions and priorities, a central theme or concern was still noticeable; namely, the promotion of greater understanding across boarders at a time when political tensions were growing.

With the geopolitical transformation resulting from the collapse of the Soviet Union, the worldwide boom of civil society, and the democratization wave that hit the former communist countries, a vast new set of philanthropic opportunities for American foundations emerged in the early 1990s.[13] Two major elements shaped this fourth period. First, the level of U.S. foundations' cross-border funding reached record levels. Second, new "megafoundations" appeared on the scene, and many adopted international agendas. Fueled by a series of years of substantial stock market rises and the consequent dramatic increase in the value of endowment assets, U.S. foundations' overseas funding rose considerably in the 1990s. In 1998 it reached $1.6 billion, which is more than twice the level of 1990. Relative to total foundation giving, overseas funding reached almost 11 percent.[14] While older foundations such as Carnegie, Ford, or Rockefeller continued to play a significant role in international grantmaking, new foundations with considerable resources have appeared on the scene over the last decade. These include the Bill and Melinda Gates Foundation, the David and Lucile Packard Foundation, and the United Nations Foundation, the last being the public foundation created by Ted Turner with an initial pledge of $1 billion. In addition to these large-scale grantmakers, several medium and small-scale foundations created in the 1990s, such as the Feinstein Foundation, the Tanaka Memorial Foundation, or the Sidney Kemmel Foundation, initiated significant cross-border funding. One reason why some of these new foundations chose to focus on international problems such as disease eradication stems from the size of the philanthropic resources involved. With annual grantmaking of over $1 billion, the Gates Foundation naturally sought to take on social problems of considerable size and importance. Early one, it chose as one of its major initiatives the eradication of polio through widespread vaccinations in the developing world. Other major American foundations, like the MacArthur Foundation and the Open Society Institute, expanded their international activities by opening multiple overseas offices and moving their grantmaking and staff closer to the issues they sought to address through philanthropy. In order to respond to the main challenges of globalization, American foundations began to focus on issues such as improving global environmental awareness and cooperation, strengthening civil society in formerly communist countries, and providing humanitarian assistance in the aftermath of natural disasters and emergency situations. American foundation giving has gotten more ambitious, systematic, and aggressive in recent years, in part because the problems and opportunities are still large and in part because the field has finally become part of the mainstream of American institutional giving.

International grantmaking has thus developed considerably over the past century and reached unprecedented levels at the end of the twentieth century. One of the most significant pieces of descriptive data about international giving is that it now stands at over 10 percent of all foundation giving—after decades of hovering around 3 percent. Historically, American foundations have always dedicated the great majority of their grants to domestic purposes. However, international grants as a percentage of total giving grew steadily in both the 1980s and 1990s, reaching 11.5 percent in 1990 and 1994, and settling at 10.9 percent in 1998 (see figure 5.1).

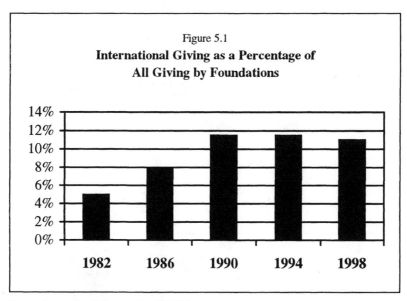

Figure 5.1
**International Giving as a Percentage of
All Giving by Foundations**

Source: International Grantmaking II, 2000.

Foundations with a long history of international activity are still the largest contributors to overseas projects. Foundations created before 1950 dedicate on average 12.4 percent of their total giving to overseas activities. Foundations created during the 1960s and 1970s allocate the least to international funding. In terms of size of grants, American foundations involved in international funding tend to support projects through a limited number of very large grants. Foundation grants of more than $500,000 represent only 3 percent of total international grants, but account for almost 38 percent of total dollars dedicated to overseas projects. Moreover, grants ranging from $100,000 to $500,000 represent 23 percent of total international grants, but account for 42 percent of total dollar amounts dedicated internationally. [15] This data confirm that international grantmaking, unlike many areas of domestic grantmaking in which large numbers of small grants dominate, is driven by fewer, larger philanthropic commitments (see figure 5.2). For those who criticize foundations for making too many small and insignificant grants in the regular programs, international giving appears to elicit an impulse to act more decisively through larger commitments. Considering that these overseas grants typically buy dollar for dollar a great deal more programmatic activity than when funds are spent at home (due to lower costs abroad), international grantmaking appears to have a number of significant advantages.

With the joint realization that many human problems span boundaries and with an appreciation that U.S. grant dollars have greater philanthropic purchasing power overseas came new actors and progenitors of international grantmaking. Throughout the twentieth century, a handful of American Foundations (Ford, Rockefeller, Carnegie, Kellogg, Andrew Mellon, Rockefeller Brothers, etc.) dominated the list of the largest international grantmakers. Today, the group of major American foundations working overseas has changed. Beyond the dominant position of the Gates Foundation, the more recently created Open Society Institute of philanthropist George Soros now ranks in eighth position, while historically prominent institutions such as the Carnegie Corporation of New York or the Rockefeller Brothers Fund have disappeared from the top ten list, now ranking respectively in the thirteenth and the nineteenth positions. It is worth noting that in 1998, the top ten foundations provided nearly 60 percent of all funding and that the Ford Foundation ($232 million in international grants) alone provided one-fifth of all overseas grant dollars and one in seven of all grants. While the institutions may have changed, the concentration of philanthropic dollars in the largest institutions has not.[16]

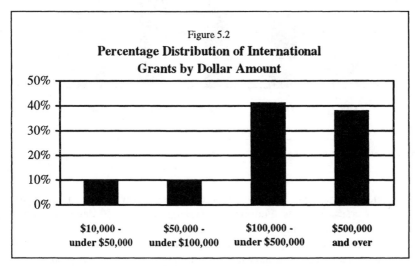

Source: International Grantmaking II, 2000

International grantmaking includes both direct overseas funding and support of U.S.-based agencies with international activities. Historically, the majority of international grants have been made to U.S.-based agencies. Only a few large American foundations with broad overseas networks have been able to allocate a substantial portion of their international grants directly to foreign organizations. With the explosion of civil society worldwide in the 1980s and 1990s,[17] some foundations worked to develop partnerships with local NGOs, cultivated relationships with intermediary organizations, and brought in new staff to increase their share of grants directly made to overseas organizations. By 1998, 42.7 percent of the total number of grants and 39.7 percent of total dollar amounts were made to overseas recipients. The remaining was directed to U.S.-based international agencies.[18]

Today, international grants allocated to overseas recipients are relatively evenly spread across four main regions of the world: Europe, Latin America, Asia, and sub-Saharan Africa. In terms of main fields of intervention, American foundations focus heavily on international development issues, health, international affairs, and education. These areas cover a wide range of activities, including relief efforts, community improvement and economic development, reproductive health care, peace and security, and higher education. Beyond the broadening of the causes supported by international grantmaking, dramatic events in the world have drawn in new funders: wars in Kosovo, East Timor, and Chechnya triggered humanitarian assistance from a host of American foundations, including some that are mainly focused on domestic issues. Health crises have also expanded the field of international giving: an important number of foundations now support research and action on AIDS overseas. The International AIDS Vaccine Initiative has received long-standing support from the Rockefeller, Starr, and Alfred P. Sloan Foundations.

In sum, American foundations are now playing a visible and multifaceted role on the international stage, using large grants to engage huge problems that span the national boundaries. Yet, as American funders direct large amounts of funds into international problems, there may be a lag between the resources devoted to non-U.S. causes and the ability of American foundations to construct plausible strategies in the increasingly complex and globalized world in which we find ourselves. At the core of this lag are difficult questions about how philanthropy's role and purpose in society are best defined and how giving strategies used at home may need adjustment when exported abroad.

*****

Beyond the minimal descriptive feature of international grantmaking set out here, a deeper question about ultimate ends lurks: What is the purpose of international foundation philanthropy? This question is a natural touch point for any examination of the current challenges that now face the field. After all, before addressing the practical questions of how foundations might go about achieving their objectives abroad, it is essential to start by asking what it is that foundations are trying to accomplish through their giving. Of course, there is no single answer to the question of what purpose international foundation grantmaking fulfills.[19] In reality, this giving represents an at times confusing assortment of purposes, each with its own logic and rationale. With some necessary simplification, it is possible to isolate four important purposes that have emerged over time as foundations have sought to define a distinctive place for themselves in society.[20] Because over 90 percent of all American foundation giving has traditionally been domestic in character, each of the four rationales has largely been worked out and developed in the U.S. context. Special challenges and obstacles await grantmakers as these purposes are pursued across borders.

Social and Political Change

One of the most common arguments for why philanthropy exists at all focuses on the ability of donors to use private funds to create social and political change. The number of the possible meanings of the term social change is stunningly broad, however. From community empowerment and organizing aimed at changing patterns of political participation to advocacy efforts aimed at tightening particular environmental laws to efforts aimed at reducing the number of abortions, the character of social change is truly in the eye of the giver. Still, using private charitable dollars to pursue public purposes is by its very nature an act that implies that the status quo should change in some way. As an agent of change, philanthropy brings with it considerable resources and, even more important, a level of freedom from both public opinion and the bottom line that limit the ability of government and business to play this role. In the domestic American context at least, the use of private funds allows philanthropy to pursue a change agenda without having to spend large amounts of time mobilizing other sources of support. Funders can even use their wealth and power to declare a particular issue of cause worth pursuing with or without a consensus among those affected. And many large foundations have done that with great commitment and energy.

Some funders have attempted to promote change by rearranging power within local communities. Mobilization efforts have at times centered on voter registration drives, such as the Ford Foundation's famous effort in the 1960s to register voters in Cleveland. This effort contributed to the election of Carl Stokes, the first African American mayor of a major American city. Ford's voter registration work eventually prodded Congress to take an interest in the activities of foundations and eventually led to regulations on the political activities of foundation donors. Still, mobilization efforts aimed at social change have proceeded apace, albeit in different guises. Many funders have purposefully defined for themselves missions related primarily to community organizing and empowerment. They have sought out nonprofit organizations whose goals are to invigorate community participation with the ultimate goal of achieving change. Other private funders have interpreted organizing more traditionally, and have supported labor organizing efforts in areas that have long been neglected.

Beyond mobilization strategies, donors have been attracted to the idea of achieving change through advocacy work, ranging from public information campaigns to ballot initiatives. Throughout the political struggle over health care reform in the 1990s in the United States private funders backed research and ads aimed at swaying public opinion one way or another on the issue of universal coverage. More recently, individual donors have used their private funds to push ballot initiatives. From financier George Soros's effort to legalize some drugs in the United States to high-tech entrepreneur Tim Draper's effort to institute a statewide school voucher system in California through a ballot initiative, donors have pursued a change agenda by supporting grassroots work aimed at changing public policy. These efforts have had a mixed record of success and have raised difficult questions about the use of philanthropic funds to advance the social change agendas of individuals, which have not always coincided with the broader public agenda. Whether attempting to achieve social and political change through mobilization or policy initiatives, donors have defined a role for philanthropy that is centered squarely on the idea of reorganizing power.

Many large American foundations are attracted to the idea of using their funds to intervene in political issues abroad, especially when these issues have global implications. Funding political change, be it through advocacy or grassroots mobilization, appears to be a relatively high-leverage proposition in that small amounts of money can purchase substantial amounts of influence and impact. When transposed to international giving, however, this political approach to philanthropy has a number of problems associated with it. Attempting to foment social and political change overseas can easily expose American foundations to criticism of inappropriate meddling or even, in some circumstances, to charges of philanthropic imperialism.[21] Since many countries have weak civil societies and governments that grant only limited freedom to nonprofit organizations, inserting foreign philanthropic funds in the middle of pitched political battles can create a backlash against local civil society actors. For this reason, American philanthropy abroad must be especially sensitive to the unintended effects of their desire to see wholesale social and political change.

There is another consideration for American foundations to consider before they attempt to shape policy or political arrangement overseas: focusing on political action may overlook the local desire for more direct forms of assistance. Since civil society can be weak in developing countries where traditions of independent action do not exist, focusing giving on generating social and political change may assume a capacity for activities and interventions not present in local organizations. After all, effecting complex advocacy, lobbying, and public information campaigns may often prove more challenging than providing direct services. In countries where nascent civil societies are just forming, asking them to play a political role may be premature and assume a level of capacity and a breadth of contacts that simply is not present. International grantmakers must also guard against putting local nonprofits in untenable situations simply because American foundations find attractive the prospect of leverage associated with policy change. Ultimately, work on social and political change must be grounded in local concerns and supported by organizations that have the capacity and expertise to carry out this kind of work. For all these reasons and others, foundations need to be careful when applying this first classic model of philanthropic action outside the American context.

Innovation

A second and very different purpose of foundation action is to locate and support important social innovations and programmatic breakthroughs. Philanthropic funds have long been viewed as social venture capital designed to be used to promote new thinking and programs. The idea that foundation grantmaking is really about producing innovation is popular among those who question the ability of government to generate new ideas and successful programs, particularly when it comes to addressing enduring social problems. On the surface, at least, foundations appear to be well positioned to be a potent force for innovation in that the freedom that foundations enjoy opens up endless opportunities. In principle, at least, the absence of strong accountability mechanisms connected to charitable giving, particularly when national boundaries are spanned, should make it possible for foundations to strike out in new and unpredictable directions. Many funders like the idea of consciously using their giving to push the frontier of ideas and practice with the goal of coming up with new ways of conceptualizing problems and responding to them. The search for innovation is a product in part of the realization that the actual solution of many important public problems requires large and expensive interventions, which few foundations have the resources to underwrite independently. However, by researching or actually developing innovative new ways of achieving a particular programmatic result, foundations can show the way to others.

When it comes to funding innovative research and pathbreaking ideas, American foundations do indeed have a strong track record if one goes back in time a bit. Many important medical breakthroughs have been achieved in research labs underwritten with private philanthropic funds. In the 1950s, the Scaife Foundation invested in the lab of Jonas Salk, though few could have predicted at the time that this support would be translated into a vaccine against polio. In other fields, including astronomy and physics, private support to universities, sometimes coupled with federal research support, has allowed basic science to progress swiftly. In the area of service innovations, foundations have over the past century helped to develop a number of innovative pilot programs in fields ranging from health to education to social services to the arts. Some of these pilot programs have shown great promise, while others, to be sure, have had more mixed results. The freedom of donors to experiment and to act quickly gives philanthropy a chance to lead, rather than follow public policy. To take full advantage of this freedom and to fulfill its function as social innovator, foundations must be willing to assume high levels of risk, evaluate carefully, and communicate widely. Whether it is has focused on breakthroughs in research or practice, philanthropy has thus been understood as a tool of innovation aimed at advancing a diverse array of fields.

International philanthropy's adaptation of the innovation function has proven more complex than one might have thought. While American foundations have regularly scoured the world for the best ideas and most significant social innovations, foundations have had less than complete success replicating and translating these innovations across borders. Perhaps the most publicized such effort involves microfinance, a movement to give small loans to poor people in order to help them create small businesses and improve their lives. While there is little doubt that the idea of microfinance has been promoted and replicated in countries around the world with significant foundation support, it remains unclear whether this replication proceeded before the underlying approaches and methodologies were fully understood and perfected. In seeking to fund innovations abroad, American foundations need to be careful not to engage in premature replication of programs based on early experiments, especially when the innovation is deeply embedded in local cultural contexts. Some of the most promising manifestations of civil society abroad may come in forms of action that are unfamiliar to outsiders and profoundly driven by local conditions and needs. Thus, as they make grants outside the United States, American foundations must not only seek out the best and most promising social innovations, but also remind themselves that what works in India may simply not be appropriate in Chile.

Redistribution

A third purpose of philanthropy is more traditional. It is not based on ambitious social and political change agendas or the relentless pursuit of innovation. A large number of foundations, particularly smaller ones with modest staffs, use their giving simply to achieve a small measure of redistribution. By giving money to nonprofit organizations that carry out services for needy populations, foundations often try to carry out small-scale redistribution. When focusing on making marginal improvements in the life conditions of disadvantaged populations, this brand of philanthropy tends to eschew programs that do not entail at least some personal responsibility and commitment on behalf of the recipient. While the impulse to help those in need is great, interest in almsgiving and unconditional charity is low. Thus, even when foundations want to use their wealth to help others, it often takes a more complex form than a simple check that can be cashed by those in need without any questions being asked. Help is most often embedded in programs and services designed to provide long-term solutions to the problems facing the poor and disadvantaged.

Redistributive giving often takes a local form, in which caring is expressed for those in the community who are less well off. The ability of foundations to execute a universal redistribution effort is limited, however, given the breadth of needs and the level of philanthropic resources available. The mismatch between needs and capacity becomes particularly imposing when the scope of giving spans national borders. Still, by transferring some funds from those with resources to those without, foundations can take a small step toward greater equality and sharing. Redistribution, albeit on a small scale, is at the heart of many of the oldest and most broadly supported social service organizations. These service providers are able to sustain themselves over long periods precisely because their missions are timeless and of broad appeal. Not surprisingly, the redistributive function of foundations giving is the least controversial of philanthropy functions.

In the context of international grantmaking, redistributive giving aimed at greater equity can take at least two major forms. The first is one that works with civil society in foreign lands to spread resources among local people. When redistribution is a local concept, the sphere of distributive justice is manageable.[22] The introduction of American dollars into other countries not only can make a difference, but the leverage these funds can generate overseas can be considerable. After all, the value of a charitable dollar—how far it will go and how much redistribution it will purchase—is far greater in Africa, for example, than in the United States. For this reason, American foundations have ample opportunity to use their funds overseas in ways that maximize impact for poor populations. When the concept of redistribution takes on a second and more expansive form, the prospects for a meaningful role for American philanthropy diminishes greatly, simply due to the resource limitations facing the field. If the goal of redistribution is to achieve global equity, foundations will have to confront the fact there is not enough money in American foundations to begin to tackle some of the gross inequities that beset the planet. Of course, foundations can and do try to make small and symbolic efforts at promoting global equity, often by funding labor movements and efforts aimed at influencing companies to pay better wages, but these efforts have had only very limited effect.

Pluralism

A fourth rationale for foundation philanthropy is the pure and unapologetic affirmation of pluralism as a civic value. The fact that hundreds of billions of dollars are applied each year to public purposes by disparate private institutions, rather than by governments, holds forth the possibility that pluralism as a core societal value is being affirmed. To be sure, without coordination or outside control, foundation philanthropy can be disorganized, unruly, and unpredictable. To some, however, this is not a problem but instead a core rationale for having a philanthropic tradition. Giving allows a multiplicity of ideas and programs to exist in the public domain, rather than a limited number of "preferred" solutions. The argument that philanthropy affirms pluralism strikes some as both inefficient and undemocratic in that private parties are acting in competing fashions rather than through a single, democratically selected course of action. Given the overlay of private interests on public needs that occur when gifts are made, these shortcomings may not be a problem. After all, with a myriad of competing conceptions of the public good struggling for supremacy in the public square, power within philanthropy is dispersed and stable.

Some worry that the ability of philanthropy to continue to affirm pluralism is threatened to some extent by the creation of a few very large private foundations that control an important percentage of all philanthropic assets. While it is certainly true that the information technology revolution created a large number of multibillionaires, the sheer size of organized philanthropy makes it hard for even the largest donors to assert a dominant position. Still, the concentration of philanthropic funds is an important concern as the Bill and Melinda Gates Foundation continues to grow by leaps and bounds. However, a little historical perspective on this development is reassuring. When the Rockefeller Foundation was created at the turn of the century, some worried that it would become a threat to the power of the federal government. Today, however, the Rockefeller Foundation is just one among a large group of billion-dollar foundations, none of which individually or collectively has the resources to challenge the power of the state. Philanthropy's ability to affirm pluralism is far more resilient than many believe. It is a field that is continuously attracting new donors, each of whom comes forward with a distinctive vision and charitable mission that takes its place among many others.

The fact that private charitable giving can be seen as an affirmation of pluralism is important because in many fields of activity there is little consensus on what issues, theories, and programs are most worth pursuing. Lacking clear consensus on most important public matters, philanthropy's role in such circumstances has come to be the promotion of a multiplicity of responses. By letting a thousand flowers bloom, philanthropy can contribute to a vibrant and diverse civil society, one in which multiple and competing conceptions of the public good coexist. Philanthropy is a counterbalance to the tendency of government toward bureaucratization. By celebrating and promoting pluralism, foundations are able to contribute to the decentralization of power in society.

As American foundations venture overseas, they have a unique opportunity to promote pluralism. In many societies in which democratic norms are weak and in which civic engagement is weak, working to expand the range and breadth of civil society actors is crucially important. Above and beyond accomplishing programmatic goals, American foundations need to have stable, diverse, and capable civil society organizations with which to work. Supporting pluralism is often tantamount to supporting capacity building and institution building. For American foundations, this sort of embracing and inclusive agenda, directed at building the number and quality of civil society actors, represents a central challenge that in many ways is a prerequisite to all three of the other grand rationales for philanthropy. Without a capable and diverse universe of civil society organizations, political change, innovation, and redistribution are very hard to achieve.

Each of the four functions of private foundations can and must be pursued across national borders. Yet the application of American philanthropic funds around the world raises special challenges related to each of these functions. Within the context of globalization, the ability of foundations to promote social change, to pursue programmatic innovation, to redistribute wealth, and to affirm pluralism is contingent on a number of new factors, many of which lie well outside the span of control of foundations. In this sense, globalization raises a set of new challenges for American foundations, especially when it comes to applying any existing rationales for philanthropy to the work of international giving.

*****

Much has been written about globalization, and there have been numerous attempts at defining this broad concept. Here, I will simply define globalization as the thickening of the networks of interdependence spanning international boundaries that accompanies increasingly rapid and inexpensive movement of information, ideas, money, goods, and people across boundaries.[23] This phenomenon has been present for centuries but has progressed with considerable intensity throughout the twentieth century, especially since the 1970s.[24] Globalization can be seen as the cause and consequence of major increases in a number of key social and economic indicators, including an explosion in the international flows of goods, services, and capital, a significant rise in human migrations, a revolution in information technology through the development of Internet and satellite technology, and a transformation of the international political system with the spread of democracy and the emergence of international and supranational organizations, such as the World Bank, the International Monetary Fund, and the European Union.[25]

Three major elements of globalization directly impact American foundations' activities. The first element is the worldwide boom of civil society as a result of the spread of democracy.[26] With the collapse of the Soviet Union, countries in central and eastern Europe transitioned from communist-type totalitarian regimes to liberal democracies. In the Middle East, pressures for political and economic liberalization have also increased in the past decades. In other parts of the world, liberal democracy has gained ground over other forms of governance. This has spurred the emergence of local civil society activists in all of these regions, a tremendous network of local actors who are now or may soon become grant recipients of American foundations.[27]

The second element is the emergence of new global needs.[28] The expansion of free trade and the liberalization of international capital markets have increased the welfare of societies around the world, but the division of the pie has not always been equal. The most vulnerable countries and populations of the globe (e.g., countries in central and southern Africa or the Middle East; low-skilled workers in industrialized countries) have been left behind with the gap between the "haves" and "have-nots" widening. For example, globalization exerts downward pressure on the wages of low-skilled workers in industrialized countries and weakens existing social safety nets. Issues such as the destruction of traditional cultures, the rapid spread of infectious diseases such as AIDS and now SARS (severe acute respiratory syndrome), and the exploitation of natural resources of developing countries have also appeared with globalization. The emergence of these new issues requires effective responses from major international actors.[29]

The third element of this new era of globalization is the dramatic democratization of technology. Inexpensive and broadly available technologies such as the Internet and the cellular phone have put an end to governments' monopolies over critical and mass information. These revolutionary technologies have also considerably augmented American foundations' and other civil society actors' ability to develop cross-border networks of supporters. This phenomenon boosts the civil society's ability to organize effectively and helps its requests get heard at both local and international level.

The combination of these three elements creates a new environment in which American foundations can thrive. Power traditionally withheld by governments is now shifting from states' hands to a myriad of transnational actors: NGOs, corporations, and international organizations.[30] This shift has created a chain of new opportunities for American foundations: global needs are more pressing in some areas of the world due to increased inequalities; information on global needs is more accessible due to the technological revolution; and a broad range of actors committed to responding to these needs has emerged due to the worldwide boom of civil society.

To take full advantage of the opening and challenge posed by globalization, American foundations must begin to think more broadly and imaginatively about the types of work they can best promote within this environment. In response to globalization, foundations could work at four different master levels to make a difference: individuals, organizations, networks, and ideas. Each of these grantmaking targets represents a distinctive theory of change or logic model for how philanthropy can shape the world, starting at the micro level and progressively moving up to the macrosocial level. All of these approaches can and should be conceived as part of nested system, with each level building upon the other.

When it comes to the individual level approach, foundations can work to train a new cadre of leaders who can act both locally and on the international stage. Having quality leaders in key civil society positions is important not just for getting things done, but also for setting the tone for the entire sector. Investing in people through professional development and training programs can be a slow and incremental approach to bringing change. However, given the pressures and changes now being put on nonprofits around the world by globalization processes, taking the time to invest in people—particularly civil society leaders—may return significant benefits. All too often those who manage nonprofit organizations are caught up in the daily struggle of locating funding, dealing with regulators, and motivating staff. Rarely do civil society leaders have time to think carefully and strategically about their work or the new context within which it will take place. Foundations can build the human capital in civil society by supporting training programs, professional development workshops, retreats, seminars, and skill-building exercises, all with the goal of improving the quality of the leadership within NGOs. By working at the individual level, foundations may be in position to see their work trickle up and across transnational civil society and have effects far beyond the small cadre of leaders they support and cultivate.

Moving up one level, foundations can focus on altering institutions and building capacity in organizations of all kinds so that they are better equipped to deal with the pressures and changes wrought by globalization. Working to increase financial stability and programmatic effectiveness of local organizations is critical to building the kind of civil society infrastructure that is needed over the long term to achieve any of the broader objectives of international grantmaking. While capacity building has become a common goal at least within some of the larger American foundations, it can also be understood as strategic response to globalization. After all, as pressures increase due to the spread of markets and opportunities, having strong and viable organizations in civil society will only become more critical, particularly in areas of the world where the finances of nonprofits will be subject to major fluctuations. Grantmakers who cross national boundaries have an opportunity through capacity-building grants to contribute to the stability and sustainability in new organizations.

Third, foundations can support the formation of transnational alliances that bring organizations together to work on common problems. By creating linkages among civil society actors, foundations might be able to create coalitions that have the size and resource base to take on some of the larger, emergent transnational problems. Working through networks is a potent tool, especially when the networks that are being forged span long-standing geographical, political, and cultural divides. Grantmakers have the ability to forge what social capital theorists refer to as "bridging ties," which allow people to connect to others that are not part of their normal circle. This form of network building can be distinguished from the creation of "bonding ties" that simply reinforce existing groups and cliques. Many funders build networks by convening nonprofits, by funding technology-driven communities, and by supporting interorganizational collaborations. As globalization increases the size and scope of many social problems, acting through networks becomes particularly appealing because it recognizes that no single organization acting alone is likely to be able to address important social problems as well as a well-organized and tightly structured coalition.

Fourth and finally, American foundations can support work that identifies subtle and emergent consequences of globalization that may otherwise be ignored. This means playing the role of researcher and policy analyst, informing and shaping the debate by introducing new ideas in the conversation. Foundations have long done this kind of work domestically by providing funding to the best thinkers in different fields and encouraging them to advance knowledge through research. When it comes to globalization, foundations could respond by funding the development of new ideas and paradigms to advance our understanding of globalization, as well as ideas about how best to cope with the effects of globalization. Working at the level of idea production would allow foundations to fashion a broad response to globalization that would potentially cut across the economic, political, and social dimensions of the process.

Each of these four theories of change has its strengths and weaknesses, and each has its place. In practice, most grantmakers—knowingly or unwittingly—apply one, two, three, or all four of these theories in their work. While there can be no meaningful claim about which of these four approaches is the most effective, it is possible to note that they can be made more or less effectively to work together. Many funders consciously build capacity and then embed organizations in strong peer networks. Similarly, grantmakers routinely develop leadership and help these individual project their voices into the world of policy and politics. The most important thing for international grantmakers to remember is that the potential for major and sudden impact increases as one moves up from micro to macro levels—from individual to organizational to network to policy levels. Before taking action the policy level, funders should be absolutely certain that they have done their homework and that their proposed course of action is the correct one. While mistakes at lower levers can be corrected easily enough, work at the policy level can be more difficult to fix and demands that the funder carry a higher burden of proof that the intervention is appropriate and needed.

As American foundations turn their attention to problems that span borders and that are shaped by globalization processes, having some clarity not just about the core rationale guiding giving, but also the method to be used, will be critical. Many of the frameworks and tools that have been helpful to grantmakers in the United States have direct application when the frame of giving shifts to the international stage. However, American foundations will need to engage in a new round of serious self-examination and learning if the transition from domestic to international grantmaking is to be smooth and successful. A useful starting point for such an exercise would be the core rationale guiding giving and the theory of change through which impact is pursued. Getting clearer about both these elements would move American foundations a lot closer to being able to respond strategically to the challenges of globalization than otherwise would be the case. And this in turn cannot help but improve the quality of international grantmaking in the years ahead.

Endnotes

[1] Robert H. Bremner, *American Philanthropy* (2nd ed.), University of Chicago Press, Chicago,1988; Waldemar A. Nielsen, *The Golden Donors: A New Anatomy of the Great Foundations*, E. P. Dutton, NY, 1985.

[2] Barry D. Karl and Stanley N. Katz, "American Private Philanthropic Foundations, 1890–1930," *Minerva* 19, 1981; Emily S. Rosenberg, "Missions to the World: Philanthropy Abroad," in Lawrence J. Friedman and Mark D. McGarvie (eds.) *Charity, Philanthropy, and Civility in American History*, Indiana University Press, Bloomington, 2003.

[3] David L. Brown, Sanjeev Khagram, Mark H. Moore, and Peter Frumkin, "Globalization, NGOs, and Multisectoral Relations," in Joseph S. Nye and John D. Donahue (eds.) *Governance in a Globalizing World*, Brookings Institution Press, Washington, DC, 2000.

[4] Merle Curti, *American Philanthropy Abroad: A History*, Rutgers University Press, New Brunswick, NJ, 1963.

[5] Sally Covington, *Moving a Public Policy Agenda: The Strategic Philanthropy of Conservative Foundations*, National Committee for Responsive Philanthropy, Washington, DC, 1997; Mark Dowie, *American Foundations: An Investigative History*, MIT Press, Cambridge, MA, 2002; J. Craig Jenkins "Channeling Social Protest: Foundation Patronage of Contemporary Social Movements," in William Powell and Elizabeth Clemens (eds.) *Private Interest and the Public Good*, Yale University Press, New Haven, CT, 1997.

[6] F. E. Andrews, *Philanthropic Giving*, Russell Sage Foundation, NY, 1950; Raymond B. Fosdick, *The Story of the Rockefeller Foundation*, Harper, NY, 1952; Judith Sealander, *Private Wealth and Public Life*, Johns Hopkins University Press, Baltimore, MD, 1997.

[7] Kevin O'Rourke and Jeffrey Williamson, *Globalization and History*, MIT Press, Cambridge, MA, 1999.

[8] Bremner, *American Philanthropy*; Rosenberg, "Missions to the World."

[9] Curti, *American Philanthropy Abroad.*

[10] Ann D. Walton and F. Emerson Andrews, *The Foundation Directory: Edition I*, Foundation Library Center, Russell Sage Foundation, NY, 1960.

[11] Sealander, *Private Wealth and Public Life.*

[12] Loren Renz et al., *International Grantmaking II: An Update on U.S. Foundation Trends*, Foundation Center in Cooperation with the Council on Foundations, NY, 2000.

[13] Jean L. Cohen and Andrew Arato, *Civil Society and Political Theory*, MIT Press, Cambridge, MA, 1997; Sanjeev Khagram, James Riker, and Kathryn Sikkink (eds.), *Restructuring World Politics: Transnational Social Movements, Networks, and Norms*, University of Minnesota Press, Minneapolis, 2002.

[14] Renz, *International Grant Making II.*

[15] Ibid.

[16] Ibid.

[17] Jessica Mathews, "Power Shift," *Foreign Affairs*, vol. 76, 1997, pp. 50–66.

[18] Renz, *International Grant Making II.*

[19] Brian O'Connell, *Philanthropy in Action*, Foundation Center, NY, 1987.

[20] Kenneth Prewitt, "Foundations as Mirrors of Public Culture," *American Behavioral Scientist*, March 42:6, 1999, pp. 987–97.

[21] Robert F. Arnove, *Philanthropy and Cultural Imperialism*, Indiana University Press, Bloomington, 1982.

[22] Michael Walzer, "The Idea of Civil Society," *Dissent* (Spring), 1991, pp. 293–304; Michael Walzer, *Spheres of Justice*, Basic Books, NY, 1984.

[23] Robert O. Keohane and Joseph S. Nye, *Power and Interdependence*, Longman, NY, 2001.

[24] Thomas L. Friedman, *The Lexus and the Olive Tree: Understanding Globalization*, Anchor Books, NY, 2000; Dani Rodrik, "Sense and Nonsense in the Globalization Debate," *Foreign Policy* (Summer), 1997.

[25] Ann Marie Slaughter, "The Real New World," *Foreign Affairs* 76, 1997, pp. 183–91.

[26] Margaret M. Meck and Kathryn Sikkink, *Activists without Borders*, Cornell University Press, Ithaca, NY, 1998; Lester M. Salamon, "The Rise of the Nonprofit Sector," *Foreign Affairs*, vol. 73, no. 4, 1994, pp. 111–24; Rajesh Tandon and Kumi Naidoo, "The Promise of Civil Society," in Kumi Naidoo (ed.) *Civil Society at the Millennium*, Kumarian Press, Hartford, CT, 1999, pp. 1–16; Walzer, "Idea of Civil Society;" Walzer, *Spheres of Justice*.

[27] For the Middle East examples see Mehran Kamrava, "The Civil Society Discourse in Iran," *British Journal of Middle Eastern Studies* (November), 2001; Mustafa K. Al Sayyid, "A Civil Society in Egypt?," *Middle Eastern Journal* (Spring), 1993. For a general discussion on the growth of liberal democracy, see Francis Fukuyama, *The End of History and The Last Man*, Free Press, NY,1992.

[28] Marc Lindberg and J. Patrick Dobel, "The Challenges of Globalization for Northern International Relief and Development NGOs," *Nonprofit and Voluntary Sector Quarterly*, vol. 28, no. 4, supplement, 1999, pp. 4–24.

[29] For further discussions on the impact of globalization around the world see Brian Tokar, *Earth for Sale: Reclaiming Ecology in the Age of Corporate Greenwash*, South End Press, Cambridge, MA, 1997; Michael Bratton, "Beyond the State: Civil Society and Associational Life in Africa," *World Politics*, vol. 41, no. 4, April, 1989, pp. 407–30; Rodrik, "Sense and Nonsense;"and Oran R. Young, *Global Governance*, MIT Press, Cambridge, MA, 1997.

[30] Mathews, "Power Shift."

Chapter 6

FOUNDATIONS IN EUROPE: ROLES AND POLICY SCENARIOS IN AN AGE OF GLOBALIZATION

Helmut K. Anheier and Siobhan Daly

From a comparative perspective, few types of organizations have received less attention by researchers and policy analysts than foundations. While cross-national studies of business firms, government agencies, and nonprofit organizations are increasingly becoming available, little is known in a systematic way about the current and future role and policy environment foundations are facing across the fifteen members states of the European Union, the ten accession countries, and other countries in the European economic area, such as Switzerland and Norway.

Perplexingly, at a time when we seem to know little about the size and scale of foundation activities, the roles and the visions that guide them, and the impact they have, policy makers from across the political spectrum are calling for greater private philanthropic involvement in fields as disparate as culture and the arts, social service, health care, and research and education. What is more, not only politicians, but also representatives of corporate interests and civic leaders, frequently stress the role foundations, along with other forms of philanthropy, could play in building and servicing civil society and the public good, both at the national and international levels.

*****

The globalization discourse provides an appropriate backdrop to the discussion of these emerging trends. At the national level, this process, in turn, has created new roles for the third sector in areas such as community renewal, social entrepreneurship and the "activation" of social capital. Yet the most significant long-term impact may well be at the transnational, global level. Some scholars argue that globalization implies the emergence of a more active citizenry that has served to diminish the importance of traditional welfare states and voluntary organizations in favor of more transnational dispersed groups and organizations that take up issues outside the framework of conventional welfare policies.

Observers have identified the emergence of an increasingly global civil society, a sphere of transnational organizations and citizen action.[1] Indeed, as Kaldor and associates[2] demonstrate, the field of global civil society has expanded significantly since the end of the Cold War; the international rule of law has become more institutionalized and provides an increasingly solid legal foundation for transnational action; and the overall level of activity of civil society has increased both in economic as well as social terms. Yet, as noted by Anheier and Leat and also Johnson,[3] the role of foundations in globalization remains unclear, as does the impact globalization has on organized philanthropy.

This chapter aims to address some of the shortcomings of what we know about foundations in Europe in the context of the wider globalization processes. In Europe, of course, the process of European integration provides the immediate background to the discussion here, and the emergence of a Pan-European sphere of operation for what are still essentially domestic organizations is very much at the heart of the phenomenon we wish to illuminate. In so doing, we draw on available data from a variety of sources, and pull in some preliminary findings of a project that looks at the visions and roles of foundations in Europe.[4] The main argument we try to develop in the chapter is that foundations remain local, domestic actors to a very large extent, and that the transnational, increasingly global sphere of philanthropic activity—despite some very important exceptions—has yet to become common fully aware of the potential of philanthropy for globalization policies. At the same time, other types of nonprofit organizations, in particular NGOs, have become international and transnational actors to an extent much greater than foundations. In a serious way, when it comes to globalization, foundations as a form are lacking behind many others, despite the many opportunities that have opened up to transnational philanthropy in recent years.

*****

The last few decades witnessed the expansion of nonprofit or nongovernmental organizations (NGOs) to levels unknown in the past, accounting for about 6 percent of total employment in OECD countries.[5] At the same time, the value of foundation assets increased significantly, and even though assets contracted in the early part of this decade, they are still at historically high levels. Never before did foundations have more resources available to them than in the course of the last ten years. However, while most foundations remain domestic organizations, some have become increasingly international in their scope and have grown into veritable global actors. European examples include the Bertelsmann Foundation, the Bosch Foundation, and the Volkswagen Foundation in Germany; the Tercentennial Fund of Sweden; the King Baudouin Foundation in Belgium; the Prince Claus Fund in the Netherlands; the Fundaçion Juan March in Spain; the Jacobs Foundation in Switzerland; the Compagnia di San Paolo in Italy; and the Gulbenkian Foundation in Portugal.

The same patterns apply to international nongovernmental organizations (INGOs),[6] and it is difficult to separate the expansion of international foundation activities from those of nonprofit organizations generally. Oxfam, Save the Children, Amnesty International, Friends of the Earth, the Red Cross, and Greenpeace have become the brand names among INGOs with significant budgets, political influence, and responsibility. Indeed, the ten largest development and relief INGOs alone have combined expenditures of over US$3 billion, which represent about half of the official U.S. aid budget.

What is more, it is difficult to underestimate the extent to which the organizational environment for philanthropy has expanded in recent decades, particularly since 1989. It now offers greater opportunities for engaging across borders than before, both in terms of resources as well as access.[7] Along with this, we suggest that the global environment for organizing over the last decade has been characterized by:

- An opening of political opportunities outside and beyond conventional national politics, due to the end of the Cold War and a superpower, the United States, being in favor of a minimalist, liberal state; the rise of a "New Policy Agenda" emphasizing the role of civil society, and which sees foundations and NGOs ever more part of an emerging system of global governance.[8]
- The development of international forms of government and interstate and interregional coordination, from the UN system to the European Union, and from Mercosur to ECOWAS, which opened up a field of foundation activities.[9]
- Major reductions in the cost of communication, in particular for telecommunication and Internet access, which increases information sharing while reducing coordination costs overall.[10] The development of communications technologies have decreased the costs of organizing and grantmaking, and thus increased the carrying capacity of the organizational environment. This made it possible for foundations to engage internationally at much lower costs than in the past.
- Generally favorable economic conditions in major world economies since the late 1940s, and a considerable expansion of populations living a relative prosperity.[11] Moreover, since the 1980s, most Organization for Economic Cooperation and Development (OECD) countries have experienced a major expansion in the number and assets of foundations.
- A value change over the last twenty-five years in most industrialized countries that emphasizes individual opportunities and responsibilities over state involvement and control. The basic argument is that the shift from materialist to post-materialist value patterns, as crude summaries of what is undoubtedly a more complex value change in developed market economies, is closely associated with the rise of cosmopolitan value, a preference for democratic forms of governance, and an appreciation of cultural diversity.[12]
- The rise in the economic importance of private nonprofit organizations in social services, health care, education and culture, which resulted in large-scale national nonprofit sectors that increasingly operate across borders. This implies a greater reliance on private philanthropic resources.[13]
- A major expansion of democracy across most parts of the world with freedom of expression and association granted in most of the world's countries, which makes it easier for foundations to operate across borders and political systems.
- The "thickening" of the international rule of law since the 1970s, which has greatly facilitated the growth of global civil society organizations, including foundation activities.[14]

It is this opening of a transnational and increasingly global "organizational space" and the greater recognition of cross-border needs (e.g., environmental protection, human rights) that continues to provide the opportunity for foundation and NGO development and growth. While none of these social factors alone, be they political, sociological, economic or technological, could have brought about the expansion in organized global civil society, it is the combination of these factors that made it possible.

*****

Unfortunately, systematic and comparable data on foundations in Europe is very incomplete, and the situation for international activities is even less solid in terms of coverage and data quality. Given the information gap that exists regarding foundations in Europe, the empirical profiling of foundations focuses on basic data about size, activities, and patterns of growth. Reflecting the diverse landscape of foundations across Europe, the results of our survey point to varied trends rather than consistent patterns in relation to the number, activities, and growth of foundations.[15]

There is great variation in the number of foundations, ranging from a high of 20,000 to 30,000 in Sweden, around 14,000 in Denmark, 11,500 in Switzerland, and 3,008 in Italy, to lows of 600 in Austria, 533 in Estonia, 338 in the Czech Republic, and 112 in Ireland. The data suggest that there are around 80,000 to 90,000 foundations in Europe (including Greece and Turkey), or, an average, around 4,500 per country. However, only foundations in the United Kingdom are almost exclusively grantmaking, and about half are in Finland and Germany. In most other countries, we find that the majority of foundations are of a mixed type. They are both operating institutions and grantmaking, thereby combining service delivery with philanthropic giving.[16]

Clearly, the economic weight of running institutions, programs, and projects tends to be more important than the actual grantmaking activities. For example, estimates of employment in German grantmaking foundations in 1995 ranged between 3,000 to 5,000 employees, whereas operating foundations employed over 90,000. The majority of German foundations, however, employ no staff at all: 9 out of 10 foundations are run and managed by volunteers only. In Scandinavia, similar results can be found: only a few of Denmark's 14,000 foundations have paid employment at all, and only 8 of the over 2,500 Finnish foundations have more than 10 full-time staff members. In Italy, over 85 percent of foundations have fewer than 10 employees, while less than 1 percent employ more than 250 people. In Poland, foundations employ more than 13,000 people, although full-time employees can be found only in a very few foundations.

Asset estimates are the most difficult data to obtain on foundations, especially cross-nationally, given the influence of different valuation measures and techniques. Irrespective of these difficulties, available estimates reveal significant cross-national variations. The assets of German foundations are EUR354 per head; the figure is higher for foundations in the United Kingdom (EUR536), and over EUR1,000 in Italy, Sweden and Switzerland. Finally, the highest per head assets are reported for Liechtenstein, with a figure that exceeds EUR12,000 because of offshore foundation assets. The high amount of assets per head for Italian foundations is a function of the privatization of the banking sector in Italy (Law 218/1990, or the Amato law). Most public savings banks were previously quasi-public, "nationalized" nonprofit organizations, and became stock corporations as a result of the 1990 reforms.[17] The shares in the privatized banks became the endowment for the new "foundations of banking origin," which, not surprisingly, have significant assets, of between EUR50 billion and EUR70 billion combined.

Foundation sectors by country can be grouped into three classes: small, medium, and large, with the middle group further divided into subcategories. Given the data situation, it is not possible to construct a strict and consistent ranking of countries in terms of foundation sector size. Yet, taken together, the various size indicators suggest three groups or clusters, and even such an admittedly crude classification involves some qualitative judgments. The relative size of the foundation sectors of European countries can be classified as follows:

• Countries with a small foundation sector—Austria, Belgium, France, Greece, Ireland, Luxembourg, and countries of central and eastern Europe.
• Countries with a medium to small foundation sector—Portugal and Spain; and countries with a medium to large foundation sector—Denmark, Finland, Germany, the Netherlands, Norway, and the United Kingdom.
• Countries with a large foundation sector—the United States, Italy, Liechtenstein, Sweden, and Switzerland.

*****

Yet, what do foundations do, and in particular, to what extent are they engaged internationally and have become transnational actors? As our data suggest, European foundations remain primarily domestic actors in traditional fields.

Indeed, two fields clearly dominate the profile of foundation activity in Europe: education and research, with an average of 30 percent and social service, with an average of 25 percent. Together, both fields account for over one-half of foundation activities so measured. In fact, education, research, and social services are the main categories of foundation activity in the countries included in the present analysis and previous analyses.[18] Adding health care, with an average of 17 percent of foundation activity, pushes the total share up to 72 percent. In other words, more than two-thirds of foundations operate in just three fields, the same fields that also dominate the nonprofit sector at large.[19]

The field of art and culture accounts for the next largest share of foundation activities. It is the most important area of activity of foundations in Spain, with 44 percent of all foundations involved in this field, and in Italy, where arts and culture account for 29 percent of foundation expenditure. It is relatively prominent in Finland, Germany, Italy, Portugal, Switzerland, the Czech Republic, and Poland. Some countries show clear concentration in one field in particular: this is the case for health care foundations in France, housing foundations in Ireland and, to a certain extent, in Estonia, international activities in the Netherlands, and cultural foundations in Spain. Such concentrations are the result of specific historical developments, such as the urgent demand for affordable housing in early twentieth century Ireland, or institutional effects, such as the prominence of large health care research foundations in France (e.g., the Institut Pasteur and the Institut Curie).[20]

However, international aspects represent a minority focus among European foundations, and the portion of foundations active across borders remains low. Virtually none of the foundations in Austria, Italy, or Portugal operate internationally. Only 4 percent of the over ten thousand German foundations have international activities; and the Netherlands, with 14 percent, remains the exception among European countries.

While some of the larger foundations such as Volkswagen Stiftung in Germany, the Tercentennial Fund in Sweden or the Compagnia di San Paolo have long made grants to recipients outside their country, they remain the exception. Of course, there are foundation networks like the Open Society network in central and eastern Europe, but these are largely funded by its founder, George Soros, from its New York base.

*****

Foundations are largely a product of the period following the World War II, and a veritable foundation "boom" seems to have set in beginning in the late 1980s. More foundations were created in the 1980s and 1990s than in the three decades before, and more of the foundations existing today were established after 1950 than prior to that date. However, this growth is not evenly spread across countries.

• *High-growth countries, such as the United States, Italy, Spain, and Portugal.* The United States experienced one of the most sustained expansions in the growth of foundation numbers as assets over the last twenty years. In Europe, with the exception of Turkey, high-growth countries are those in which foundation law underwent a major reform: in Italy, Law 218/1990, or the Amato law; in Spain, the Foundation Act (1994); and in Portugal, Law 460/1977, with the proven effect that foundations increased sharply in number. In Portugal, where 56 percent of all foundations were established after 1980, and Spain (over 90 percent of cultural foundations and 70 percent of educational foundations), the rapid growth could also be a delayed effect of the democratization in the 1970s, when both countries shed their autocratic regimes. The high growth is also a reflection of the rapid economic development of the countries of southern Europe, in particular Portugal and Spain.

• *Medium-growth countries, such as Finland, Germany, Greece, Switzerland, and the United Kingdom.* With the exception of Belgium and Greece, these are countries with already sizable foundation sectors, and recent growth rates of twenty to thirty new foundations per decade add to a relatively high base. Finland, Germany, Switzerland, and the United Kingdom are high-income countries with stable political systems. We can assume that the foundation boom of recent years is in large measure a function of political stability and economic prosperity, amplified by a more self-confident middle class. Greece has a small foundation sector, and the expansion is probably the result of increased economic prosperity and greater political stability.

• *Low-growth countries, such as Austria, Belgium, and France.* All three countries have relatively small foundation sectors. The relatively few foundations in France are, on average, older, with one-half predating the postwar period, and with fewer foundations being established during the expansion period which began in the 1980s. Similarly, growth rates have changed little in Austria and Belgium over the last four decades, even though a slight upward trend is discernable. The reasons for the slow growth are legal and procedural, as the establishment of foundations in France or Belgium is highly regulated and complicated, providing relatively few incentives for potential founders.

*****

As we have seen, European foundations are primarily domestic actors, although the societies in which they operate have become increasingly international, even "Europeanized." What role, then, could foundations play in a Europe that has changed significantly over the last decade?

The literature on foundations has identified a number of roles for foundations. Prewitt[21] identifies four basic functions for foundations; redistribution, efficiency, social change, and pluralism. Less is known about the extent to which foundations in Europe actually aspire to, and fulfill these roles. However, evidence gathered by our researchers through analysis and interviews with a sample of foundation representatives in each country allows us to probe deeper into how foundations view their role in society and how their aspirations relate to their activities in practice.[22] Further interviews with members of umbrella organizations, experts, and policy makers also provide valuable observations of how relevant external actors articulate the roles of foundations in Europe.

"Roles" are understood as the normative expectations stakeholders have as to the purpose and performance of foundations. Altogether, seven roles were considered; complementarity, substitution, redistribution, innovation, social and policy change, preservation of traditions and cultures, and pluralism. The comparison of the countries included in the analysis in relation to each of these roles reveals insightful findings regarding the goals and aspirations of foundations in Europe.

- COMPLEMENTARITY. *This role is concerned with the extent to which foundations serve otherwise undersupplied groups under conditions of demand heterogeneity and public budget constraints.*

There was a broad consensus across the cases included in the analysis that the complementarity role is one that is generally fulfilled by foundations such as in Poland, Switzerland, the United Kingdom (UK), Italy, Sweden, Germany, and Hungary.

- SUBSTITUTION. *This role expects foundations to take on functions otherwise or previously supplied by the state. In this role, foundations substitute for state action, and foundations become providers of public or quasi-public goods.*

There is a general reluctance on the part of the foundations to assume this role, as is evident in Poland, Ireland, Belgium, Austria, Germany, the UK, and the Czech Republic. Perhaps reflecting a more general theme, this assumption is underpinned in Switzerland by concerns that this role may curtail the freedom of foundations and tie their activities to official guidelines. In Italy, this reluctance appears rooted in the belief that the state should retain responsibility for public welfare.

- REDISTRIBUTION. *The idea that the major role of foundations is to engage in, and promote, redistribution of primarily economic resources from higher to lower income groups.*

Overall, the response to the suggestion that the role of foundations is to redistribute wealth was one of negativity and indifference. Only two foundations in Belgium, which are engaged in grantmaking on a large scale, identified with this role. In contrast, this was not seen as a key role for foundations in Britain, Denmark, and Germany, nor is it one that foundations were willing to admit to. Similarly, in Poland, Hungary, and Switzerland, representatives indicated their awareness of this role, but also displayed a general reluctance to give it priority. In the Czech Republic, foundation representatives preferred to see redistribution as a rather banal feature of foundation giving, but not one that should be considered a fully fledged role for foundations in Czech society.

- INNOVATION. *Promoting innovation in social perceptions, values, relationships, and ways of doing things has long been a role ascribed to foundations.*

This was by far the most popular role that the foundations wished to be associated with. Nonetheless, this role raises more fundamental questions across countries as to what constitutes innovative behavior by foundations. In Sweden, some of the interviewees puzzled over whether this role applied to foundations that focus on a new field or use new methods; or foundations that seek to promote innovation as part of their mission statement, such as those involved in funding research; or, simply, to foundations that work in an innovative way. Furthermore, in the UK, for example, although foundation representatives were able to point to examples of innovation on the part of foundations, some also questioned the underlying meaning of the term and whether patterns of foundation grantmaking actually reflected this role. Similarly, in Austria, policy makers and experts were skeptical of whether foundations are engaged in innovative activities, with the possible exception of those involved in funding research. Examples of innovation tend to point to some specific examples of activities with which foundations are engaged, such as new approaches to social care pioneered by the Caritas Socialis Private Foundation in Austria or the support the Rural Areas Support Foundation gives to the rural environment and economy in Poland. In Germany, "innovative" foundations tend to share two characteristics in common; first, their openness to horizontal networking and collaboration with other parts of civil society; and second, the emphasis they place on reviewing their goals and activities at regular intervals. But, what is perhaps more generally apparent about the examples of innovation suggested by the country reports is that they indicate rather abstract links with the complementarity and substitution roles, given that the nature of innovative behavior involves doing what the government does not do or, indeed, does not have the funds to do. For example, in Denmark, the majority of the representatives from the eight foundations interviewed stressed their wish to promote new ways of thinking and to engage in risk taking in areas where neither governments nor markets act. This point of view was echoed in the Italian and the Swedish research. The question of what meaning underlies innovation is provocative and underpins all of the roles in which foundations engage.

- SOCIAL AND POLICY CHANGE. *Promoting structural change and a more just society, fostering recognition of new needs, and empowerment of the socially excluded.*

Overall, the foundations acknowledge the importance of this role. Sweden poses an exception to this trend; there, many representatives identified associations with this role, rather than foundations. Although it is not given as much precedence as complementarity and innovation, there is evidence to suggest that foundations have sought to take a more active position in general and political debate: for example, the Avenir Suisse in Switzerland, through its research and projects seeks to influence and partake in political decision making. In Germany, this role is associated with the larger foundations, such as the Bertelsmann Foundation, which sees itself as being engaged in processes of reform that aim to combat social stagnation. This role is also associated with the larger foundations in Denmark, such as the Egmont Foundation, and in Hungary, notably with the Soros Foundation. These examples suggest that financial and personnel resources are fundamental to foundations being able to aspire to this role, a point which was also stressed in the Hungarian case. Underlining the links between innovative actions and social and policy change, some foundations in Belgium, such as the King Baudouin Foundation, argued that their innovative activities have gained a positive reaction from the state. Although one other foundation claimed to play a key role in stimulating political decision making, no activities could be identified to support this claim.

In eastern Europe, the nature of this role posed a particular dilemma for some foundation representatives who sought to articulate it in terms that did not reflect links with the communist past. Representatives from the Czech Republic did not articulate their desire for a "decent" or "civil" society in terms of a "just" society, given its associations with the communist regimes. For similar reasons, some foundations were reluctant to speak of the "empowerment" of the socially excluded. Indeed, foundations that tend to be funded by Western sources were found to be more likely to support the rights of particular social groups, such as the Roma minority.

- PRESERVATION OF TRADITIONS AND CULTURES. *Opposing change, and preserving past lessons and achievements that are likely to be swamped by larger, social, cultural and economic forces.*

This role was not awarded substantial importance in the countries considered. However, its importance is broadly acknowledged in relation to the cultural field in Austria, Switzerland, Germany, and Poland. What is more, in Italy this role is awarded particular salience among foundations, given the apparent decrease in state interest and funding of culture and the arts.

- PLURALISM. *Promoting experimentation and diversity in general; protecting dissenters/civil liberties against the state; challenging others in social, economic, cultural, and environmental policy.*

As evidence of their role in the promotion of pluralism, the foundations tend to point to their very existence and the broad range of activities in which foundations are engaged. However, in Germany, the research points to the role of some foundations in "building bridges" between different societal spheres. For example, community foundations such as the Bürgerstiftung Hamburg present opportunities for collaboration that otherwise may not be possible.

This role has particular resonance in the eastern European context, but one that is largely driven by a foreign-influenced agenda. In the Czech Republic, the promotion of pluralism is awarded primary importance by all but one of the foreign-funded foundations included in the sample. For other foundations, it forms one of many goals among which they divide their resources. This is a role to which policy makers and representatives from umbrella organizations also attach much importance. To a certain extent, this is reflected in the Polish context, where the promotion of pluralism tends to be associated with those whose life experiences are connected with anticommunist movements. For example, the promotion of this role in Poland is associated with the Helsinki Foundation of Human Rights, which was founded by members of the Helsinki Committee who had conspired against the communist regime. It is also dependent on funding from foreign sources. Yet, in Hungary, one foundation representative did question whether foundations that are dependent on state funding can aspire to this role.

*****

Leat and I argue[23] that the impact of globalization forms part of the most significant changes in the environment of foundations; "the redefinition of the role of the state in pursuit of public benefit." The analysis of the roles of foundations points to the challenges and dilemmas that the changing role of the state in different countries poses for foundations. We have identified three key themes that represent how foundations both contribute to the discourse on public policy, and react to it, while also taking into account the broader context of the effects of globalization.

The interviews conducted in Sweden raised the issue of how the roles foundations articulate are influenced by the environment in which they operate. In other words, whether we label a foundation as engaged in innovative activities, or complementarity, or substitution, is determined by the broader societal context in which it functions. The analysis of the roles and visions of foundations across our selection of European countries suggests that foundations are currently struggling with the challenge of reacting to widespread changes in governance. The discussion of the roles of foundations indicates the discrepancy that exists between the roles foundations tend to allocate themselves and how government representatives tend to view their role, or potential role. This has implications for the strategies and activities foundations can pursue in practice. Perhaps reflecting the impact of globalization very clearly, the orientation of Danish social policy since 1998 toward a policy of involving citizens, business enterprises, and voluntary organizations was an issue for some foundations. One foundation, A. P. Möller, felt that the state's expectations of foundations were becoming more visible, but that this, in turn, raises questions surrounding whether this means that foundations risk entering the political arena by acting where the state used to act or is unwilling to act. Particularly in relation to the fulfillment of the complementarity and substitution roles, the foundations face the expectations of governments, on the one hand, and the need to consider their ability and to refine their willingness to assume roles in specific areas, on the other. The extent to which this challenge can have a negative impact on the ethos and goals of foundations is evident in Estonia. Although foundation representatives rated complementarity as the least popular role in a questionnaire, they revealed in interviews that complementing the functions of the government formed a substantial part of their everyday work program. Although there have been calls from national governments and the European Union to involve foundations and, more broadly the third sector in certain policy areas, the research has revealed a lack of understanding on the part of government representatives in some countries as to what foundations are and what they do. There is much work to be done on either side in order to refine and articulate the roles of foundations (and the implications thereof) in the context of government plans for public sector reform.

Growing trends towards the contracting out of public services by governments to nonprofit organizations has generated increased demands for better transparency and accountability within the nonprofit sector.[24] Despite the state of flux surrounding foundations' roles and visions, our research also sought to probe deeper into what foundation representatives view as the immediate priorities and challenges facing foundations. In this way, it is possible to gain an insight into what is the best way forward for foundations in responding to calls for greater transparency. The following common themes emerged.

Management issues concerning the internal governance, monitoring, evaluation, and accountability of foundations were identified as immediate challenges for foundations. In both Switzerland and Britain, for example, many of the experts and foundation representatives interviewed underlined the need for foundations to become more transparent so as to generate a more visible and positive image. In Germany, the issue of transparency among foundations is a source of debate and some controversy. On the one hand, the demand that foundations become more transparent is linked to the view that the future of foundations lies in a number of important and innovative projects. Transparency is believed to be necessary in order to give legitimacy to foundation initiatives and activities. On the other hand, such a "radical" vision of civil society is rejected by some foundation representatives. Although the need for greater transparency was broadly acknowledged, some foundations, such as Quandt and Hypo-Kulturstiftung, were keen to emphasize their autonomy and their need to only be accountable to the sector's supervisory bodies, as opposed to being democratically accountable.

- It should be noted that the perceived lack of understanding on the part of the general public as to what foundations do was noted as a concern by several foundation representatives in each of the countries included in the analysis.
- There appears to be a general consensus among foundation representatives that collaboration among foundations, ranging from the sharing of financial resources to the sharing of expertise, is fundamental to helping foundations to reach their full potential. As indicated above, the need for collaboration also extends to foundations and the corporate sector. However, in Denmark, the general preference for cooperation among foundations extends to informal networking, rather than the formation of a national umbrella organization.
- The British research reported foundation representatives' frustration and irritation at having to articulate their roles to the extent that one interviewee remarked that "if you go by practice the foundations don't have a distinctive role." To a certain extent, the evidence suggests that foundations are also in a state of flux in relation to defining their role in society. The disdain for roles such as redistribution and the preservation of traditions and cultures, contrasted with the enthusiasm with which the majority embraced the role of innovator, suggests that foundations are conscious of their image and looking for ways of appearing more forward looking.

*****

The discussion of "Europe" provides interesting perspectives into foundations' "worldview." With the exception of a minority of foundations that are engaged in cross-border giving, foundations tend to identify themselves as national, rather than European or international, actors. For instance, in terms of representation, foundations in the UK tend to look toward the Association of Charitable Foundations and the Community Foundation Network rather than to the European Foundation Centre (EFC). Indeed, only the larger foundations tended to be aware of the EFC, they cited an absence of orientation toward Europe and the cost of membership as reasons for not choosing to join the EFC. Yet two Community Foundation network members did show awareness of the EFC through its Community Philanthropy Initiative. There are signs that this situation is changing.

- In Austria, the 4 Pfoten Foundation provides an example of how some foundations are beginning to recognize the impact of European Union policy on some of the areas in which foundations operate, which in this case is animal welfare. To this end, they have established an international umbrella organization, 4 Pfoten International, to coordinate the activities of similar organizations in different countries.
- In light of the need for greater collaboration among foundations, some foundation representatives in Ireland pointed to the benefits to be derived from the peer group interaction that is facilitated by organizations such as the EFC. Similarly, in Switzerland, some foundation representatives noted the opportunities for collaboration that Europe provided, although all the indications are that this potential has not been utilized. In Italy, all of the foundations interviewed reacted positively to increased international cooperation among foundations. This was viewed as essential to processes of transferring "best practices," fund-raising, and learning from the experiences of foundations operating in different countries.
- Although European issues did not appear to feature on the radar of Polish respondents, the findings from the Czech Republic and Hungary indicated the types of opinions prevalent on the likely impact of EU membership on foundations in these countries. These opinions varied between fears that it will lead to excessive bureaucratization and constraints on the activities of foundations to anticipation of the increased funding possibilities it is hoped membership of the EU will provide. But, overall, they did not perceive any changes to their roles or visions in accordance with joining the EU. The exception to this trend is the NROS Foundation in the Czech Republic, which is essentially an implementing agency for EU Phare programs.

*****

In two ways, foundations and other civil society groups are a response to these needs: first, in terms of collective action, they lobby for better access and conditions for some group or another; second, they respond to demands for services of many kinds and act as service-providing organizations. Indeed, with respect to, in particular, direct service provision and financing, we find that policy developments affecting the role of foundations at the international level are closely related to domestic debates about welfare reform.[25] In this respect, the policy prominence of philanthropic institutions is closely linked to two developments with roots in domestic policies in developed countries that have now spilled over into the international arena, especially at the OECD, the World Bank and the European Union.

The first development is the rise of *new public management approaches* as part of the modernization of welfare states. At the international level, new public management is replacing conventional development assistance policies and seeks to capitalize on the comparative efficiency advantages of nonprofit organizations through public-private partnerships, competitive bidding, and contracting under the general heading of privatization.[26] Foundations would play the role of providing capital and supporting innovations in service delivery.

Prompted in part by growing doubts about the capacity of the state to cope with its own welfare, developmental, and environmental problems, political analysts across the political spectrum have come to see NGOs as strategic components of a middle way between policies that put primacy on "the market" and those that advocate greater reliance on the state.[27] Together with bilateral donors, many developing countries are searching for a balance between state-led and market-led approaches to development, allocating more responsibility to NGOs, and seeking out contributions from philanthropic institutions.

The basic argument for a greater nonprofit role in both developing and developed countries is based on public administration, which suggests that nonprofits, with the help of foundations, are efficient and effective providers of social and other services that governments may find costlier and more ineffectual to offer themselves. As a result, cooperative relations between governments, foundations, and nonprofits in welfare provision have become prominent features in many countries, such as the United States, Germany, France, and the United Kingdom, resulting in policies that are exported to the international level.[28]

The second development is *social capital approaches*. As a somewhat amorphous set of policies and recommendations, they seek to regain or reinvigorate a sense of community, social cohesion, and collective responsibility in advanced market economies.[29] NGOs and other philanthropic institutions are linked to a neo-Tocquevillian concept of a "strong and vibrant civil society characterized by a social infrastructure of dense networks of face-to-face relationships that crosscut existing social cleavages such as race, ethnicity, class, sexual orientation, and gender that will underpin strong and responsive democratic government."[30] This perspective has now become relevant internationally in the form of World Bank–sponsored social capital projects, or corporate social responsibility programs whereby transnational corporations team up with INGOs to tackle environmental, social, and economic problems. The foundations' role is to support the generation and sustainability of social capital and functioning communities.[31]

In contrast to the basically neoliberal role foundations assume under new public management, the neo-Tocquevillian approach emphasizes their social integrative and participatory function as well as their indirect contributions toward community building, both nationally and internationally. Norms of reciprocity and trust are embodied in transnational networks of civic associations. Put simply, the essence of the neo-Tocquevillian approach at the international level is this: global civil society creates transnational social capital, which is good for political stability and international business. Thus, whereas the manifest function of global civil society may be in keeping political or business interests in check, as the classical liberal position would have it, its latent function is what ultimately matters: it is a mechanism that creates social cohesion across borders, a general principle of societal constitution based on individualism, communal responsibility, and self-organization in a post-nation-state world. According to such neo-Tocquevillian thinking, foundations and NGOs are to form the social infrastructure of civil society. They are to create as well as facilitate a sense of trust and social inclusion that is seen as essential for the functioning of some form of modern society that seems to outgrow national boundaries.

Indeed, as Kendall and I report, the relationship between interpersonal trust and membership in voluntary associations is a persistent research finding cross-nationally. The 1999–2000 wave of the European Value Survey[32] shows for twenty-eight of the thirty-two participating countries a positive and significant relationship between the number of associational memberships[33] held and interpersonal trust.[34] The summary of results from the European Value Survey reveals a striking pattern. Respondents with three or more memberships were twice as likely to state that they trust people as those holding no memberships. Overall, there is almost a linear relationship between increases in membership and the likelihood of trusting people.

Could it be that this connection also applies to the transnational level and serves as a principle of transnational community building and activism, as some have suggested?[35] The main argument seems compelling: continued participation in voluntary associations, local, national, or international, creates greater opportunities for repeated "trust-building" encounters among like-minded individuals, an experience that is subsequently generalized to other situations, such as business or politics.

Whereas the social capital policy argument for greater use of NGOs and foundations is essentially an extension of domestic policy debates into the transnational arena, the nexus between transnational corporations (TNCs) and philanthropy is in its modern form of more recent origins, although many historical examples of business and civil society relations have been documented.[36] Given that over one-third of the world's one hundred largest "economies" are TNCs, there are many "points of contact" between global businesses and global civil society organizations, in particular INGOs like Greenpeace, the World Wildlife Fund, Oxfam, and World Vision, and foundations such as MacArthur, Mott, Ford, and Bertelsmann—the global brand names of civil society. TNCs and philanthropic institutions work together not only addressing global problems (e.g., environmental degradation, malnutrition, and low skills and education levels), but also many local issues in failed states and areas of civic strife and conflict.

Yet it is not only in the developing world that global businesses and philanthropy are developing partnerships. In some ways as a backlash to, in other ways as an implication of, neoliberal policies and "lean states," public opinion in Europe's developed market economies is expecting greater corporate responsibility and "caring" about the societies in which they operate. Increasingly, as Oliviero and Simmons point out, this goes beyond adherence to principles of corporate governance and some core of conduct; it implies greater emphasis on service delivery to employees and their communities (e.g., educational programs and child care), addressing negative externalities of business operations (e.g., pollution and resource depletion), and maintaining the public good (e.g., health and sustainability).

These policy developments suggest that foundations and NGOs are part of the transformation of societies from industrial to postindustrial societies, and the transition from a world of nation-states to one of transnational, even globalizing economic/social systems with weak political integration. In this context, civil society institutions such as NGOs are meeting needs and demands, both old and new, and are redefining and developing partnerships with other institutions, be they governments or business firms. What are the implications of such partnerships for the wider societies in which we life in, and the kind of welfare system involved? The following four options cast separate roles for foundations in a globalizing world.

- *New public management.* Foundations work with NGOs as the set of well-organized, corporate entities that take on tasks and functions previously part of the state administration and international organizations, but which are now delivered through competitive bidding processes and contractual arrangements that try to maximize the competitive advantages of nonprofit providers in complex regional, national, and international social markets under state/IO tutelage.

- *The mellow weakness scenario.* Foundations are encouraged to operate in areas or problem fields that national and international politicians find either too costly relative to payoffs (actual or opportunity costs) or inopportune to tackle themselves, which allows them to pretend that "something is being done." In a loosely centered political arena, foundations are the fig leaf for a political world unwilling to solve its problems in a serious way.[37]

- *The corporate scenario.* As corporate foundations grow they expand their role to include local and global civil society. Corporations use extended social responsibility programs to provide, jointly with nonprofits, services that were previously in the realm of government agencies (e.g., health care, child care, pensions, and a wider variety of community services) and the international community.[38] Such a role for corporate foundations is of great interest in both developed and developing countries. The corporate scenario is closest to the neoliberal model of globalization.

- *Social capital scenario.* Foundations become agents of a self-organizing "quasi-state" apparatus of the twenty-first century and function as part of a benign civil society, with high levels of individualism, participation, and transnational "connectivity," that prevent social ills or detect and correct them before they become "global social problems." Well-coordinated foundations operate at arm's length, with and by a minimalist, technocratic state, both nationally and internationally. Foundations and NGOs function as a source of dissent, challenge, and innovation, as a countervailing force to government and TNCs—a sector that serves as a social, cultural, and political watchdog keeping both market and state in check, a sector that creates and reflects diversity and pluralism and dynamism of the modern world.

These are caricatures, of course, but each "vision" rests on very different assumptions and as strikingly different implications.

*****

Foundations have a rich and long history in Europe. The European foundation landscape is varied and complex, and increasingly dynamic and changing. In recent decades, foundations have grown in number across most European countries; their policy importance has generally increased, both domestically as well as internationally; and they are beginning to cooperate across borders with a wider range of institutions and at levels much higher than in the past.

Most important, foundations are part of the general reorganization of modern societies that involves a reappraisal of the role of the state, more reliance on markets, and a greater emphasis on individual responsibility. Foundations, as private institutions for public benefit, are increasingly attractive to policy makers across the political spectrum. However, they remain largely domestic actors, and are only beginning to move onto the international and transnational stage. This chapter has outlined some of the options for foundations in the process of globalization, and it will be of great importance to monitor which of the roles and scenarios suggested here will prevail over others.

Endnotes

[1] H. K. Anheier, M. Glasius and M. Kaldor (eds.), *Global Civil Society 2001*, Oxford University Press, Oxford, UK, 2001.

[2] M. Kaldor, H. K. Anheier, and M. Glasius, "Global Civil Society in an Era of Regressive Globalisation," in M. Glasius, M. Kaldor, and H. K. Anheier (eds.) *Global Civil Society Year Book 2003*, Oxford University Press, Oxford, UK, 2003.

[3] H. K. Anheier and D. Leat, *From Charity to Creativity: Philanthropic Foundations in the 21st Century*, Comedia, York, 2002. Also, P. Johnson *Global Social Investing: A Preliminary Overview*, available at: www.tpi.org. (2001).

[4] The project, *Visions and Roles of Foundations in Europe* is directed by Helmut K. Anheier and managed by Siobhan Daly. It is located at the Centre for Civil Society, London School of Economics, and includes researchers from twenty-four countries; Austria, Belgium, the Czech Republic, Denmark, Estonia, Finland, France, Germany, Greece, Hungary, Ireland, Israel, Italy, Liechtenstein, the Netherlands, Norway, Poland, Portugal, Spain, Sweden, Switzerland, the United Kingdom, and the United States. The project also includes a separate analysis of the European Union, and a comparative view from the United States. The project was launched in October 2001. For more information on the project, including the project's methodology, visit the Web site at http://www.lse.ac.uk/ccs.

[5] L. M. Salamon, H. K. Anheier, R. List, S. Toepler, S. W. Sokolowski and Associates, *Global Civil Society: Dimensions of the Nonprofit Sector*, Institute for Policy Studies, Center for Civil Society Studies, Johns Hopkins University, Baltimore, MD, 1999.

[6] H. K. Anheier and W. Seibel, *The Nonprofit Sector in Germany*, Manchester University Press, Manchester, UK, 2001.

[7] J. Clark, "Trans-national Civil Society: Issues of Governance and Organisation," issues paper prepared as background for a seminar on transnational civil society, London School of Economics, June 1–2, 2001. See also, L. Kriesberg, "Social Movements and Global Transformation" in J. Smith, C. Chatfield, and R. Pagnucco (eds.) *Transnational Social Movements and Global Politics: Solidarity beyond the State*, Syracuse University Press, Syracuse, NY, 1997.

[8] M. Edwards and D. Hulme (eds.), *Beyond the Magic Bullet: NGO Performance and Accountability in the Post–Cold War World*, Macmillan, London, 1995.

[9] Kriesberg, "Social Movements and Global Transformation."

[10] Clark, "Trans-national Civil Society." Also J. Naughton, "Contested Space: The Internet and Global Civil Society," in H. K. Anheier, M. Glasius and M. Kaldor (eds.) *Global Civil Society 2001*, Oxford University Press, Oxford, UK, 2001.

[11] A. O. Hirschmann, *Exit, Voice, and Loyalty: Responses to Decline in Firms, Organizations and States*, Harvard University Press, Cambridge, MA, 1970. See also Kriesberg, "Social Movements and Global Transformation."

[12] R. Inglehart, *Culture Shift in Advanced Industrial Society*, Princeton University Press, Princeton, NJ, 1990. Also J. W. Van Deth and E. Scarbrough (eds.), *The Impact of Values*, Oxford University Press, Oxford, UK, 1995.

[13] Salamon, et al. *Global Civil Society*. See also H. K. Anheier and R. List, *Cross-Border Philanthropy: An Exploratory Study of International Giving in the United Kingdom, United States, Germany and Japan*, Charities Aid Foundation, West Malling, Kent, and Centre for Civil Society, London School of Economics, London, 2000; H. K. Anheier, "The Third Sector in Europe: Five Theses," Global Civil Society Working Paper 12, Centre for Civil Society, London School of Economics, London, 2002.

[14] M. Keck and K. Sikkink, *Activists Beyond Borders: Advocacy Networks in International Politics*, Cornell University Press, Ithaca, NY, 1998.

[15] The preliminary findings from the countries included in the present analysis should provide an indication of the extent and nature of the empirical information about foundations that the European-wide network of researchers working on *Visions and Roles of Foundations in Europe* will be able to provide.

[16] The data reported in this section draw on a comparative analysis by Helmut Anheier and J. Kendall (eds.), *Third Sector Policy at the Crossroads: An International Nonprofit Analysis*, Routledge, London, 2001, which itself uses data from individual country reports in Bertelsmann Foundation, *Foundations in Europe: Society, Management, Law*, London, 2001. The data are updated and expanded by information provided by the staff at *Visions and Roles of Foundations in Europe*.

[17] G. P. Barbetta (ed.), *The Nonprofit Sector in Italy*, Manchester University Press, Manchester, UK, 1997.

[18] Anheier and Kendall, *Third Sector Policy at the Crossroads*.

[19] Salamon, et al. *Global Civil Society*.

[20] E. Archambault, M. Gariazzo, H. K. Anheier, and L. Salamon, "France," in L. M. Salamon, H. K. Anheier, R. List, S. Toepler, S. W. Sokolowski, and Associates, *Global Civil Society: Dimensions of the Nonprofit Sector*, Institute for Policy Studies, Center for Civil Society Studies, Johns Hopkins University, Baltimore, MD, 1999.

[21] K. Prewitt, "The Importance of Foundations in an Open Society," in Bertelsmann Foundation (ed.) *The Future of Foundations in an Open Society*, Bertelsmann Foundation Publishers, Gütersloh, Germany, 1999. For literature on foundations, see H. K. Anheier and S. Toepler (eds.), *Private Funds—Public Purpose: Philanthropic Foundations in International Perspectives*, Plenum, NY, 1999.

[22] Given the practical impossibility of surveying all existing foundations in the different countries, each of the researchers was asked to purposefully select a number of foundations to help illustrate the broader picture in their country, without aiming to be representative in a statistical way. Further information on the project methodology is available at the project Web site: http://www.lse.ac.uk/ccs.

[23] Anheier and Leat, *From Charity to Creativity*. See also Johnson, *Global Social Investing*.

[24] Anheier and Leat, *From Charity to Creativity*.

[25] Anheier and Kendall (eds.), *Third Sector Policy at the Crossroads*; and N. Deakin, *In Search of Civil Society*, Palgrave, Basingstoke, UK, 2001.

[26] E. Ferlie (ed.), *The New Public Management in Action*, Oxford University Press, Oxford, UK, 1996. See also K. McLaughlin, S. P. Osborne, and E. Ferlie (eds.), *New Public Management: Current Trends and Future Prospects*, Routledge, London, 2002.

[27] A. Giddens, *The Third Way*, Polity Press, Cambridge, UK, 1998; European Commission, *Promoting the Role of Voluntary Organisations and Foundations in Europe*, Office of Official Publications of the European Communities, Luxembourg, 1997; European Commission, *The Commission and Non-Governmental Organisations: Building a Stronger Partnership*, Discussion Paper, European Commission, Brussels, 2000.

[28] For a general overview see L. M. Salamon, *Partners in Public Service: Government-Nonprofit Relations in the Modern Welfare State*, Johns Hopkins University Press, Baltimore, MD, 1995. Specifically, for the United States, see L. M. Salamon, *The Tools of Government: A Guide to the New Governance*, Oxford University Press, NY, 2002; for Germany, see H. K. Anheier and W. Seibel, *The Nonprofit Sector in Germany*, Manchester University Press, Manchester, 2001; for France, see E. Archambault, *The Nonprofit Sector in France*, Manchester University Press, Manchester, UK, 1996. Last, for an overview of the United Kingdom, see W. Plowden, *Next Steps in Voluntary Action*, Centre for Civil Society, London School of Economics, and NCVO, London, 2001; and Strategy Unit, *Private Action, Public Benefit: A Review of Charities and the Wider Not-for-Profit Sector*, Cabinet Office, London, 2002.

[29] R. D. Putnam, *Bowling Alone: The Collapse and Survival of American Community*, Simon and Schuster, NY, 2000; R. D. Putnam (ed.), *Democracies in Flux*, Oxford University Press, Oxford, UK, 2002. See also C. Sirianni and L. Friedland, *Civic Innovation in America: Community Empowerment, Public Policy, and the Movement for Civic Renewal*, University of California Press, Berkeley, 2000.

[30] B. Edwards, M. W. Foley and M. Diani, *Beyond Tocqueville: Civil Society and the Social Capital Debate in Comparative Perspective*, University Press of New England, Hanover, NH, 2001, p. 17.

[31] For a discussion on the World Bank, see P. Dasgupta and I. Serageldin (eds.), *Social Capital: A Multifaceted Perspective*, World Bank, Washington, DC, 1999. For a discussion on transnational corporations, see M. B. Oliviero and A. Simmons, "Who's Minding the Store? Global Civil Society and Corporate Responsibility," in M. Glasius, M. Kaldor and H. K. Anheier (eds.) *The Global Civil Society*, Oxford University Press, Oxford, UK, 2002.

[32] Besides Britain, the EVS covers the following countries: France, Germany, Austria, Italy, Spain, the Netherlands, Belgium, Denmark, Sweden, Iceland, Northern Ireland, Ireland, Estonia, Latvia, Lithuania, Poland, the Czech Republic, Slovakia, Hungary, Romania, Bulgaria, Croatia, Greece, Russia, Malta, Luxembourg, Slovenia, Ukraine, Belarus, and the United States. The countries in which the positive relationship between trust and memberships in voluntary associations either does not exist or is weak are Romania, Russia, Ukraine, and Belarus. See L. Halman, *The European Values Study: A*

Third Wave, Source Book of the 1999/2000 European Values Study Surveys, Tilburg University Press, Tilburg, the Netherlands, 2001.

[33] This includes memberships in health and social welfare associations, religious/church organizations, education, arts, music or cultural associations, trade unions and professional associations, local community groups and social clubs, environmental and human rights groups, youth clubs, women's groups, political parties, peace groups, and sports and recreational clubs, among others.

[34] Measured by the following question: "Generally speaking, would you say that most people can be trusted or that you need to be very careful when dealing with people?"

[35] M. Lindenberg and C. Bryant, *Going Global: Transforming Relief and Development NGOs*, Kumerian Press, Bloomfield, CT, 2001, chap. 1, 3, 5.

[36] Oliviero and Simmons, "Who's Minding the Store."

[37] W. Seibel, *Funktionaler Dilettantismus: Erfolgreich scheiternde Organisationen im Dritten Sektor, zwischen Markt und Staat*, Nomos, Baden Baden, 1994.

[38] C. Perrow, "The Rise of Nonprofits and the Decline of Civil Society," in H. K. Anheier (ed.) *Organizational Theory and the Nonprofit Form. Report No. 2. Centre for Civil Society*, London School of Economics, London, UK, 2001.

Chapter 7

GLOBALIZATION AND
THE CIVIL SOCIETY SECTOR

Lester M. Salamon

A "global associational revolution" appears to be under way around the world, a massive upsurge of organized private, voluntary activity in virtually every region of the globe—in the developed countries of North America, western Europe, and Asia; throughout central and eastern Europe; and in much of the developing world.[1] To be sure, voluntary activity and voluntary organizations are by no means new phenomena. Mutual assistance and charitable institutions have long operated in societies throughout the world, the product of religious impulses, social movements, cultural or professional interests, sentiments of solidarity and mutuality, altruism, and, more recently, government's need for assistance to carry out public functions. Yet the number and variety of such organizations seem to have grown enormously in recent years. The global associational revolution that appears to be under way at the present time may, in fact, prove to be as significant a development of the late twentieth and early twenty-first centuries as the rise of the nation-state was of the late nineteenth and early twentieth centuries.

*****

That this development is taking place, and taking place now, is hardly an accident. The contemporary rise of the nonprofit, or civil society, sector is the by-product of a striking coming together of a variety of historical trends. Many of these trends, moreover, are closely related to the broader contemporary phenomenon of globalization, the growing international connectedness of people and institutions. Indeed, the rise of the civil society sector is both a consequence and a cause of globalization. More precisely, many of the forces driving the contemporary process of globalization are also contributing to the growth of the civil society sector internationally, and civil society institutions are in turn adding new dimensions to the whole phenomenon of globalization.

The purpose of this chapter is to examine these interrelationships between the growing civil society presence throughout the world and the broader phenomenon of globalization. To do so, the discussion falls into three parts. The first part analyzes the factors that seem to lie behind the recent growth of the civil society sector internationally and shows how they relate to the forces contributing to growing globalization. The second part documents the scale and character of the civil society sector that has emerged as a consequence of these forces in countries throughout the world, drawing on a new body of research recently completed under the auspices of the Johns Hopkins Comparative Nonprofit Sector Project, which the present author directs. Finally, the third part looks briefly at the special subset of civil society organizations operating at the cross-national level, since these display especially sharply the relationship between globalization and civil society. The central conclusion that emerges from this analysis is that globalization involves more than a shift in the relative positions of nation-states and corporations. A powerful citizen sector has also emerged in this process and is laying claim to an expanded voice on both the national and international stages.

*****

That the past twenty to twenty-five years have witnessed a dramatic growth both in the attention paid to civil society organizations and in the scale and importance of these institutions seems to be due to a host of different factors. What is striking about these factors, however, is how closely they parallel the forces that have also been responsible for the parallel growth of globalization.

Communications Technology

Foremost among these factors have been the recent dramatic breakthroughs in information technology and expansion of literacy. These changes have affected the growth of civil society organizations in a number of different ways. In the first place, they have increased the demand for them. Improved communications have awakened people to the realization that their circumstances may not be immutable, that opportunities may be better elsewhere, and that change is possible. This has stimulated citizen activism; sparked gender, environmental, and ethnic consciousness; and prompted heightened interest in human rights—all of which in turn have further stimulated the growth of civil society organizations. Coupled with the general economic prosperity in the major world economies since the late 1940s, advanced communications has helped to foster a broader value change emphasizing human rights, individual freedoms, environmental protection, and related lifestyle issues,[2] all of which have helped prompt interest in organizations through which these values can be pursued.

Not only has new communications technology helped stimulate the demand for civil society organizations, but also it has helped increase the supply of them. Just as advanced telecommunications have made it possible for corporations to organize production across much wider geographic boundaries, so, too, they have made it far easier for citizens to join together to meet common needs and to press common demands on public or private authorities. Communication is the lifeblood of organization, just as it is of commerce. It makes it easier to concert action, to sustain contact, and to create a sense of belonging. As communications has improved both within countries and between them, organizations have become far easier to build and maintain.

Neoliberalism and New Public Management

The ideas of empowerment and human rights transmitted by advanced communications have not been the only ones prompting the growth of civil society organizations. Also at work has been a broader set of neoliberal economic theories that the new communications technologies have also helped to spread. These ideas gained widespread visibility with the election of Margaret Thatcher in the United Kingdom and Ronald Reagan in the United States, and they came to inspire the "structural adjustment" policies of institutions such as the World Bank and the International Monetary Fund. At the center of this body of thought has been a profound questioning of the capability of states, at least on their own, to cope with the interconnected social welfare, developmental, and environmental problems of our day. The state stands accused in these theories of stifling initiative, creating unresponsive bureaucracies, failing to mobilize grassroots energies, and generally absorbing escalating shares of national income to the detriment of more efficient private investment.

Although the central thrust of this neoliberal agenda has been to reduce the functions of the state and expand the role of the market and the private business sector, it has also given new prominence to the nonprofit sector and philanthropy. This is so because neoliberal politicians and theorists have needed an explanation for how social welfare problems would be dealt with once government spending was cut and government social welfare protections eliminated, and the nonprofit sector and philanthropy have provided a convenient one.[3] Initially, this took the form of trumpeting the potentials for private philanthropy, both individual and corporate, to fill in for the shrinking state. As the financial impossibility of this became apparent, however, a frantic search began for a "middle way" between sole reliance on the market and sole reliance on the state to cope with public problems—a search that is evident in Prime Minister Tony Blair's emphasis on a "Third Way" in the United Kingdom, Gerhard Schröder's "New Middle" in Germany, and strategies emphasizing empowerment of the poor and "assisted self-reliance" in the developing world."[4] Former French prime minister Lionel Jospin's summary declaration "Yes to a market economy, No to a market society" seems to summarize the prevailing sentiment well.

Because of their unique combination of private structure and public purpose, their generally smaller scale, their connections to citizens, their flexibility, and their capacity to tap private initiative in support of public purposes, civil society organizations have surfaced as strategically important potential partners in the effort to fashion such new solutions. Having played a critical part in the initial "neoliberal" project, they have therefore taken their place as well as "a basic part," as one close observer has put it, "of the politics of the third way," though some continue to insist on a sharp distinction between empowerment-oriented citizen action and assistance-oriented nonprofit organizations that presumably function as instruments of domination instead.[5]

The Social Capital Emphasis

Also contributing to the attention civil society organizations have recently attracted is the recent interest in "social capital," those bonds of trust and reciprocity that have been found to be critical preconditions for democracy and economic growth.[6] Fears about a decline, or general insufficiency, of such trust have come to be a major preoccupation in countries throughout the world, leading to increased interest in civil society organizations as a way to help remedy the deficit. Very likely contributing to the popularity of this argument, particularly among policy makers, has been its assignment of responsibility for a wide range of social ills not to underlying inequalities of power or economic opportunity, but to the lack of supportive social ties among the disadvantaged. In the developed countries, this line of argument has provided a convenient explanation for rising levels of crime and poverty.[7] Similar arguments have had great appeal in the developing world as well where they offer an explanation for widespread poverty and under-development that focus on shortcomings among the people of less developed regions rather than on such factors as unequal terms of trade, globalization, or the power of entrenched elites.[8]

Social Entrepreneurs

The fact that new communications technologies helped spark increased interest in civil society organizations among disadvantaged populations and neoliberal elites alike, and that they eased the problems of forming such organizations, is still not sufficient to explain the global associational revolution that has taken place in recent years. Also at work was an increase in the supply of "social entrepreneurs" willing to come forward to form such organizations.[9] For this, an unusual confluence of developments seems to have been responsible. One of these was the considerable economic growth that occurred in the world economy in the 1960s and 1970s, with all regions sharing in the expansion, especially central and eastern Europe and the developing world, where growth was particularly strong. What is important about this growth for our purposes here is the contribution it made to the creation of a sizable professional middle class of doctors, lawyers, scientists, educators, and engineers in many parts of the world. Because of the repressive political regimes in many of these countries, however, many of these educated elites found themselves increasingly frustrated politically and socially. Following the oil crisis of the early 1970s, moreover, many of them found themselves economically frustrated as well. In this climate, many seem to have turned to nongovernmental organizations as vehicles through which to give meaning to their lives. Such middle-class leadership was critical to the emergence of private, nonprofit organizations in Latin America, Asia, Africa, and central Europe during this period.[10] As Andras Biro, a Hungarian activist put it: "We are witnessing an escape from the enforced immaturity of the socialist system. For the first time in 40 years we are reclaiming responsibility for our lives."[11] In the process, these educated elites helped convert the demand for civil society organizations into an actual supply of them.

External Actors

Finally, a variety of external actors has also played crucial roles in moving the process of civil society development along. The significant expansion of grassroots nonprofit organizations in much of Latin America in the 1970s and 1980s, for example, was triggered in important part by the post–Vatican II effort of the Catholic Church to counter the influence of the Castro Revolution in the region by forming Christian "base" communities through which liberal clerics could aid the rural poor. Western charitable foundations as well as religious organizations committed to grassroots democracy and empowerment of the poor have also played major roles, delivering important financial assistance to the new nongovernmental organizations taking shape in many developing regions. In recent years, moreover, multinational corporations eager to ensure a "license to operate" in faraway lands and multilateral organizations like the World Bank that have come to recognize the need to engage citizen energies to implement their development agendas have also entered the scene.

These external actors have provided especially tangible evidence of the impact of globalization on the recent growth of civil society. In turn, however, civil society organizations have also had an impact on globalization. According to one line of theory, in fact, the progress of globalization has been importantly fueled by a particular set of transnational nongovernmental organizations whose "primary concern" is the propagation of an integrating global culture of universalism, individualism, rational voluntary authority, and world citizenship.[12] These transnational organizations have been credited, in turn, with the creation of counterpart organizations, in particular nations that have carried their message of globalization forward.

In short, many of the same factors driving the broader phenomenon of globalization—increased communications, neoliberalism, growing individualism, expanded education, and the extended reach of transnational organizations themselves— are stimulating the development of civil society around the world. In this sense, globalization and the "global associational revolution" are opposite sides of the same coin. Even as globalization has stimulated a global civil society movement in opposition to globalization, it has paradoxically been responsible in important part for the fact that such a movement could exist.

*****

The upshot of this set of forces has been the establishment of a civil society sector that is global in reach and substantial in both size and composition. Unfortunately, however, clear recognition of this reality has lagged badly behind.

Despite its growing presence and importance, the civil society sector has long been the lost continent on the social landscape of our world. Only recently has it attracted serious attention in policy circles or the press, and academic interest has long been equally tepid. Even now, social and political discourse remains heavily dominated by a "two-sector model" that acknowledges the existence of only two social spheres outside of the family unit—the market and the state, or business and government. This has been reinforced by statistical conventions that have kept this "third sector" of civil society organizations largely invisible in official economic data.[13] Even the most basic information about these organizations—their numbers, size, activities, economic weight, finances, and role—has therefore been lacking almost everywhere, while deeper understanding of the factors that contribute to their growth and decline has been almost nonexistent. As a consequence, the civil society sector's ability to participate in the significant policy debates now under way has been seriously hampered and its potential for contributing to the solution of pressing problems too often challenged or ignored.

*****

To help fill the resulting gap in basic knowledge about the third sector internationally, we launched an ambitious international project—the Johns Hopkins Comparative Nonprofit Sector Project—in 1991. Initially focused on thirteen countries—

eight developed and five developing—this project has since been extended to include over forty.[14]

Objectives

The principal objectives of this project were (1) to *document* the scope, structure, financing, and role of the civil society sector in these countries for the first time in solid empirical terms; (2) to *explain* why this sector varies in size, composition, character, and role from place to place and identify the factors that seem to encourage or retard its development; and (3) to *assess the impact* these organizations are having and the contributions they make, as well as the drawbacks they entail. In addition, the project sought to conduct its work in a way that would (4) *improve awareness* of this set of institutions; and (5) build *local capacity* to carry on the work in the future.

Approach

To pursue these objectives, we formulated an approach that was:
- *Comparative*, covering countries at different levels of development and with a wide assortment of religious, cultural, and political traditions. In particular, work has been undertaken in over forty countries, representing all the inhabited continents and most of the major religions of the world. To date, data have been generated in thirty-six of these, including sixteen developed countries in North America, western Europe, and Asia, and twenty developing and transitional countries in Latin America, Africa, the Middle East, South Asia, and central and eastern Europe.
- *Systematic*, utilizing a common definition of the entities to be included and a common classification system for differentiating among them.
- *Collaborative*, relying extensively on local analysts to root our definitions and analysis in the solid ground of local knowledge and ensure the local experience to carry the work forward in the future.
- *Consultative*, involving the active participation of local civil society activists, government leaders, the press, and the business community in order to further ensure that the work in each country was responsive to the particular conditions of the country and that the results could be understood and disseminated locally.
- *Empirical*, moving wherever possible beyond subjective impressions to develop a body of reasonably solid empirical data on this set of organizations.

Definition

Given the comparative and empirical nature of this inquiry, it was imperative to develop a common definition of the entities of interest to us.[15] For this purpose, we adopted a bottom-up, inductive approach drawing on the actual experiences of the broad range of countries embraced within our project. Out of this process emerged a consensus on five structural-operational features that defined the entities at the center of our concern. In particular, we defined the civil society sector as the set of (a) *organizations*, whether formal or informal and whether registered or not, that are (b) *private*, that is, not part of the institutional apparatus of the state; (c) *non-profit-distributing*, that is, they that do not distribute profits to their owners or directors and are not primarily commercial in purpose; (d) *self-governing*, that is, able to put themselves out of business if they so choose; and (e) *voluntary*, that is, staffed and supported by people as a matter of choice and not as a matter of legal obligation.

While not without its grey areas or borderline cases, this definition has now been tested in countries throughout the world and found to be workable in identifying a set of institutions that is sufficiently broad to encompass the great variety of entities commonly considered to be part of the third or civil society sector in both developed and developing countries, yet sufficiently sharp to be able to distinguish these institutions from those in the other two major sectors—business and government. Most organized forms of citizen action are covered by this definition, including not just formal service organizations but also social clubs, professional organizations, social movements, and community-based cooperatives engaged in community development work, such as the *stokvels*, or revolving credit associations, in Africa. Intentionally excluded, however, are government agencies, private businesses, and commercial cooperatives and mutuals.[16] For the sake of convenience, we will generally use the term "civil society organizations," or "civil society sector" to refer to the institutions that meet this fivefold structural-operational definition.

Methodology

Armed with this definition, our local associates and we drew on a variety of data sources to generate estimates of the scope and composition of the set of institutions so defined. These included (a) official economic statistics (e.g., employment surveys, population surveys); (b) data assembled by umbrella groups or intermediary associations representing various types of civil society organizations or industries; specialized surveys of civil society organizations, including hypernetwork sampling surveys; and population surveys, focusing particularly on giving and volunteering.

*****

Out of this work has come a variety of findings that challenge conventional beliefs about this civil society sector internationally.[17]

A Major Economic Force

In the first place, this work has made clear that the civil society sector constitutes a sizable economic presence in countries throughout the world. This is evident most clearly in the human resources this set of organizations mobilizes. With religious institutions included, the civil society sector in just the thirty-six countries for which we have collected reliable data engaged a cumulative total of 46 million full-time equivalent workers as of the mid- to late 1990s, or an average of 4.4 percent of the economically active population of these countries. This is at least ten times more people than are employed in the utilities and textile industries in these countries, five times more people than work in the food manufacturing industry, and 20 percent more people than work in transportation and communications. Put somewhat differently, if the nonprofit sector in these countries were a separate national economy, its expenditures would make it the seventh largest economy in the world, ahead of Italy, Brazil, Russia, Spain, and Canada, and just behind France and the United Kingdom.

Significant Volunteer Presence

Of these 46 million full-time equivalent (FTE) civil society organization workers, over 20 million, or 44 percent, are volunteers. In fact, of course, the actual number of volunteers exceeds this number by a substantial margin since most volunteers work only part-time. We estimate that 132 million people engage in some volunteer activity in these thirty-six countries, or about 10 percent of the adult population, on average.

Great Variations Among Countries

While the civil society sector is a sizable force in a wide range of countries, it varies from a high of 14.4 percent of the economically active population in the Netherlands to a low of 0.4 percent in Mexico, with a high degree of diversity in between these poles (see figure 7.1). Interestingly, when measured relatively, the United States does not have the largest civil society workforce in the world, as is commonly assumed. Indeed, three other countries of the thirty-six for which we now have data record relatively larger civil society sector workforces and all of these are in western Europe. Also notable is the fact that the civil society sector is relatively larger in the more developed countries than in the less developed and transition countries, even when account is taken of volunteer effort, though there are considerable variations within both groups of countries.

Not only do countries vary considerably in the overall size of their civil society sectors, but also they vary in the extent to which these organizations rely on paid as opposed to volunteer workers. While volunteers comprise 44 percent of the combined civil society organization workforce in the countries we studied, this figure varies considerably among individual countries—from a low of under 20 percent in Hungary, Israel, Brazil, and Egypt to a high of over 70 percent in Sweden and Tanzania. This reflects the different historical traditions of these countries. In Sweden and Norway, for example, a strong tradition of social movements and volunteer sports leads to a high level of volunteer mobilization, whereas Hungary is still suffering from the residual effects of enforced volunteering under Soviet-style communism.

Composition

Civil society organizations are not simply places of work, whether paid or volunteer, of course. What makes them significant are the functions they perform, and these functions are multiple.[18] Indeed, some analysts argue strongly in favor of differentiating the empowerment functions of the civil society sector from its service functions on grounds that they represent very distinct phenomena.

In practice, however, drawing these distinctions is far from easy, particularly since many organizations perform more than one function. Nevertheless, we can make a rough approximation of the composition of this set of organizations by grouping organizations according to their principal activity, and then assessing the level of effort each such activity absorbs. To this end, we developed the International Classification of Nonprofit

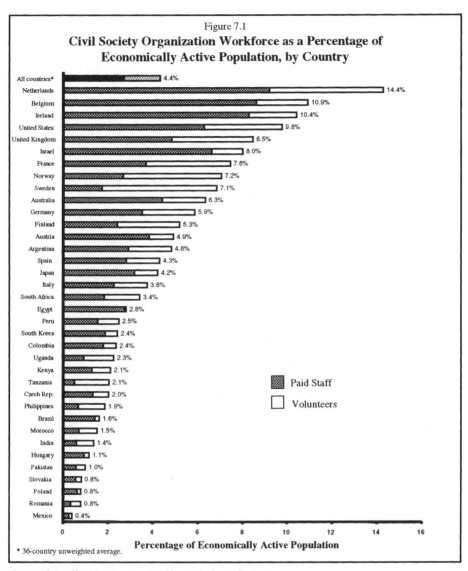

Figure 7.1
Civil Society Organization Workforce as a Percentage of Economically Active Population, by Country

All countries* 4.4%
Netherlands 14.4%
Belgium 10.9%
Ireland 10.4%
United States 9.8%
United Kingdom 8.5%
Israel 8.0%
France 7.6%
Norway 7.2%
Sweden 7.1%
Australia 6.3%
Germany 5.9%
Finland 5.3%
Austria 4.9%
Argentina 4.8%
Spain 4.3%
Japan 4.2%
Italy 3.8%
South Africa 3.4%
Egypt 2.8%
Peru 2.5%
South Korea 2.4%
Colombia 2.4%
Uganda 2.3%
Kenya 2.1%
Tanzania 2.1%
Czech Rep. 2.0%
Philippines 1.9%
Brazil 1.6%
Morocco 1.5%
India 1.4%
Hungary 1.1%
Pakistan 1.0%
Slovakia 0.8%
Poland 0.8%
Romania 0.8%
Mexico 0.4%

Paid Staff
Volunteers

Percentage of Economically Active Population
* 36-country unweighted average.

Source: Johns Hopkins Comparative Nonprofit Sector Project.

Organizations based on the International Standard Industrial Classification, but with additional detail to accommodate the range of activities in which nonprofit organizations are typically involved.[19] We then grouped these activities into two broad groups—service functions and expressive functions—and calculated the extent of civil society organization effort that goes into each as reflected in the amount of paid or volunteer workforce time. When this is done, it reveals that nearly two-thirds (64 percent) of civil society organization workforce time is absorbed in essentially service functions, chiefly the traditional social welfare services of education (23 percent of the workforce), social services (20 percent), and health (14 percent). At the same time, at least one-third of the effort is concentrated in the sector's more expressive activities, such as culture and recreation (19 percent), business and professional representation (7 percent), and civic advocacy and environmental protection (6 percent). If the organizations engaged in "development" work are treated as part of the "expressive" functions rather than the service ones (on the ground that they involve empowerment activities and not simply service delivery), the expressive functions swell to 40 percent of the effort and the service ones shrink to 57 percent (see figure 7.2).

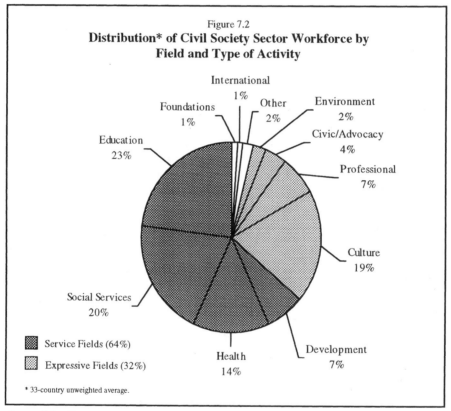

Figure 7.2
Distribution* of Civil Society Sector Workforce by Field and Type of Activity

International 1%
Foundations 1%
Other 2%
Environment 2%
Civic/Advocacy 4%
Professional 7%
Education 23%
Culture 19%
Social Services 20%
Development 7%
Health 14%

Service Fields (64%)
Expressive Fields (32%)

* 33-country unweighted average.

Source: Johns Hopkins Comparative Nonprofit Sector Project.

While the dominance of service functions seems to hold for most countries, it is by no means uniform. Thus, for one thing, "development" work absorbs a substantially higher proportion of civil society organization energies in the developing countries than in the developed ones (16 percent versus 5 percent); and in the African countries this figure reaches 25 percent of the nonprofit workforce effort. This suggests an especially marked grassroots component of the civil society sector in these developing regions, particularly in Africa.

Even among the developed countries, moreover, significant differences are apparent. Thus, social services are especially prominent among the service offerings of civil society organizations in western Europe, whereas health services are more prominent in the United States, Japan, Australia, and Israel. Even more dramatically, in the Nordic countries and in central Europe the "expressive" functions of the civil society sector are more prominent than the service ones. This likely reflects the far more dominant role of the state in providing human services in these countries and, in the Scandinavian context, the vibrant heritage of citizen-based social movements and citizen engagement in advocacy, sports, and related expressive fields. Clearly, different societies have made different choices about how they handle crucial social functions, which makes the civil society sector an instructive vantage point from which to observe broader social realities.

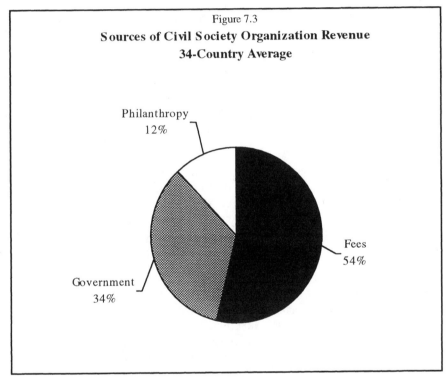

Figure 7.3
Sources of Civil Society Organization Revenue
34-Country Average

Philanthropy
12%

Fees
54%

Government
34%

Source: Johns Hopkins Comparative Nonprofit Sector Project.

Revenue Sources

How is this civil society activity financed around the world? Perhaps the most striking conclusion that emerges from the empirical record is that far less of it comes from private philanthropy than is widely believed. Rather, the dominant source of civil society organization revenue in the thirty-four countries for which revenue data are available is fees and charges.[20] Over half (54 percent) of civil society organization income comes, on average, from such commercial sources (see figure 7.3). In second place as a source of income for civil society organizations around the world is government. Public sector payments account on average for 34 percent of civil society revenue in the thirty-four countries studied. Private philanthropy—from individuals, corporations, and foundations combined—plays a decidedly smaller role in the financing of global civil society activity, accounting on average for 12 percent of the total.

Fee income is a particularly important source of civil society sector revenue in Latin America, Africa, and central and eastern Europe, as well as in the United States, Australia, and Japan. By contrast, public sector support is the most important source of income for the civil society sector in western Europe. South Africa is the only developing country in which fee income is less important than government funding, reflecting the post-apartheid policy of supporting civil society institutions as a means of strengthening democracy and public participation.

This picture of civil society sector finance changes significantly, however, when volunteer time is factored into the equation and treated as a part of philanthropy. When this is done, philanthropy's share of total sector support increases from 12 percent to 30 percent, edging government out of second place as a source of revenue. This demonstrates how much more important contributions of time are to the support base of third sector institutions as compared to contributions of money. This is particularly true in less-developed regions, where monetary resources are limited. But it also holds in the Nordic countries as well, where volunteer work is particularly marked.

Recent Trends

Not only is the civil society sector quite large in a significant range of countries around the world, but also its scale and presence appearing to be expanding, both absolutely and in comparison with the other sectors. Evidence of this is the growth in the recorded number of such organizations. The number of associations formed in France,[21] for example, increased from approximately 10,000 per year in the 1960s and early 1970s to 40,000 to 50,000 per year in the 1980s and 1990s. Similar striking growth was recorded in the number of civil society sector institutions in Italy in the 1980s, as new forms of "social cooperatives" took shape to supplement strained state social welfare institutions.[22] Developments in central and eastern Europe and in much of the developing world were even more dramatic since they often started from a smaller base.

The number of organizations is a notoriously imperfect variable through which to gauge the growth of this sector, however, since organizations vary so fundamentally in size and complexity. What is more, the apparent growth in numbers of organizations may really reflect a change in legal procedures for registering entities that previously existed in a more informal state. Regrettably, however, reliable time series data on the more tangible dimensions of the civil society sector have been lacking for all but a handful of countries. The data that are available, however, mostly pertaining to developed countries in the early 1990s, are revealing. What these data show is that for the seven countries on which valid time series data could be assembled, civil society employment increased from an average of 3.5 percent of nonagricultural employment in 1990 to 4.5 percent in 1995. Put somewhat differently, employment in the civil society sector grew by an average of 29 percent in these seven countries between 1990 and 1995, whereas overall employment grew only by 8 percent during the same period. At the same time, volunteering and membership rates expanded as well. In fact, despite talk of increased "bowling alone," all of the countries reported increases in volunteering and membership affiliation rates.[23]

Regional Patterns

In short, the civil society sector has become a major social and economic force in countries throughout the world. At the same time, the size, composition, and character of this sector differ markedly from place to place. While the differences are partly country-specific, there are also broad regional differences. Thus, for example, among developed countries there is a more or less distinct "Anglo-Saxon pattern" characterized by a sizable civil society sector extensively oriented toward services and financed mostly by fees and philanthropy; a "Nordic pattern" characterized by a relatively small civil society paid workforce but a sizable volunteer presence and an orientation toward expressive functions;[24] and a "western European pattern" characterized by a sizable civil society, heavily engaged in service activities, mostly comprised of paid workers, and heavily supported by government.[25] These patterns suggest that the civil society sector is deeply rooted in the broader social structure of each society—in the pattern of class relationships, religious traditions, and historical evolution that exists.[26] This "social origins approach" to explaining the evolution of civil society makes clear that while globalization may have stimulated a worldwide expansion of civil society, it has hardly been powerful enough to overwhelm the varied structures that determine what shape this civil society phenomenon will take in particular places.

*****

Not only has the civil society sector emerged as an increasingly significant actor at the national level in countries throughout the world, but also it has emerged as a major force at the international level as well. In part, this has been a *product* of globalization, of the extension of communications technology and the heightened interconnectedness of people and processes. Nationally based civil society organizations formed around particular occupations or industries or interests have consequently found it useful—indeed, necessary—to follow the globalization of these occupations, industries, and interests by forging global links with their counterparts in other countries. In part also, however, the growth of transnational civil society organizations has been a *reaction* against globalization. As national corporations have gone global by outsourcing crucial production functions, organizations concerned about environmental protection, worker rights, human rights, child labor, and other matters have had to go global as well, forging links with counterpart organizations in other countries in order to combat some of the perceived ill effects that globalization might otherwise have. This process has been encouraged, moreover, by the series of high-profile international conferences sponsored by the United Nations and other international bodies over the recent years, such as the Rio Conference on the environment in the early 1990s and the Beijing Conference on Women later in the decade. These events have provided venues for civil society activists from different parts of the world to forge alliances and build networks through which to concert action on a global scale.[27]

The upshot is a significant expansion in the number and activism of transnational civil society organizations. According to the Association of International Organizations' *Yearbook of International Organizations*, some eighteen thousand international nongovernmental organizations and internationally oriented nonprofit organizations were registered as of 2001, an increase of two thousand over the previous decade.[28] This probably understates the extent of globalization within the civil society sector, however, for numerous less formal networks and linkages have also emerged.

Many of the resulting organizations are highly complex, moreover, rivaling in their scope and complexity the multinational corporations with which they increasingly interact. Amnesty International, for example, has more than 1 million members, subscribers, and regular donors in over 140 countries and territories. Care International employs over ten thousand professional staff.

Increasingly, these civil society networks are coming to constitute an independent force on the international scene, challenging governments and for-profit corporations, mobilizing constituencies across national boundaries to lobby for national policy changes, and establishing linkages with international organizations such as the World Bank, the United Nations Development Program, and others. One common tactic is for civil society activists in one country to appeal to colleagues in other countries or at the international organization level to put pressures on their own governments to protect human rights, promote environmental protection, outlaw land mines, or pursue other objectives. The same tactics are used to pressure corporations to refrain from practices in far-off lands that might be frowned upon in their own home countries by threatening to expose these practices in their home markets. This has led many corporations to seek partnerships with civil society organizations to avoid such confrontations and ensure a sufficient "license to operate." This, too, has helped promote global ties among civil society organizations.

*****

Recent international developments have focused new attention on the civil society sector around the world and also helped to stimulate the growth of these organizations both domestically and internationally. The upshot is a greater appreciation of the enormous scale of this set of institutions and the considerable contributions they make to both national and international life. As the process of globalization has progressed, the civil society sector has taken its place as an increasingly important, and increasingly prominent, social, economic, and political force.

The global civil society sector and the broader process of globalization, if not offspring of one another, are at least next of kin, each with its own origins and growth paths, but each also affected by the origins and growth paths of the other. As such, their mutual interactions are important to chart and understand, both to comprehend how we have gotten to where we are and to foresee where we are going. It is my hope that this chapter has provided some useful markers along this road.

Endnotes

This chapter draws heavily on Lester M. Salamon, S. Wojciech Sokolowski, and Regina List, in L. M. Salamon, S. W. Sokolowski, and Associates (eds.) "Global Civil Society: An Overview," *Global Civil Society: Dimensions of the Nonprofit Sector*, Volume 2, Kumarian Press, Bloomfield, CT, 2004.

[1] Lester M. Salamon, "The Rise of the Nonprofit Sector," *Foreign Affairs*, 73:4, 1994, pp. 111–24.

[2] R. Inglehart, *Culture Shift in Advanced Industrial Society*, Princeton University Press, Princeton, NJ, 1990.

[3] Lester M. Salamon and A. Abramson, "The Nonprofit Sector," in J. Palmer and I. Sawhill (eds.) *The Reagan Experiment: An Examination of Economic and Social Policies under the Reagan Administration*, Urban Institute Press, Washington, DC, 1982, pp. 219–43; J. Howell and J. Pearce, *Civil Society and Development: A Critical Exploration*, Lynne Rienner, Denver, CO, 2001.

[4] J. P. Lewis and N. T. Uphoff, *Strengthening the Poor: What Have We Learned?* Transaction Books, New Brunswick, NJ, 1988.

[5] A. Fowler, "Civil Society Research Funding from a Global Perspective: A Case for Redressing Bias, Asymmetry, and Bifurcation," *Voluntas*, 13:14, 2002.

[6] J. Coleman, *Foundations of Social Theory*, Harvard University Press, Cambridge, MA, 1990.

[7] R. D. Putnam, *Bowling Alone: The Collapse and Survival of American Community*, Simon and Schuster, NY, 2000.

[8] M. Edwards and D. Hulme (eds.), *Beyond the Magic Bullet: NGO Performance and Accountability in the Post-Cold War World*, Macmillan, London, 1996.

[9] E. James, "The Non-profit Sector in Comparative Perspective," in W.W. Powell (ed.) *The Non-profit Sector: A Research Handbook*, Yale University Press, New Haven, CT, 1987.

[10] Barnett Baron, "An Overview of Organized Private Philanthropy in East and Southeast Asia," Paper prepared for delivery at the John D. Rockefeller 150th Anniversary Conference, Pocantico Hills, NY, 1989; Michael Bratton, "Beyond the State: Civil Society and Associational Life in Africa," *World Politics*, 41, no. 4 (April), 1989, pp. 407–30.

[11] Lester M. Salamon, *Partners in Public Service: Government-Nonprofit Relations in the Modern Welfare State*, Johns Hopkins University Press, Baltimore, MD, 1995.

[12] J. Boli and G. M. Thomas, "World Culture in the World Polity: A Century of International Non-governmental Organization," *American Sociological Review*, 62 (April), 1997, pp. 171–90.

[13] The System of National Accounts (SNA), the guidance system for international economic statistics, essentially assigns the most important nonprofit institutions to the corporate or government sectors based on their principal source of revenue. See Lester M. Salamon and Helmut K. Anheier, "Nonprofit Institutions in the Household Sector," in *Household Accounting Experience in Concepts and Compilation*, vol. 1, United Nations, NY, 2000, pp. 275–99; Lester M. Salamon, Gabriel Rudney and Helmut K. Anheier, "Nonprofit Institutions in the System of National Accounts: Country Applications of SNA Guidelines," *Voluntas*, vol. 4, no. 4, 1993, pp. 486–501.

[14] For further detail on this project and the findings summarized here, see Lester M. Salamon, S. Wojciech Sokolowski, and Associates, *Global Civil Society: Dimensions of the Nonprofit Sector*, vol. 2, Kumarian Press, Bloomfield, CT, 2004.

[15] For further detail on the alternative definitions of the nonprofit sector and their limitations, see Lester M. Salamon and Helmut K. Anheier, "In Search of the Nonprofit Sector: The Question of Definitions," in Lester M. Salamon and Helmut K. Anheier (eds.) *Defining the Nonprofit Sector: A Cross-national Analysis*, Manchester University Press, Manchester, UK, 1997.

[16] Since data on the large mutual and cooperative institutions is fairly readily available, those interested in the broader social economy definition, which includes these entities, can easily add them to the data reported here to generate a picture of the broader social economy. For a discussion of the social economy concept, see Jacques Defourny and Patrick Develtere, "The Social Economy: The Worldwide Making of a Third Sector," in J. Defourny, P. Develtere, and B. Foneneau, (eds.) *L'economie sociale au Nord et au Sud*, DeBoeck, Brussels, 1999.

[17] Salamon, Sokolowski and Associates, *Global Civil Society.*

[18] R. Kramer, *Voluntary Agencies in the Welfare State*, University of California Press, Berkeley, CA, 1981.

[19] Helmut K. Anheier and Lester M. Salamon, "Nonprofit Institutions and the Household Sector," in United Nations Statistics Division (ed.) *The Household Sector*, United Nations, NY, 1998, pp. 315–41.

[20] Revenue data could not be collected in Egypt and Morocco.

[21] E. Archambault, *The Nonprofit Sector in France*, Manchester University Press, Manchester, UK, 1996.

[22] P. Barbetta (ed.), *The Non-profit Sector in Italy*, Manchester University Press, Manchester, UK, 1997.

[23] Anheier and Salamon, "Nonprofit Institutions and the Household Sector."

[24] T. Lundstrom and F. Wijkstrom, *The Nonprofit Sector in Sweden*, Johns Hopkins Nonprofit Series, no. 11, Manchester University Press, Manchester, UK, 1997.

[25] For further detail on these patterns, see Salamon, Sokolowski, and Associates, *Global Civil Society.*

[26] Anheier and Salamon, "Nonprofit Institutions and the Household Sector."

[27] M. Keck and K. Sikkink, *Activists Beyond Borders: Advocacy Networks in International Politics*, Cornell University Press, Ithaca, NY, 1998; A. Florini, *The Third Force: The Rise of Transnational Civil Society*, Carnegie Endowment for International Peace and Japan Center for International Exchange, Washington, DC and Tokyo, 2000; J. Clark, *Worlds Apart: Civil Society and the Battle for Ethical Globalization*, Kumarian Press, Bloomfield, CT, 2003; D. Korten, *Getting to the Twenty-first Century: Voluntary Action and the Global Agenda*, Kumarian Press, Hartford, CT, 1990; M. Lindenberg and C. Bryant, *Going Global: Transforming Relief and Development NGOs*, Kumerian Press, Bloomfield, CT, 2001; L. Kriesberg, "Social Movements and Global Transformation," in J. Smith, C. Chatfield and R. Pagnucco (eds.) *Transnational Social Movements and Global Politics: Solidarity Beyond the State*, Syracuse University Press, Syracuse, NY, 1997.

[28] Union of International Organizations, *Yearbook of International Organizations: Guide to Civil Society Networks*, Union of International Organizations, Brussels, 2001; Boli, and Thomas, "World Culture in the World Polity."

Chapter 8

GLOBALIZATION AND THE THIRD SECTOR: THE CANADIAN EXPERIENCE

Kathy Brock with David Brook and Janice Elliott

Globalization has penetrated the very institutions and patterns of interaction that give structure and meaning to our daily lives. While it is easy to analyze the link between global events and processes and international nongovernmental organizations (INGOs), it is not as easy to discern the impact of globalization on domestic NGOs or of domestic institutions on global trends. Are global forces changing the way that organizations practice philanthropy? Is there a homogenizing effect on philanthropic organizations worldwide or are important differences emerging between philanthropic organizations in different countries? How have the forces of globalization affected the relationship between civil society and the state? To what degree are global institutions and systems altering local values, institutions, goods, and services? These questions take on a particular urgency as the effects of globalization are felt more strongly than at any other time in world history. The impact of global forces on civil society is only beginning to be understood as citizens, economies, nations, and societies become increasingly interconnected. Answers to the questions posed above deepen the understanding of globalization and its impact on humankind on the local, national, and international levels. While much has been written on the contours of globalization on the international level, less is known about its specific impact on civil society, philanthropic organizations, and their relationship with the state in particular nations or about the effects of domestic institutions of particular nations on the process of globalization. This chapter contributes to those answers by examining the effects of globalization on the civil society sector in Canada.

*****

Civil society and philanthropic organizations are not passive victims of global economic powers or trends. On the contrary, this chapter argues that charitable, nonprofit, and philanthropic organizations are exerting pressure and influence on world events in ways that are often unrecognized, underappreciated, or overshadowed by the role of corporate capitalism on the world stage. To reach this conclusion, this chapter begins with an exploration of the concept of globalization, isolating key components that relate to the role of civil society and philanthropic institutions most directly. Using data from a qualitative survey of leading figures in the nonprofit sector in Canada, this paper probes the effects of globalization on the operation of civil society organizations and local values and social systems, the practice of philanthropy both domestically and internationally, and the relationship between those organizations and the Canadian state.[1] While globalization offers the benefits of homogenization, it also promotes local distinctiveness in critical areas to social, economic, and political life. Globalization is an evolving phenomenon with a decidedly different character in the current era.[2] While some political scientists trace globalization back to the Greeks and successive imperial regimes, as Wolf Schäfer notes in this volume,[3] other observers, especially economists, locate its zenith between the 1880s and 1920s when the industrial world arose.[4] According to Thomas Friedman's popularization of the phenomenon, "If you compared the volumes of trade and capital flow across borders, relative to GNPs, and the flow of labor across borders, relative to populations, the period of globalization preceding World War I was quite similar to the one we are living through today."[5] However, even Friedman distinguishes the current era of globalization by the degree and intensity of the forces knitting the world together, by the number of countries and people affected by the phenomenon, by falling costs of technology rather than transportation, and by the centrality of the United States in forging an open international trading system.[6] In his scholarly tract, Peter Dickens emphasizes the distinctiveness of the current era of globalization, noting that the previous period of international economic integration was shallow and effected through trade and the movement of capital across borders by firms rather than by the deeper functional integration of economic activities across borders by transnational firms in the current period.[7] Commentators also distinguish this era of globalization from the Cold War era since the latter was predominantly characterized by division between superpowers, and internationalization.[8]

What are the leading characteristics of the current process of globalization? Definitions of globalization are hotly contested[9] but most agree that globalization is about interconnectedness, interdependence, and a reduction of the perception of spatial realities. As Bruce Mazlish and Raymond Grew pointed out during the opening session of the conference, globalization is a process that is not unidirectional and one that links the local and the global. Friedman captures one dimension of this process when he argues that "it is the inexorable integration of markets, nation-states and technologies to a degree never witnessed before—in a way that is enabling individuals, corporations and nation-states to reach around the world farther, faster, deeper and cheaper than ever before, and in a way that is enabling the world to reach into individuals, corporations and nation-states farther, faster, deeper and cheaper than ever before."[10] However, as Grew observed, globalization cannot just be reduced to neoliberal elements. Instead, it must be understood as extending to the common experiences of social groups, the diffusion of technology and knowledge, the connections people—as well as businesses and nations—form, and to the new and varied cultural encounters. The process of globalization is not reducible to a neoliberal, corporate experience, but must be understood in its fullest sense as an economic, political, social, cultural, and psychological phenomenon.

This broader definition of globalization is embraced and elaborated by David Held. After reviewing leading authors on globalization, he emphasizes the "growing magnitude or intensity of global flows such that states and societies become increasingly enmeshed in worldwide systems and networks of interaction."[11] He mentions the material component explicitly, capturing the supporting structures: "flows of trade, capital and people across the globe . . . facilitated by different kinds of infrastructure—physical (such as transport or banking systems), normative (such as trade rules) and symbolic (such as English as a lingua franca)—which establish the preconditions for regularized and relatively enduring forms of global interconnectedness."[12] But like Grew, Held suggests that globalization is more than this: it affects social time and geographic space by embedding the local in the regional and interregional and global. Local occurrences can have global effects and vice versa, much more quickly and to a greater degree than ever before. Distance "shrinks," borders "disappear," and connections multiply and strengthen, signifying a cognitive shift.[13]

The new level of interconnectedness doesn't necessarily imply harmony. While the benefits of globalization might include advanced communications, more choice in both economic and social goods, and the saving of human life through the extension of medical practices and new technologies, the effects of globalization might be negative, uneven, or neutralized within countries. Held observes that interconnectedness can cause local resentments, reactionary politics, and xenophobia, and for the significant segment of the world population who remain outside these new connections and benefits, there is a deepening sense of division and a need to contest the process.[14] The negative effects of globalization can be varied and range from the impoverishment and depopulation of local communities as corporations or factories relocate to optimize competitiveness and unemployment rises, to the homogenizing and demoralizing effects of the global export/import of popular culture and products on vibrant subnational cultures, to the destabilization of political regimes hostile to dominant world powers, to the rise and export of terrorism and fear between countries.[15] The extension of the benefits of the global economy and democratic institutions to previously authoritarian or liberal states may be stymied by the reproduction of the harmful behaviors of repressive regimes unless the democratic ideals of tolerance and compromise are embraced within those states. National and subnational experiences of the positive and negative effects of the process of globalization will be tempered by local conditions and norms.

Much of the literature considers globalization in terms of nation-states and corporations, and only lately civil society. Usually these civil society analyses focus on the antiglobalization movements, including individuals protesting in Seattle, Quebec City, and Davos against global governance and multilateral trade and investment talks, or on the collective action of individuals and groups in forcing international agreements (and compliance) on trade concessions, labor standards, the environment, land mines, human rights, or even, potentially, a world parliament to replace the UN.[16] While these aspects of globalization are significant, less has been written about the institutional branch of civil society in the process of globalization. The changing role of international nongovernmental organizations with regard to the democratization and the global economy was highlighted during discussions at the conference. However, domestic civil society organizations and philanthropic foundations are both profoundly affected by global trends in their operations within their nations, and are exerting an influence on the course of world events. Four areas of activity capture the embedding of domestic civil society organizations and philanthropic foundations in the global process.

First, new demands and pressures are compelling civil society organizations to assume new roles and relationships with the public. In addition to their traditional roles as service providers and benevolent agencies, civil society organizations are required to act as mediating and bridging institutions to constrain the negative effects of globalization. This can be achieved either by facilitating or by tempering the process of globalization.

An adherent of the former approach, Thomas Courchene suggests that the shift of power away from the nation-state reorders relations with citizens,[17] requires civil society to move beyond engaging citizens in the community, and forces political life to play "a critical mediating role in terms of the societal implications arising from the forces of GIR [globalization and the knowledge/information revolution]. Not to put too fine a point on this, they are actively engaged in a process of 'embedding GIR' domestically. That is, they are part and parcel of the process to ensure that international economic integration does not lead to domestic social disintegration."[18] It is important that these organizations maintain their independence from government if they are to successfully meet citizen needs in an increasingly resource competitive environment. Equally important is their integration into the production and employment sector if they are to develop and sustain the human capital necessary for countries like Canada to function effectively in the new global order.[19]

To perform a mediating role, civil society organizations may wish to remain independent from the realms of production and employment. For example, Anthony Giddens argues for an independent civil society that enlivens public debate and mediates the effects of a globalized economy. Unlike Courchene, Giddens emphasizes the role of organizations in generating "creative and energetic strategies to cope with social problems" rather than in the production of human capital to improve the national competitive edge.[20] Civil society organizations would play a critical role in constraining the market and in ensuring social justice as new inequalities emerge.[21] In his view, a vibrant civil society would act as a counterbalance to the economic sector by forcing issues onto the public agenda and ensuring a robust public debate. In a similar vein, from a very different ideological perspective, Jamie Swift also concludes that civil society organizations are critical to integrating society. He focuses on the marginalized and argues that civil society can help make political institutions more democratic and the market serve social justice if actors recognize the divisions in society and the economy and act to change them, a slow process at best.[22]

Civil society organizations may face difficulties in sustaining their current activities, let alone expanding their role as integrative and mediating institutions for society. Both Courchene and Giddens stress that the sector must have the requisite resources and support from the state to fulfill this role. Increased responsibilities, constrained resources, and competition with the private sector for public contracts and services might jeopardize the ability of civil society organizations to serve the public or play an integrative role.[23] Moreover, Josephine Rekart argues that global pressure towards neoliberal polices such as commercialization in social welfare and reduction in state functions will ultimately erode the values of the sector, making it function more like the state and business.[24] In contrast, Robert Reich argues that civil society organizations have moved more toward this model as civic participation has been commodified.[25] He suggests that the critiques offered by Robert Putnam and others that citizen participation is declining and community is crumbling fail to realize that the basis of participation has changed.[26] Citizens shop for the best deals that suit their needs. Governments and civil society organizations must position themselves to attract the labor and capital necessary to sustain their operations. This entails the professionalization of staff, adopting a more policy-focused orientation, and being able to speak the language of business.[27] One effect of globalization might be to "rationalize" the sector by forcing out smaller, less competitive, or direct-action organizations at the very time that a diversity of organizations is required to enable the sector to play an integrative function in society and mediate the negative effects of globalization.

Second, just as globalization has meant a process of interconnectedness for business and nations, civil society has become more connected across borders. In his conference presentation, Salamon traced the rise of a global civil society and increasing awareness of local issues as global. In their multicountry project, Tadashi Yamamoto and Kim Gould Ashizawa note the challenge posed by powerful civil society organizations to governments as they connect across borders as well as within states.[28] Like James Rosenau, they suggest that networks and collaboration among civil society organizations are the most effective means of ensuring a stronger civil society, the embrace of democratic values, and better governance.[29] Rosenau maintains that networks of organizations have undermined civil authority but also disaggregated it to new collectivities operating on more horizontal forms of governance.

One of the chief means of connecting globally has been the establishment of the World Wide Web and the Internet. Through this medium, citizens may connect, organizations may share and borrow ideas and best practices, and causes may mobilize citizens. Certainly, the antiwar demonstrations during the 2003 U.S. war on Iraq illustrated the power of the Internet in mobilizing and coordinating citizen activities. However, as Ronald Shaiko and Robert Putnam point out, the Internet has posed a dilemma for the sector. While the new information technology is useful in attracting new members and informing current members, it has a downside. Members recruited through "the Net" tend to be passive rather than active; self-selecting rather than more broadly focused; and virtual rather than directly engaged. Moreover, undifferentiated access to current members and the public reduces the incentive to join.[30] The Internet also poses serious questions of access and exclusion both within Canada and across the world by sharpening the divide between affluent, English-speaking, geographically accessible citizens and poorer citizens who live in remote areas or do not speak English as a first language or at all.[31] By bringing messages and images to communities that clash with local culture and values, the Internet produces new tensions as well as a homogenization effect.[32] Finally, the flow of information is unprecedented and must be managed.

Third, the embeddedness of civil society in the process of globalization is evident in the changing practices of philanthropy. Helmut Anheier asks whether the amalgamation of private sector companies and the movement of corporate headquarters to financial centers will negatively impact upon philanthropy and the ability of nonprofits to raise funds to do their work.[33] Reich suggests that affluent citizens will make choices that become a sorting mechanism for society: they will live in communities with fewer social services; their children will attend better schools; and they will be less inclined to subsidize the needier elements of society.[34] Like the fictitious Mrs. Kravitz, they will be drawn to establish foundations or help causes that are trendy or socially significant rather than ones designed to assist less-fashionable causes.[35] In Canada, this trend is detectable in the 2000 National Survey of Giving, Volunteering and Participating, in which wealthier and less affluent citizens alike indicated a growing preference to give to causes that affect them directly rather than services aimed at the poor or needy and are more likely to give to health organizations rather than social service organizations.[36] While Peter Frumkin captures the extensive tradition of philanthropic giving by U.S. foundations to international causes, the discussion of his paper indicates that the Canadian tradition of philanthropy has not been as strong or developed. Thus, these recent developments in philanthropic practices may be more worrisome in Canada, where the monies are more coveted than in the United States, which has more corporations, a higher per capita affluent population of givers, and an established tradition of giving to diverse causes.

Finally, globalization is influencing the way that civil society and the state relate to one another. According to the Giddens and Courchene models, the state should provide financial support to assist the sector in modernizing and participating in the policy process but should remain independent from the sector. Others question whether the sector should adopt an adversarial, collaborative, or partnering approach to the state, with most concluding that the approach is dependent on the nature of the organization and issues. Commentators, such as Amory Starr, argue that that corporations and political and bureaucratic elites have conspired in the process of globalization, with corporations achieving more power and influence. To offset the effects of global corporate hegemony and genocide, the social justice groups should join forces with the state.[37] In a more moderate vein, David Cameron and Janet Gross Stein argue that citizens and civic groups desiring more responsive policies will find their influence is best exercised not on corporations or through international nongovernmental organizations but on their own governments, which can then make representations singly or jointly on the global stage. They argue that international organizations are unlikely to achieve the openness and accountability citizens demand despite the emphasis on new forms of governance. The state provides more points of access, and is more accountable to its citizens.[38] Like David Cameron and Janice Gross Stein, David Held and Anthony McGrew also "bring the state back in" at this time of global erosion of state functions, arguing that the state is important in achieving cosmopolitan social democracy. However, they are more optimistic than Cameron and Gross Stein about the new institutions of global governance and maintain that political power is being reconfigured in an increasingly multilayered system that is more open to civil society influence.[39]

In assessing the power of the state, Rekart, Yamamoto, and Ashizawa caution that constrained state resources and continuing tensions between the state and civic groups limit the ability and willingness of the state to take action on behalf of civic group demands. In their multicountry study, Yamamoto and Ashizawa warn that powerful civil society organization may rival or challenge the state producing resistance and weakening the state in the process.[40] As Balmurli Natrajan points out in this volume, cultural norms and practices may influence the ability of the state to maneuver and to respond to civil society demands. The importance of the state to civic groups may be dependent on specific contexts.

*****

These four areas outlining the impact of globalization on civil society and philanthropy raise important questions regarding how citizens will be governed and served in the future. However, is such an assessment accurate? How do practitioners and leaders in civil society experience globalization? Are they cognizant of its effects on a daily operational level? To these questions, we now turn. Interviews and discussions with leading figures from civil society in Canada illuminate the extent to which the global has penetrated and transformed the local, which in turn influences the global. Civil society organizations are not passive recipients of global influence but active players in the process.

Data were gathered from interviews and roundtables conducted with forty leaders from civil society organizations and a few selected representatives from business and government with extensive experience with civil society organizations. The sample was small to allow for extended answers to a qualitative survey consisting of five open-ended questions drawn from a literature review of globalization and civil society.[41] The roundtables allowed brainstorming on previous answers and provided feedback on preliminary findings. The leaders were selected according to three sets of criteria: familiarity with the concept or experience with globalization issues; type of organization; and place or space. While the first criterion biased the results toward a pool more knowledgeable about globalization than is generally the case in the sector, it was justified given the small sample and the type of information sought by the interviewers. The organizations were diverse, covering the following characteristics: volunteer-based and nonprofit, umbrella, religious, gender, cultural, racial, disabled, sports and recreational, foundations, philanthropic, food banks, large, small, service, and advocacy. Place and space referred to efforts to ensure that the pool of respondents covered international, national, provincial, local, and regional organizations in Canada. Given the different configuration of the social economy, Quebec was overrepresented, with five of the respondents representing organizations.

Leaders in the civil society sector in Canada differed over the precise meaning of globalization but moved quickly to a broader definition of globalization that included the social and human dimensions of the process as well as the economic basis.[42] Individually and then collectively at the roundtables, leaders dismissed a neoliberal economic version of globalization as primarily affecting business and then the state. While they acknowledged that this was the popular understanding of globalization, they thought reducing the process to a global economic phenomenon missed its essence. They were more comfortable with the approach outlined above in the works of Joseph Stiglitz, Charles Derber, and Raymond Grew. For these scholars, the process of globalization was intimately intertwined with the areas where civil society organizations are active: universal human rights, social justice, equality, poverty alleviation, and the environment, among other things. As one person described it, "Globalization is about people—what it means in terms of benefits and costs to citizens." A few leaders commented that a definition of globalization should capture the colonial dimension inherent in the assertion of Western, largely American, values over other cultures and the disorienting impact this can have on communities and the social fabric as well as the uneven effect of the benefits and costs of technology and the market mentality.

The leaders tended to think that a more expansive definition of globalization was important. If the narrower market definition of globalization as the "quicker and easier movement of goods, services, people technology and money over borders around the world" is accepted, then it privileges business and Western economic principles while appearing to be value neutral or amoral. A broader definition included the activity of international and domestic civil society organizations, which leaders believed were important in bringing a sense of morality and direction to a process that had been driven by corporations. Some leaders though that the narrower definition of globalization implied an inevitability to the process that missed the fact that people had alternatives to accepting a new global governance, international trade regulations, and other multinational agreements that eroded local values. They argued that any understanding of globalization had to capture the tension between corporate goals and citizen values expressed in the street protests and direct action groups. Others suggested that the broader definition also captured the positive role that civil society organizations play in ensuring that the benefits of the economic order are shared widely and ill effects mitigated among citizens. The view of civil society organizations as mediating and bridging institutions was embedded in this definition of globalization.

*****

Leaders believe that globalization is exerting new pressures on the role of civil society organizations. A dominant theme in the interviews and roundtables was that the exchange of ideas across the globe and the flow of information through new technologies was empowering to leaders and organizations. However, for every advantage of interconnectedness there was a disadvantage. Both advantages and disadvantages affected the role of organizations as well as local values.

Primarily in the leaders' minds was the sharing of information. A key advantage to the Internet and computerization of civil society organizations was that information was readily available, thus obviating the need for original research in many cases. One leader identified the Internet as an important source of critical perspectives and counterintelligence on prevailing dogma that was essential for organizations to form independent and informed positions on issues. For others, the information provided by other organizations served a more practical function. One leader explained: "We are vigilant about information. We try to reinforce the education part of our mandate, and we hold training sessions with all of our member groups in order to counter private sector governance models which are spreading within the sector." Some leaders noted that the information available on the Web could save time and improve the quality of decisions in core functions. For example, when an executive director was searching for a name or a background on a potential employee or a method of addressing a new issue, "the Internet could provide the information within minutes if not seconds." The Internet may be used to establish an objective value of labor on the international market that assists in human resources functions. For example, where there is a dispute between a symphony's board of directors and musicians over pay, an independent standard may be ascertained over the Web. The Web is also useful in recruiting talent internationally by providing a convenient forum for advertising positions and establishing competitive pay scales.

There are costs to "being connected." The number one cost identified by leaders was time. Many organizations lack the person-hours to expend on tracking issues on the Internet. The consensus was that while the Internet provided wonderful learning opportunities, the amount of information on almost any topic required more sifting and sorting than most organizations could afford. The information accessible through the Internet and e-mails was exciting, but as one leader said, "We are overloaded with information and demands for support from causes all over the world. We would need one full-time staff member just to read the e-mails and respond. At one point, we were on so many Listservs that it was impossible to keep track of everything. And we don't have the resources to do so."

Being connected could be both energizing and enervating. One roundtable concurred that the Internet could be very useful in identifying causes and mobilizing support but that it can overtax sympathies, leaving people feeling exhausted from exposure to so many worthy causes. For organizations and executive directors, "It's hard to discriminate between demands as well. Do we help this cause or that one? There are so many." While the World Wide Web allows people to cross racial and national lines to build ties and support or to compare experiences, it can exclude whole groups of people and critical issues. Building positions on issues internationally requires careful attention to what information is available; and if important information is missing, the most carefully devised work will come to naught. Too often, leaders commented, the flow of information allows issues to be identified as needing attention, but often does not provide solutions or means for dealing with them.

The dual edge to advanced communications and information technology was evident with respect to resources, skills, and language. If organizations lack current technology or the necessary skills and knowledge, they may miss opportunities available to more affluent organizations. For example, the Internet readily provides organizations with access to government policies, programs, and funding opportunities, but organizations require the skills and knowledge to know where to look and the capacity to download forms or information. In the process of posting information, governments have downloaded the responsibility for awareness of new opportunities to organizations. If organizations do not speak English, the lingua franca of the Internet, as mentioned above, complications arise. Quebec leaders said language was a barrier to information access but had the positive effect of insulating their provincial organizations from global pressures, particularly cultural ones. Leaders of organizations serving new Canadians said that their members had trouble accessing government information critical to their status in Canada. On the global level, leaders viewed the homogenizing effect of English on the Web as a form of linguistic imperialism. Some leaders thought language had become divisive with English as the language of business and Spanish as the language of human rights. Both excluded the other from important debates and new developments particularly when communication across the divide was critical to foster economic policies that were efficient and just. Leaders thought civil society had an obligation to bridge these differences since business was unlikely to be aware of the divide.

The time and energy costs affected the roles and values of civil society organizations in their communities, whether domestic or international. Some leaders thought that the role of organizations was being shifted from direct service on a local level to information trafficking. Time spent on the computer, whether searching for information or answering e-mail requests from similar organizations in other jurisdictions was time lost for face-to-face contact with people their organization served on a daily basis—the real strength of the sector. International requests received by e-mail could steal precious time and resources from domestic causes. Information could be shared and facts acquired, but, as one respondent suggested, this process of knowledge accumulation erodes time for thinking and solid reflection. The erosion of time for developing innovative approaches to social problems presents a threat to the future development and sustainability of civil society.

The role of organizations has shifted from local concerns to global issues. Organizations felt pressure to build coalitions or reach out to other organizations on pressing issues. Even representatives associated with food banks or community tables, a seemingly local concern, noted that they felt an obligation to join with other organizations in tracking and participating in multilateral trade negotiations, since decisions in areas like agriculture could affect local supplies of food. Reflecting on the emerging connections between organizations across borders, one person observed that the voluntary sector had not been as effective as it should be in building coalitions to deal with difficult social problems. Other leaders thought the sector could be more active in crossing the state-business-citizen and linguistic divides due to globalization.

The easier and more frequent movement of people and ideas around the globe is also affecting local values. Civil society leaders believed that the amount of traveling done by Canadians introduces them to new ideas and experiences, creating a more cosmopolitan outlook. The way of conducting business has changed as well: a businessperson might be located in a small community and yet the business may be worldwide, facilitated through the Web and travel. A new dynamic is created that can inspire local economies. Culture is becoming less heterogeneous as ideas and music flow back and forth and as dominant Western cultures spread their messages, needs, and expertise. These exchanges are not always felicitous or welcome. For example, one leader cited the case of teenagers in eastern Europe who watch reruns of *Dallas* and "then want out of the village. They leave their culture, language, country for a better material world that they have seen in those shows." Another suggested that Fiji is worried about the impact of "schlock TV from Australia and the U.S." Leaders suggested that a generational gap exists on this issue, with the younger generation more readily accepting a "no-border" approach to business and culture than baby boomers. A few leaders feared that maintaining the "Canadian way" of leadership or Canadian values on social issues was becoming more difficult. In particular, they believed that the U.S. leadership styles and values are eroding our differences as the North American economy becomes more regionalized. Others said the sector had a duty to ensure that local culture and communities continued to thrive.

Canadian civil society leaders identified two particularly intriguing developments for the role of civil society in this "smaller, faster world." First, the information transfer was not one way—from industrialized Western nations to less-affluent nations, or from north to south. Many developing nations had implemented policies and practices that could address challenges faced by social groups in Canada and other Western industrialized nations. Civil society should facilitate the responsible import and implementation of best practices from other nations. Second, and conversely, leaders identified a responsibility of Canadian organizations to the rest of the world. The consensus style of leadership, respect for difference common in the civil society sector, and the practice of participatory action research in the Canada sector qualified it as a model for the sector in less-affluent or developing nations in which democratic traditions and liberal individualism were less prevalent. One leader summarized this duty:

> Canadian nonprofits are world leaders and don't know it. What are Canadians really good at? It is not being peacekeepers. The world doesn't see us that way. Models of civil society in Canada are size appropriate and possible to replicate elsewhere. For example, Canadian community foundations development plans are being used around the world. This is in contrast with the U.S. There the models are too big, too complex to be replicated. The Canadian Centre for Philanthropy program, Imagine [a program aimed at securing partnerships between business and civil society organizations], can be replicated in other countries. These models are successful and work well elsewhere. Canadians are world leaders. We need to make our models available to others. This is what the movement of goods, services, people, and technology can mean to the nonprofit sector here.

In short, Canadian civil society organizations serve as an ambassador to the world. During the roundtable discussions, leaders worried that globalization also meant that actions by the United States and Britain toward Iraq and the Middle East and the ambivalent position of the Canadian government were undermining the perception of Canadian organizations as neutral or helpful. These trends, contended the civil society leaders, may compromise the ability of Canadian organizations to perform a vital international function.

*****

Leaders were especially concerned with the changing nature and character of philanthropy in Canada. There were two dimensions to this concern. First, the operation and nature of Canadian philanthropic foundations are changing in response to global pressures. Second, the movement of corporate headquarters is having an impact on giving and the practice of corporate philanthropy, as the literature suggested.

One of the most striking effects of globalization on Canada concerns the growth and nature of philanthropic foundations. By comparison with the United States, this sector has been small and underdeveloped. Canadian foundations have been less active in fostering research, education, and development abroad, with the exception of institutions like the Kahanoff Foundation, whose mission is international. This is changing with a remarkable increase in the number of foundations and umbrella organizations.[43] Foundations have become an integral part of the process of community development in Canada. Private foundations are playing a greater role in research, economic development, and social issues. Several leaders observed that actors in the philanthropic sector are transforming in many ways to resemble their American counterparts, although we still have a long way to go given the continued reliance of organizations and citizens on governments for funding and services. They believed that a key challenge is to engage in "different kinds of resource building, to create a culture of philanthropy, to build an indigenous philanthropic movement."[44]

Canadian philanthropic foundations are now a part of the global structure of giving. Leaders said that foundations are now playing a significant role in "diasporic giving." Immigrants to Canada will trust foundations to receive and distribute their money to communities in their former country, whereas they would not trust governments, corporations, or community officials to perform this function. One foundation head remarked, "We, the foundations, are a series of trusts. We are developing relationships with other foundations in other countries throughout the world so that people can make a donation to their village and know that the money will get there." While one leader wondered if this trend was good or bad for giving in Canada, this leader thought that the "globalization of philanthropy is real, and very positive. We need to think differently about how money is given now. People are motivated differently than in the past. It is no longer checkbook charity. There is an opportunity for foundations because they should be the vehicle for global philanthropy." Canadian foundations are able to help flow dollars from affluent countries to needier countries in a more sustained way than ever before. Domestic foundations have accepted a role in alleviating regional and global inequality that is more similar, albeit not as developed, to U.S. foundations.

Globalization has restructured domestic economies like the Canadian one with tremendous implications for the practice of corporate philanthropy. Although the effects vary from region to region,[45] leaders allowed some generalizations. First, the movement of corporate headquarters to larger financial centers and corporate amalgamations shrink the donor pool, causing more competition among community and private foundations as well as civil society organizations for fewer corporate dollars. Second, the loss of main corporate offices in Canada has meant that there is "much less independence and autonomy on the part of corporate Canada to act independently on philanthropy decisions." Third, corporate amalgamations and mergers have consolidated headquarters in major centers, centralizing corporate giving policies and limiting the discretion of local managers to allocate dollars to community causes. Fourth, companies owned and headquartered outside Canada often misunderstand the context for giving in Canada. One leader gave the example of U.S. corporate lawyers not knowing that in Canada donor liability is limited to the amount given, whereas in the United States liability is unlimited. Fifth, scandals like Enron hit closer to home in this era of globalization. While "trust is the most important currency of the sector," scandals like Enron spill over onto the sector. One person even suggested, "Not-for-profit boards are perceived as the worst kinds of boards," thus affecting whether affluent individuals and corporations will give to organizations.

Sixth, the loss of Canadian ownership of corporations and movement of corporate headquarters out of the country has affected the effectiveness of corporate philanthropy. As one respondent explained:

> One of the consequences of globalization is that corporate decision makers look at the country level rather than at the community level. This can be blinding to those with the ability to make a difference; that is, to governments and donors. They make decisions without understanding the neighborhood, the fabric of the community. They look at issues with lightning speed. For example, they see the world from the corporate office in New York City. They see that there are poor and dying in a country but also the rich and so balance it out. Then they make their decision on this level. For example, last year a U.S. foundation spent $25 million on the environment . . . But they didn't do it well. How could they know what will make a difference to the local community priorities or the local First Nations' priorities? The decision was emotional. They had flown over and seen the effects of clear-cutting and were reacting to that. They don't get to what people want.

Another leader summed it up: "The way money is given out does not always foster local development and independence." Leaders suggested that civil society organizations could provide the bridge between corporate decision makers who wish to effect positive change in a community and the local residents.

Many organizations have begun to serve in this capacity as mediating and bridging institutions. One leader observed that networks and partnerships could be very effective in taking on this onerous task of educating corporate decision makers. She said:

> Policy being developed at the global level can have negative effects for local communities just as it can have very positive impacts as well. Many donors and recipients are working together in a collaborative process to develop policies and programs that are more suitable for the local communities. For example, the Education for All (EFA) initiative by UNESCO involves the donor and recipient countries working

together to provide education in communities that suit their needs. They have developed mechanisms for involving civil society organizations.

This regional model of cooperation can also be applied domestically to achieve the ends identified by the previous speaker.

Seventh, the flow of dollars to communities has changed as well. As governments engage in the process of attracting capital businesses identified by Reich, the nature of partnerships has changed. One leader explained: "This model is now government giving to the private sector giving to the community. It is no longer just a deal between governments and for-profits. Civil society is more involved. Civil society is needed to establish trust within communities." Another commentator observing the same trend suggested that this new flow of money has affected priorities and values. Government money is filtered through corporate systems of values and priorities are often determined at a multinational level, rather than through domestic public sector values and priorities. As a result, there is pressure on communities and civil society organizations to adapt to the new values and priorities. This causes tension within organizations trying to remain faithful to members, their mission, and local cultures and values.

Leaders identified two positive effects of globalization on philanthropy. First, the need to approach distant corporate actors without a personal attachment to a community has meant that civil society organizations have adopted more rigorous standards of accountability, both to present a solid image to a corporation when seeking funds and to justify the expenditure of any funds received. Second, as the links with communities are weakened, corporations are compelled to justify their operations. Corporations are now "building trustmarks rather than trademarks" and adopting social audits or "the triple bottom line." According to one commentator, "There is a link with globalization here. Corporations are seen as bad. Shell has a social audit because of its South African reputation. Major companies are moving into social audits. CCP/Imagine is helping this. The Conference Board is developing benchmarking. More companies are moving this way." Corporate social responsibility has become an important means of putting a kinder, gentler face on capitalism. Corporations are realizing that one consequence of the pressure they applied to governments to scale back and reduce regulations has been that they must now accept some responsibility for the gaps left where government services used to be. As one person said, there is a new "form of noblesse oblige." Civil society organizations have among the highest levels of trust with the public and can serve as a conscience to business and as a partner in arrangements that improve the image of business while securing resources for causes. Thus, one positive consequence of globalization (corporate social responsibility and social audits) is to bring dollars back into communities to offset the negative effects of globalization—the consolidation of the corporate sector, the loss of headquarters, and the loss of dollars to communities.

*****

How has globalization affected the relationship between the state and the sector? While a minority of respondents said there had been no change in their relationship or that the real change was in the relationship of governments to citizens, most leaders felt that the pressures of globalization were altering their relationship with government in important ways. Perhaps most significantly, globalization is changing how governments behave and how organizations relate to them.

> To be effective in applying for support from these governments, organizations need to know what is happening elsewhere, the pressures on government, and where they fit in that picture. They need social data to go to government to be persuasive, but there is no money for organizations to engage in research and data collection. We need to develop this capacity to be effective with government. Until we have the social data, the relationship with government won't improve. We don't know what to ask for and how to build the case. For example, when there are people with illnesses, how do we get the cost analysis? What is necessary is much more obvious in countries where people are starving.

Leaders felt frustrated by the new requirements in an era of scarce resources. Sector leaders do question the relevance of the federal government and nation-state. Increasingly, the choice for leaders is whether to engage at the national level or to pursue issues through the corporate sector or transnational bodies and movements. One leader commented that despite its recent massive undertaking to redefine its relationship with the voluntary sector, the federal government is perceived as largely irrelevant to the sector. While much of the basis of that argument lies in the constitutional allocation of authority for social institutions to the provinces, a portion may be traced to the public alienation from government as part of the effects of the transfer of powers away from the state in a globalized era identified by the globalization scholars.

Sector leaders share the concerns of some of the scholars mentioned above that governments are shifting from a focus on developing the welfare state and caring to neoliberal values and competitiveness. To obtain a competitive advantage, governments are investing in the advantaged classes rather than the needier elements of society. The gap between those benefiting from globalization and those bearing the costs is widening. Two examples given by leaders suffice to illustrate this. Governments offer tax cuts to the affluent and to corporations to attract new business and investment rather than increasing funding for social programs that assist people adversely affected by economic restructuring. Governments will offer high-end skills development to create a more competitive workforce rather than remedial-skills training or literacy programs for the more disadvantaged and most vulnerable workers. Consequently, organizations either follow the government lead and forsake the most vulnerable or attempt to assist these elements of society with increasingly constrained resources. Leaders thought the sector should attempt to influence or moderate government policies here. The shifting focus of governments has affected the ability of the sector to perform its role as service provider and social integrator. One leader cautioned:

> The charitable sector used to do the extras. These organizations did service delivery as well as innovative programs for communities. Now, the need for service delivery is so great that they must focus there. They don't have the time and opportunity for innovation as a result. While they are playing a larger role than before, it is not necessarily the one they want. There is a critical role that the nonprofit sector plays and we don't want the charitable sector just to replace government as it withdraws from areas. It must retain its unique role. We need a

balanced civil society that we have defined in Canada. Canada has always had a nice mix of government, civil society, and the corporate sector. Each has its own role. This is why the quality of life issues are surfacing now. We have to figure out how to attract investment in healthy communities. This involves protection of the social, economic, and other bases of a strong community life.

These leaders confirm the need to maintain a distinction between the roles of government and the sector and to ensure that the sector has the resources to buffer the negative effects of globalization, as well as to remain a social innovator.

The experiences of leaders also indicate that tensions between the voluntary sector and governments are rising even as they attempt to work together more closely. A signal of this tension is the linguistic shift away from "advocacy" organizations to "public policy" organizations. One person wryly observed that governments are nervous when you begin to speak about advocacy: "With advocacy comes the fear of social activism. But you can't build social capital if you are afraid of people speaking out. How interested is government in democracy?" A vital role of civil society is to act as a conscience and critic of government, and yet governments seem increasingly nervous about that role in an era of mass media and instant communication. Many organizations that collaborate with governments will only speak privately or suppress public criticism of government policy in order to maintain a good relationship. In this way, they begin to mirror the behavior of corporations that they criticize. All the while, citizens, particularly the young, become impatient with this cozy discourse and take to the streets, distancing themselves from both government and sector organizations. Disillusionment with both sectors grows. Globalization can have the ultimate effect of impoverishing democratic discourse.

Leaders also lamented the lack of perception within governments of the changing role of civil society in the era of globalization. Many organizations perceive a need to create coalitions, learning networks, and international alliances to combat problems that transcend boundaries. Most governments have been slow to recognize this shift and secure the new resources required to sustain this work. Governments are only beginning to learn to collaborate among themselves to serve as a better partner to the sector in addressing multijurisdictional issues. Canadian leaders were adamant that government failure to protect noneconomic interests meant that civic organizations should play a larger role in trade negotiations to forge the link between trade and human rights policy. Although the civil society representatives commended the Canadian government for including sector leaders at the table in international trade negotiations, they observed that there was still a lot to do. In contrast to Maude Barlow who believes that civil society organizations have limited effects in trade negotiations, sector leaders thought their concerns had influenced negotiations.[46] In general, leaders commented that governments fail to realize the extent to which they have abdicated their exclusive role as rule maker. The sector has assumed this function, making relations between governments more complex and, at times, strained.

Finally, sector leaders confirmed that the growing importance of local governments and city regions in this era of globalization was having a considerable impact on the role of civil society in policy development. Sector organizations and local governments are increasingly acting as partners in addressing social problems with mixed results. In the words of one leader, "City-based organizations with advocacy as part of their mandate have more opportunity to participate in the [policy] debate now. They contribute something unique. Still, it hasn't strengthened the sense of community in general. If you look at the winners and losers from the global economy, you can see that communities are incredibly stressed as a consequence of globalization." The sector is no longer just responding to government or to society needs; it has assumed the responsibility of helping to define and shape the governing structures and community needs. In significant ways, globalization has empowered civil society organizations.

*****

The relationship between civil society and globalization is a complex one. Understandings of globalization are as varied among civil society leaders as the assessments of the impact of the changes sweeping the globe. Many see the forces of globalization and the information revolution as setting limits on organizations and increasing their burdens. Organizations struggle to meet social needs of communities that are adversely affected by the movement of capital, corporate relocations, and the new competitiveness of corporations and governments. They must cope with information overload and demands from abroad that borrow on the scarce resources and time of organizations and their leaders. Many leaders viewed their organizations as disproportionately bearing the costs of globalization, while others saw the process of globalization as empowering. Globalization brought new opportunities with increased flow of information, the ability to forge ties across borders to combat social ills and injustices, and the sharing of knowledge and resources. They also identified their service as social mediators and integrators as important and worthy of continued development. Leaders also identified new roles for the sector. As governments downloaded services (contracting out) or retrenched, civil society was emerging as a rule maker in key areas of policy. No longer could government dictate rules. In addition, the sector is assuming a part on the world stage. Canadian organizations are exporting ideas and models of operation to other countries. Canadian foundations are playing an increasingly important role in the redistribution of wealth and the flow of money across borders.

The effect of globalization on civil society is somewhat paradoxical. At the same time that organizations are being integrated into the world community, civil society is beginning to recognize itself as an independent and coherent entity within Canadian political, social, and economic life. As organizations reach out across borders to similar organizations and activities, they are also beginning to forge links within Canada across subsectors. Mobilization on the global stage has provided an impetus to local activity. On a more somber note, as one leader pointedly argued, the role of the sector is being elevated in response to global trends largely as the result of the foresight of sector leaders, but conjectured whether this activity is sustainable. The growth of civil society and philanthropic foundations, and the need for resources to meet the challenges posed by globalization requires imagination, a new understanding within government, and the cooperation of all sectors.

Endnotes

[1] The authors wish to acknowledge the generous support of the Community Engagement Division, Social Development Directorate, Human Resources Development Canada for this project and to thank voluntary sector leaders for their time and interest.

[2] This statement is contentious. Some writers maintain that it is new, since previous periods of economic expansion lacked the technological sophistication, speed, and depth of penetration of the current phase, inter alia. See, for example, K. Ohmae, *The Borderless World: Power and Strategy in the Interlinked Economy*, Harper Business, NY, 1990; Jessica Mathews "Power Shift," *Foreign Affairs* vol. 76 , 1997, pp. 50–66.

[3] See for example, Mohammed A. Bamyeh, *The Ends of Globalization*, University of Minnesota Press, Minneapolis, 2000, pp.12–58. Marc Raboy comments that globalization could be used to describe the process begun by the arrival of Europeans in their lands; see "Communication and Globalization: A Challenge for Public Policy," in David Cameron and Janice Gross Stein (eds.) *Street Protests and Fantasy Parks: Globalisation, Culture and the State*, University of British Columbia Press, Vancouver, 2002, pp. 109–40.

[4] For example, Paul Hirst locates it between 1890 and 1914 in "The Global Economy: Myths and Realities," *International Affairs*, July 73:3, 1997, and in Paul Hirst and Grahame Thompson *Globalization in Question: The International Economy and the Possibilities of Governance*, (2nd edition), Polity Press, Cambridge, UK, 1999, by tracing the roots of manufacturing multinationals and international business and trade.

[5] Thomas L. Friedman *The Lexus and the Olive Tree: Understanding Globalization*, (revised edition), Anchor Books, NY, 2000, p. xvi. Friedman provides a personalized look at the effects of globalization through his travels throughout the world. In an absorbing account of the effects of the integration of capital, technology, and information on rich and poor nations, Friedman captures the need to strike a new balance between local and international forces. He argues for a politics of sustainable globalization that balances economic gains against social safety nets.

[6] Ibid., pp. xvii–xix.

[7] Peter Dicken, *Global Shift: Transforming the World Economy*, (3rd edition), Paul Chapman, London, 1998.

[8] Friedman, *Lexus and the Olive Tree*, p. 9. Compare Hirst and Thompson, *Globalization in Question*, p.196, who concede that the international economy has changed significantly but is not borderless.

[9] For an overview of the various definitions offered by technological enthusiasts, marxisant pessimists, pluralist pragmatists, and skeptic internationalists, see Vic George and Paul Wilding, *Globalization and Human Welfare*, Palgrave, Houndmills, UK, 2002, pp. 1–24.

[10] Friedman, *Lexus and the Olive Tree*, p. 9.

[11] David Held and Anthony McGrew (eds.), *The Global Transformations Reader: An Introduction to the Globalization Debate*, Polity Press, Cambridge, UK, 2000, p.3.

[12] Ibid.

[13] Ibid., pp. 3–4.

[14] Ibid.

[15] During the August 2003 blackout in Ontario and the eastern United States caused by the failure of the electricity power grid, the immediate concern of political spokespersons in both Canada and the United States was to reassure citizens that it was not due to a terrorist act. In the wake of 9/11 [the terrorist attack on the World Trade Center in New York City, September 11, 2001], most Canadians shared the U.S. fear of aggression by internationally operating terrorist organizations. For a discussion of the effects of 9/11 on civil society and public policy, see Ann Capling and Kim Richard

Nossal, "The Third Sector Meets the National Security State: The Anti-Globalization Movement in Canada after 9/11" in Kathy L. Brock (ed.) *Delicate Dances: Public Policy and the Nonprofit Sector*, McGill-Queen's University Press, Toronto, 2003.

[16] See, for example, Charles Derber, *People Before Profit: The New Globalisation in an Age of Terror, Big Money and Economic Crisis*, St. Martin's Press, NY, 2002, esp. pp. 160–9. Derber discusses both the role of NGOs and a world parliament as proposed by Richard Falk and Andrew Strauss. He challenges the ideas that the current trends of globalization are inevitable and beneficial for both rich and poor nations. He examines the inequities generated by the global economy, then calls on activists and civil society not to fight against globalization but rather to press for a more democratic brand of globalization that will result in social justice and economic stability. Like the leaders interviewed in this paper, Derber emphasizes the opportunities in a global order that have not been sufficiently explored. See also Friedman, *Lexus and the Olive Tree*, pp. 327–47, who emphasizes individuals not organizations; Joseph E. Stiglitz *Globalisation and Its Discontents*, W.W. Norton, NY, 2002, pp. 54–5; Ronald J. Deibert, "Civil Society Activism on the World Wide Web: The Case of the Anti-MAI Lobby," in David Cameron and Janice G. Stein (eds.) *Street Protests and Fantasy Parks: Globalisation, Culture and the State*, University of British Columbia Press, Vancouver, 2002, pp. 88–108.

[17] Thomas J. Courchene, *A State of Minds: Toward a Human Capital Future for Canadians*, Institute for Research on Public Policy (IRPP), Montreal, 2000, pp. 6–7, 17, 18–19, 21–2, 25–6, 30–1. Courchene tackles the question of how to ensure Canadian competitiveness in a global economy. In contrast to authors like Barlow and Clarke, Courchene argues that an open federal state can achieve both economic prosperity and social justice. A key, and controversial, component of his argument is that Canadians will have to think of some functions of social institutions as part of the production and employment of human capital and thus as essential components of global competitiveness. To ensure prosperity and quality of life, Canada will have to become a "state of minds."

[18] Ibid., p. 115.

[19] Thomas J. Courchene, "Great Expectations: The Ideal Characteristics of Non-Profits," *Alternative Service Delivery Project Research Bulletin* 3, Canada West Foundation, Calgary, 2000, pp. 116, 118–9; Thomas J. Courchene "Social Dimensions of the New Global Order," in Richard P. Chaykowski (ed.) *Globalization and the Canadian Economy*, School of Policy Studies, Kingston, Ont, 2001, pp. 61–104, esp. pp. 82–3. Courchene outlines a positive rather than reactive role for NGOs on the international trade front as well.

[20] Anthony Giddens, "Introduction," in Anthony Giddens (ed.) *The Global Third Way Debate*, Polity Press, Cambridge, 2001, pp. 7–8; Anthony Giddens, *The Third Way: The Renewal of Social Democracy*, Polity Press, Cambridge, 1998, pp. 81–6, esp. p. 84.

[21] Anthony Giddens, *The Third Way and Its Critics*, Polity Press, Cambridge, 2000, pp. 64–5.

[22] Jamie Swift, *Civil Society in Question*, Between the Lines and South Asia Partnership, Toronto, 1999.

[23] See, for example, Kathy Brock, "The Role of Government in Ensuring Voluntary Sector Accountability," paper presented to the Thirty-first Annual ARNOVA Conference, November 14–16, 2002, Montreal, Quebec, Canada; Josephine Rekart,

Public Funds, Private Provision: The Role of the Voluntary Sector, University of British Columbia Press, Vancouver, 1993, esp. pp.147–54; Chris Pinney, "Building· Civil Society Towards a New Framework for Corporate Social Responsibility and Civil Society—Business Coordination and Partnership," discussion paper of the Canadian Centre for Philanthropy's Imagine Program, CIVICUS Corporate Engagement Project, August 11, 1999 and Lester M. Salamon, *Global Civil Society: Dimensions of the Nonprofit Sector*, Johns Hopkins Comparative Nonprofit Sector Project, Baltimore, MD, 1999. Cf. Pete Hudson, who reaches a similar conclusion for Britain in "The Voluntary Sector, the State and Citizenship in the UK," in Dave Broad and Wayne Antony (eds.) *Citizens or Consumers? Social Policy in a Market Society*, Fernwood, Halifax, 1999, pp. 212–24.

[24] Rekart, *Public Funds, Private Provision*, p. 154.

[25] Robert Reich, *The Future of Success*, Knopf, NY, 2001, pp. 195, 198–202.

[26] Robert D. Putnam, *Bowling Alone: The Collapse and Revival of American Community*, Simon and Schuster, NY, 2000; cf. Susan J. Pharr and Robert D. Putnam, *Disaffected Democracies: What's Troubling the Trilateral Countries?* Princeton University Press, Princeton, NJ, 2000.

[27] Ibid., pp. 208–9; cf. Kathy Brock, "State, Society and the Third Sector: Changing to Meet the New Challenges," *Journal of Canadian Studies* 35:4 (Spring), 2001; Ronald Shaiko, *Voices and Echoes of the Environment: Public Interest Representation in the 1990s*, Columbia University Press, NY, 1991, pp. 88–91.

[28] Tadashi Yamamoto and Kim Gould Ashizawa, "Overview," in Tadashi Yamamoto and Kim Gould Ashizawa (eds.) *Governance and Civil Society in a Global Age*, Japan Centre for International Exchange, Tokyo, 2001, pp. 17–20, 25–9.

[29] Ibid., pp. 28–9; cf. James N. Rosenau, "Governance in a New Global Order," in David Held and Anthony McGrew (eds) *Governing Globalization: Power, Authority, and Global Governance*, Polity Press, Cambridge, UK, 2002, pp. 76–86. In this collection of essays, the authors examine the emerging system of global governance to understand how global affairs are being regulated. The volume combines theoretical approaches to global governance with empirical studies ranging from humanitarian interventions to global finance. As a whole, the book provides insight into the limits of the shift of power from national governments to multinational organizations, with particular authors calling for more democratic global public policies.

[30] Shaiko, *Voices and Echoes*, p. 171; Putnam *Bowling Alone*, pp. 169–80.

[31] See, for example, United Nations Development Programme, "Globalisation with a Human Face," reprinted in David Held and Anthony McGrew (eds.) *The Global Transformations Reader*, Polity Press, Cambridge,UK, 2000, p. 346.

[32] John B. Thompson "The Globalisation of Communication," in David Held and Anthony McGrew (eds.) *The Global Transformations Reader: An Introduction to Globalization*, Polity Press, Cambridge, UK, 2000, pp. 212–13.

[33] Helmut K. Anheier and Regina List (eds.) *Cross-Border Philanthropy: An Exploratory Study of International Giving in the United Kingdom, United States, Germany and Japan*, Center for Civil Society Studies, The Johns Hopkins University Institute for Policy Studies, and Charities Aid Foundation, Baltimore, MD, London, 2000; Helmut K. Anheier and Stefan Toepler (eds.), *Private Funds—Public Purpose: Philanthropic Foundations in International Perspective*, Plenum, NY, 1999.

[34] Reich, *Future of Success*, pp. 198–202.

[35] In *Barney's Version*, Knopf, Toronto, 1997, pp. 162–3, Mordecai Richler satirizes this type of thinking when Duddy Kravitz rushes into Barney's consultation with his doctor: "Duddy explained that his millions notwithstanding, never mind his donations to the Montreal Symphony Orchestra, the art museum, the Montreal General Hospital, McGill, and his whopper of an annual cheque to Centraide, he was still unable to crack Westmount society to his wife's satisfaction." His solution was to find a disease: "There has to be a disease out there not yet spoken for, something for which I could register a charitable foundation, organise a ball at the Ritz . . . and everybody would have to turn out." But it can't be any disease: "Listen from my wife it has to have some class." This distinction between first-tier and second-tier causes for the very wealthy is also captured in Jane Stanton Hitchcock's tough portrayal of New York society in *Social Crimes*, Hyperion, NY, 2003.

[36] Michael Hall, Larry McKeown and Karen Roberts *Caring Canadians, Involved Canadians: Highlights from the 2000 National Survey of Giving, Volunteering and Participating*, Ministry of Industry, Canada, 2001, p. 22. Health organizations receive 41 percent of donations while social service organizations receive 20 percent. The increase in tendency to give to causes directly affecting donors is slight but significant and will require attention in future surveys.

[37] Amory Starr, *Naming the Enemy: Anti-Corporate Movements Confront Globalization*, Zed Books, London, 2000, pp. 8–9, 225–6. Starr examines the three basic types of social movements that are challenging the new global capitalism and defending local culture, land, and autonomy. She warns the intellectual left to be careful in identifying "the enemy."

[38] See David Cameron and Janice Gross Stein (eds.), *Street Protests and Fantasy Parks: Globalisation, Culture and the State*, University of British Columbia Press, Vancouver, 2002, pp. 156–7. Cameron and Stein's collection of essays focuses on the consequences of globalization for culture and society. The volume contends that while society and economy are becoming more integrated, the state is still vital in ensuring a healthy and vibrant democracy. Citizens and organizations should view it as a natural ally in allaying some of the effects of globalization.

[39] David Held and Anthony McGrew, *Globalization and Anti-Globalization*, Polity Press, Cambridge, UK, 2002, pp. 9–24, 130–6. Held and McGrew discuss global trends as they affect governance, culture, economics, inequalities, and ethics. They conclude their analysis with an argument that globalization is not a singular phenomenon but involves multiple, overlapping political processes. Common ground may be found by political groupings and civil society movements in the idea of a cosmopolitan social democracy that offers a basis for social justice and economic progress.

[40] Yamamoto and Ashizawa, "Overview," pp. 17–20, 25–9.

[41] The interview protocol consisted of the following questions: (1) What does globalization mean to you? (2) Do you feel that globalization presents opportunities for your organization? If yes, what are they? Are there examples where globalization is strengthening your organization or helping it to work better? (3) Do you feel that globalization presents challenges, issues, or problems for your organization? If yes, what are they? Are there examples where globalization is making your work more difficult? (4) Is there a link between the impact of globalization on the corporate community in general, or on corporations that you deal with, and their relationship with your organization or on the voluntary sector more generally? Does the loss of corporate

headquarters to other countries impact on your organization? If so, in what ways? (5) Has globalization changed your relationship with governments (at any level), the private sector, donors, or others? Respondents were provided the interview protocol with the definition of globalization and five sets of questions in advance of the interview.

[42] We provided the following definition of globalization in the interview protocol: "Globalization is a term that is widely used today. It has different meanings and definitions for different people, but a basic definition might be something like: *The term "globalization" means the quicker and easier movement of goods, services, people, technology and money over borders, and throughout the world.* Some examples of the impact of globalization might include the ability for organizations to learn from similar organizations in different regions of the world or, a decreased ability to raise money in a corporate sector that is increasingly dominated by a small number of companies."

[43] Organizations such as Community Foundations Canada or Philanthropic Foundations Canada.

[44] This was identified as particularly important in Quebec, where patterns of private giving are not as ingrained as in other parts of Canada. One person gave the example that while someone in Ontario will instinctively give $100 if asked for a donation, someone is Quebec is more likely to give $50 with the same spirit of generosity and goodwill. As the Quebec leader explained, "When you think back, people used to donate through the church and it wasn't big amounts, just twenty-five cents so the gap today is bigger."

[45] When probed specifically on the impact of corporate mergers and the relocation of corporate headquarters to the United States and other countries, the opinions of civil society leaders across the country diverged. Commentators from Alberta were more optimistic than those in similar organizations from other provinces were. One Alberta respondent informed the survey that the loss of corporate headquarters was partially offset by the number and spirit of entrepreneurs in Calgary. Another said that the loss of headquarters had affected donation strategies with the shift from "corporate donations people," as they were called fourteen years ago, to "community investment offices." Both identified a strong working relationship between the voluntary and corporate sectors. For example, alliances between the two can enhance the attractiveness of corporations to socially conscious recruits. Atlantic Canada leaders noted that corporate headquarters had, in their history, been more likely to be located in central Canada, so this development was less important to them. Quebec leaders observed that they had previously experienced a loss of headquarters to Ontario and that this had provided an impetus to indigenous Quebec businesses. One Quebec leader said that the advantage of large corporations was that they were familiar with mediating institutions like the United Way, so smaller organizations still benefited from corporate largesse whether Canadian or American. A few people noted that there was a difference within provinces as well: urban centers were more likely to be affected by the loss of headquarters than rural areas, since corporate headquarters had tended to be located in larger centers.

[46] Maude Barlow and Tony Clarke, *Global Showdown: How the New Activists are Fighting Global Corporate Rule*, Stoddart, Toronto, 2001, pp. 91–3. Barlow and Clarke examine the actions of citizens' groups around the world that are challenging trade liberalization. They document the claim of these groups that trade liberalization is not creating a world market with fair access but deepening the inequality of the distribution

of wealth between rich and poor nations. This argument reverberates with the experiences of some of the civil society leaders interviewed for this study.

GLOBALIZATION OF CULTURE AND TECHNOLOGY

BEYOND HOMOGENIZATION VERSUS HETEROGENIZATION: DIFFERENCE AND CULTURE IN GLOBALIZATION

Balmurli Natrajan

Much of the extant scholarship on globalization may be said to operate with a "disciplinary vision" of globalization, a *vision* that is derived from a historical *division* of labor within the university, especially that between economics and politics, and between both these disciplines on the one hand and sociology and anthropology on the other. Thus, although globalization (like all other social realities) is transdisciplinary (i.e., neither multi- nor interdisciplinary), debates on globalization tend to be typically divided into the standard format of economic, political, and cultural scholarship, each dominated respectively by economists or business and management studies specialists, political scientists, and anthropologists, communication studies, or cultural studies specialists. This disciplinary division of labor, relying heavily on disciplinary *habitus*,[1] produces a vision that analytically divides the phenomenon of globalization into three prominent axes: economic, political, and cultural. The problem with this vision is that analytical divisions very easily assume the status of the empirical, giving rise to three somewhat delinked or at least discrete phenomena: economic globalization, political globalization, and cultural globalization. Each of these then becomes the object of study for specialists working within such a disciplinary vision of globalization. Not surprisingly, debates on *economic* globalization tend to be primarily about the extent and character of market relations around the globe (built on the tropes of commodities and interests); debates on *political* globalization tend to be primarily about the demise, growing obsolescence, or persistence and roles of the state (built on the tropes of governance and power); and debates on *cultural* globalization tend to be primarily about the growing homogenization or heterogenization of the world (based on the tropes of difference and identity). The result is that we tend to think of globalization as if commodity flows and economic interests were not dependent on issues of power and identity, and that matters of governance were somehow independent of matters of commodity flow and cultural difference.

*****

That such a disciplinary vision (with respect to globalization) pervades our everyday lives was brought home to me in the following interaction that I had with a student. In the fall semester of 2002, a student who had previously taken one of my introductory anthropology courses on globalization approached me with a request from him and some of his friends in the Economics Club to offer a higher-level course on globalization in conjunction with the Department of Economics. I was delighted at the prospect of such a team-taught course and asked him what he had in mind. He said:

> Students would like to have the class organized around debates on globalization. Further, as students of economics they would be concerned that although the major debates and protests around globalization were around issues of culture and people's identities, the course should also clarify facts about markets and democracy.[2]

The comment was sincere and from a good student who obviously felt that it was important to understand the phenomenon of globalization. Yet its neat vision of globalization based on the division of the cultural, economic, and political needs to be examined. In such a vision, cultural globalization concerned *debatable* issues of identity, while economic globalization was somehow placed beyond discourse in the realm of *facts* of the market, as was political globalization in the *fact* of democracy.

Visions of globalization such as my students' seem to be defiantly durable in the face of the much referred to academic goal of approaching the study and teaching of globalization (and society in general) as a multidimensional phenomenon in which economy, politics, and culture intersect and shape each other. Looking to the available texts and readers on globalization only reinforces this vision. For example, even the available readers on globalization (where one could hope to find some overlap between these axes) are neatly organized into separate sections devoted to economic, political, and cultural globalization![3] The following figure presents the topics covered in each of the sections in one of the better and more popular readers on globalization for introductory students.

Figure 9.1
Common Typology of Globalization

DIMENSION	KEY PHENOMENA/TOPICS/DEBATES
Economic globalization	Trade liberalization, commodity chains, labor conditions and wages, global investment, poverty
Political globalization	States vs. markets, democratization, international/global movements, NGOs and civil society, human rights, security and conflicts
Cultural globalization	Media and informational regimes, identity, fundamentalism
Other	Environmentalism

Based on Frank Lechner and John Boli (eds.) *The Globalization Reader*, Blackwell, Malden, MA, 2000.

It is quite clear that some assumptions need to be made in choosing to place media and informational regimes in the cultural section rather than the political or economic section, and such examples of assumptions underlying what may be called the social organization of "categories of reality" can be argued to exist for all the entries in the table. What is interesting to me is that some of the choices actually appear almost *natural* (thus, global investment seems to naturally belong to economic globalization while identity naturally belongs to the cultural) and *discrete* (there indeed seem to be not one but *three* globalizations). Although this particular text was very good in presenting every topic as a debated and debatable one, it is not unreasonable, given its particular organization of topics, to expect students to carry in their heads static (and realist) representations of analytical boundaries between the economic, the political, and the cultural.

The challenge then is to work against disciplinary habits in order to truly approach an understanding of globalization beyond disciplinary visions. Such an alternate vision needs to consider its major weakness in the disciplinary vision above—the lack of an integrated vision of globalization as a *social* phenomenon and consequently either a very weak or ill-formed notion of "society" in the theories of globalization. We are only left with three globalizations, none of which seem to have much to say about what Antonio Gramsci calls "civil society" or what Karl Polanyi calls "active society."[4] Consequently, an alternative vision must be based on a view of globalization as the most recent form of capitalism that is historically structured, dialectical, and uneven.[5] It must be viewed as structured rather than "mere random encounters [since it has established] entrenched and enduring patterns of global interconnectedness,"[6] including the ways in which state, market, and (civil) society impinge upon and shape each other constantly; it must be viewed as dialectical in its transformations in order to grasp the fact that it is filled with contradictions that tend to be "resolved" not in mechanical ways; and finally, it must be viewed as uneven because its effects are distributed unevenly across space and time, and its basis may be arguably said to actually depend upon some kind of unevenness. I approach the task of constructing such an alternative "framework" by considering the issue of the so-called cultural globalization as my entry point to this discourse, rather than as a privileged and foundational basis for understanding globalization. The reason for this is that underlying a "disciplinary" vision of globalization lies the fact that the notion of "culture" itself gets defined and used in ways that promote its separation from things economic or (to a lesser extent) political. I will focus primarily on the ongoing debate of cultural homogenization versus heterogenization in the globalization literature.

To grasp the sense of the concept of culture used in this debate, we need to raise a seldom-asked question: Why does it appear so desirable and even ethical (for scholars and policy makers alike) to show and ensure that globalization allows "cultural" differences to exist?[7] From another perspective, in the jargon of disciplines, we can observe that the "convergence" problem in political science refers to the (desirable) trajectory of more and more nation-states becoming liberal democracies, while in the economic literature this "convergence" thesis takes the form of seeing how different economies from the south move toward approximating ideal-type free-market models. In stark contrast, in the cultural field, convergence is fiercely combated as a desirable. As I will argue below, this is due to the fact that *difference* seems to be exclusively associated with *cultural* spaces and the *cultural* dimension of globalization (rather than with economic and political dimensions). Addressing this problem of the relationship between difference and the concept of culture is essential to any framework constructed to understand globalization as a structured and dialectical phenomenon.

In the first part of this chapter, I use some major positions from the debate on cultural globalization to delineate the ways in which scholars debating globalization use the concept of culture. Here I consider two influential "visions" of globalization—as disjunctive cultural flows, and as complex connectivity. In the next part, I argue for a notion of culture that will allow for a different view of globalization without the attendant problems of compartmentalization. Finally, in the last part, I introduce the notions of "distinctive difference" and "domesticated difference" as possible elements to be considered in any framework for understanding globalization.

*****

In their masterful compendium on globalization, Frank Lechner and John Boli introduce the sections on cultural globalization with what is probably one of the clearest statements of the nature of the debates (although the quote highlights only one side of the debate).

> Cultural globalization is probably the most familiar form [of globalization] for most people. Everyone knows that prominent *icons* of popular culture, like Coca-Cola, blue jeans, rock music, and McDonald's Golden Arches, can be found "everywhere." We are also all aware of the seeming sameness engendered by the diffusion of such *cultural objects and genres*. Add to the list Hollywood movies, French philosophizing, and Japanese organizational techniques that have been widely adopted by American and European companies, and it is easy to believe that cultural globalization inevitably acts as a universal solvent that will dissolve all *cultural differences* in a dull and colorless homogeneity throughout the world.[8]

This may be taken as a classic form of the "cultural homogenization" thesis of globalization. It brings to mind images of quintessential globalized spaces in which people who are *culturally different* meet but are unable to signify their differences anymore. The icons and cultural products and genres that they operate with in their everyday lives have become the same. Arguments on this side of the debate have been put forth by a number of scholars, mostly from the field of media and communication studies, almost all of whom have given us a number of creative tropes and concepts to understand globalization. Thus, the works of H. Schiller and C. J. Hamelink give us the concept of cultural imperialism, and the work of Sean MacBride and Colleen Roach the concept of a world informational order.[9] In the general form of the argument, globalization in its cultural dimension is argued to be characterized by informational and symbolic transactions, and since the production and distribution of these units of culture is mostly controlled by advanced capitalist (American or European) institutions and industries, it follows then that the world is in danger of losing its cultural differences and moving toward a cultural homogeneity. Adherence to a cultural homogenization argument in turn implies some form of acceptance of the related concepts of Americanization, Westernization, and/or commodification, the last mentioned being a more direct attempt at relating globalization to modernity and capitalism, including, specifically, the vision of the McDonaldization, Disneyfication, or Wal-Martization of the world.

The key point to note here is that the shared use of cultural products is taken to be a sign of cultural sameness. Cultural identity, in other words, seems literally embodied within cultural products. As we can see, the cultural homogenization or sameness in question is one of cultural "difference" and its rapid or gradual erasure. It is not difficult to see that the challenge to this thesis must address the issue of difference and cultural products. Does the sharing of cultural products make us culturally the same? To this, we have a slew of scholars who have answered in the negative, key ones being John Tomlinson, Arjun Appadurai, Jonathan Friedman, and Jan Nederveen Pieterse.[10] Two of these are anthropologists, one a sociologist, and one a media/cultural theorist. All of them bring to the debate a sharp critique of the use of culture within the homogenization arguments. According to these scholarly lines of thought, which have been gathered under the banner of cultural heterogenization, globalization does not lead to the erasure of cultural differences. On the contrary, these scholars argue that globalization seems to itself actively generate cultural differences in social spaces. It may even be argued that globalization actually protects and even produces difference. Cultural identities are in no danger of becoming homogenized.

Although many of them admit to the global commodification of values and tastes emanating from Euro-American sites and shaping the global flows of goods (and ideas) as a fact of globalization, they do not agree with the conclusion of the homogenization scholars. For a start, these scholars (along with many others) point to the *multidirectionality* of the flow of cultural goods. Thus, in addition to the fact of Levi's, Coca-Cola, and McDonald's moving from the West to the rest of the world, these scholars point to the flow of cultural products from non-Euro-American sites into parts of the metropolitan West, including such goods as World Beat music, Indian curry, Japanese productions of Western classical music, acupuncture, and even yoga. In fact, it is in this context of the counterflows of cultural goods that Tomlinson speaks of the decline of the West's self-assured assumption of "cultural superiority." The West is no longer hegemonic in these narratives; at least not as far as cultural issues go.

But the critical point on the side of the heterogenizers is the useful distinction they make between cultural identity and cultural products. Unlike the homogenizers, for these scholars the latter does not exhaust the former. This is because culture is about meaning production, and in Tomlinson's words, "culture should be distinguished from its technologies via which cultural representations are transmitted."[11] In support of this argument, many examples of the lack of correlation between the sharing of cultural products and the attendant cultural identities are pointed out. These include the much-touted fact that Coca-Cola has acquired various meanings in different settings around the world—meanings that indicate active differences in interpretive modes of behavior and identities—or that the television show *Dallas* is interpreted in radically different ways by different people in various parts of the world, or that Filipinos who sing old American popular songs in the Philippines do not construct the rest of their lives as Americans, even nostalgically, or—in the even more widely circulated image used by Thomas Friedman in *The Lexus and the Olive Tree*—that the Kayapo people of Brazil use cell phones and cable television to monitor the extraction of gold from their traditional lands to ensure their rights.[12]

This distinction between cultural identity and cultural products has moved the debate onto more nuanced planes for theorizing globalization from the vantage point of culture. Three related and well-theorized "visions" of globalization are Appadurai's globalization as "disjunctive global cultural flows," Tomlinson's globalization as the experience of "complex connectivity," and Nederveen Pieterse's globalization as "hybridization." All three of them build upon the concept of "deterritorialization" as a core cultural element of globalization. I shall briefly discuss the main thrusts of the first two scholars in this section and the third in the next in order to distill the sense of "culture" in their models.

In his influential essay "Disjuncture and Difference in the Global Cultural Economy," (1990)[13] anthropologist Arjun Appadurai refers to the changes brought about by globalization in the realm of what he calls variously "cultural dealings," "cultural transaction," or even more evocatively the field of "cultural gravity." Such a focus allows Appadurai to settle on "global cultural flows" as the trope for representing globalization. Further, he calls for us to move beyond the homogenization-heterogenization debate and recognize the complex character of cultural globalization as *disjunctive* global cultural flows, the disjuncture being between economy, culture, and politics, for which he has given us the now famous five scapes—ethnoscapes, technoscapes, financescapes, mediascapes, and ideoscapes.[14] Global cultural flow then occurs "in and through the growing disjunctures" among these scapes. Appadurai builds his flow model by acknowledging the twin phenomena of "deterritorialized contexts" and "social imagination" as central forces of the global culture today. He rightly points out that in globalization not only do people, goods, capital, ideas, and images move at faster speeds on a greater scale and in larger volume, there are also simultaneously *imagined worlds*, that is, the multiple worlds that are constituted by the historically situated imaginations of persons and groups spread around the globe."[15]

While Appadurai explains his flow model quite tightly, I do not see as clearly why these flows are *cultural*, especially since he does not give any sense of his use of that term in that essay. It is only in the later work *Modernity at Large* (1996) that one gets a clear sense of what Appadurai means by culture. Here he builds on the idea of social imagination as being constitutive of human subjectivities and argues that people and images are "in simultaneous circulation" in modernity. He uses this vision to argue against the idea of cultures as strictly delineated, definable entities (a task performed by many anthropologists working on issues of delinking the identity of culture to place; for example, Akhil Gupta and James Ferguson, as well as James Clifford).[16] This sets up the stage for Appadurai's specific use of the concept of culture as "the process of naturalizing a subset of differences that have been mobilized to articulate group *identity*" (my emphasis). Culture thus comes to be very inextricably linked to "difference" and the "mobilization of group identities."[17] It may then be fair to reason that although the image of flows that are so prominently placed in Appadurai's model of globalization may have had a fair role to play in his sense of culture, the various scapes of flows cannot be collectively termed *cultural* if culture is used in the above sense. Nevertheless, the negative critique (from Tomlinson) that culture should not be confused with cultural products is supplemented here with a positive critique that associates culture with cultural identity through difference. We turn once again to Tomlinson to see how the sense of culture gets slightly more nuanced.

The cultural and media theorist John Tomlinson has also contributed to the development of the key concept of deterritorialization (of culture from place), a concept that seeks to explain how cultural differences exist and shape our experiences of globalization.[18] In his 1999 work *Globalization and Culture*, Tomlinson uses a number of examples from ordinary everyday life activities of people in an age of globalization to characterize the "phenomenal worlds" that we make and exist within as increasingly characterized by "the weakening or dissolution of the connection between everyday lived culture and territorial location." Thus he correctly observes that

> people probably come to include distant events and processes more routinely in their perceptions of what is significant for their own personal lives. This is one aspect of what deterritorialization may involve: the ever-broadening horizon of relevance in people's routine experience, removing not only general "cultural awareness" but, crucially, the processes of individual "life planning" from a self-contained context centered on physical location or politically defined territory.[19]

Classic examples for Tomlinson include the growing awareness and experiences of being linked to distant parts of the world, and different people than one's local community, during mundane activities such as buying or eating food, watching television, searching for a job, shopping, or walking on the streets. Globalization, in other words, transforms the experience of locality itself. And it is an ambiguous experience, bringing with it fears of vulnerability and risk as well as excitement and expansion of cultural horizons.[20] Such a transformed experience of the local is new in the sense that it moves us beyond a feeling of "proximity" (which existed long before globalization due to long-distance trade) to a feeling of "connectivity," which is dependent upon decreasing what he calls "sociocultural distance" and actually enabling the *cultural* experiences of globalization. Tomlinson's rich repertoire of concepts does indeed aid an understanding of globalization as "complex connectivity."

Like Appadurai's, Tomlinson's vision of globalization also derives closely from his sense of the term *culture*. In *Globalization and Culture* (as in his earlier work on cultural imperialism), Tomlinson carefully distinguishes culture from economics and politics. So, for him, culture refers to "the ways in which people make their lives, individually and collectively, meaningful by communicating with each other," whereas the economic realm deals with material goods and the political with power. He further refines his use of culture in the following manner: "This is the sense of the cultural dimension that I want to stress, with the emphasis on meanings as ends in themselves, as distinct from simply instrumental meanings."[21]

Finally, Tomlinson acknowledges his own affinities to Serge Latouche's existential view of culture as a "response to the problem of being," although he is careful to associate his sense of culture with ordinary mundane activities such as going to the restaurant, the supermarket, the sports club, or the street corner, rather than "specialized existential discourses." At this point, one may wonder how a trip to the supermarket addresses the "problem of being" or qualifies as a *cultural* activity in Tomlinson's sense of producing meaning in life *as an end in itself* rather than instrumentally by enabling the buying of food necessary to sustain life.

One may gather, then, that such a sense of culture is needed to build his vision of globalization as complex connectivity because sociocultural distance is another way of speaking of cultural differences and identity. If Appadurai's vision of globalization is built upon a sense of culture as tied to difference and the mobilization of group identities, then Tomlinson's sense of culture as producing meanings successfully places those identities outside the realm of economics and politics. But although deterritorialization is a valuable insight into the workings of globalization, and both Appadurai and Tomlinson produce visions of cultural globalization that take us beyond the model of sameness put forward by the homogenization theorists, I argue that the peculiarly dematerialized understanding of culture in their respective visions makes *cultural* globalization appear only linked to identity, not interests and power.[22] These are influential visions that unfortunately aid the compartmentalized ideas of globalization spoken of in the introduction to this chapter, which cause the debates about globalization to exist only around culture, not economics, *because* the sense of culture used here has been emptied of economics and power, and meaning becomes only about noneconomic and nonpolitical existential narratives of life. While we have usefully moved from equating culture with cultural products or tying it to places, we have in this process idealized it by emptying it of power and economy. There is meaning underlying utility, and power is almost always in need of clothing—power seeks to be hegemonic rather than nakedly coercive. Conversely, such a sense of culture also empties economics and politics of culture. The concept that economics is all about the market, politics is about power, and culture is about meanings does not allow for a synthetic understanding of culture as the basis of economy and politics. Since one should not stop with a critique, I offer what could be termed a construction in the next section.

*****

Consider the following advertisement that appeared in the *New York Times* as part of a series of ads against globalization in 1999 before the World Trade Organization (WTO) protests in Seattle. The ad is boldly titled "Global Monoculture" and accuses the WTO of "homogenizing global cultures and values," (along the lines of the movie *Demolition Man*).

> A few decades ago, it was still possible to leave home and go somewhere else: the architecture was different, the landscape was different, the language, lifestyle, dress, and values were different. That was a time when we could speak of cultural diversity. But with economic globalization, diversity is fast disappearing. The goal of the global economy is that all countries should be homogenized.[23]

Familiar terms by now? But the most interesting part of that ad is the following:

> For these agencies and corporations, *diversity* is not a primary value: efficiency is. Diversity is an enemy because it requires differentiated sales appeal. What corporations love is creating the same values, the same tastes, using the same advertising, selling the same products, and driving out small local competitors. Mass marketers prefer homogenized consumers. They also prefer places with low wages, cheap resources, and the least restrictive environmental and labor laws.

It is easy to dismiss this ad as failing to understand that "differentiated sales appeal" is indeed the hallmark of globalization viewed economically as flexible specialization under what David Harvey calls the "condition of postmodernity," and therefore concluding with the heterogenization theorists above that cultural diversity is indeed not viewed as the enemy by capitalist interests in the age of globalization. Such a position would place those among us who lean toward the heterogenization argument ironically against the sponsors of that series of ads who call themselves "50 non-profit organizations that favor democratic, localized, ecologically sound alternatives to current practices and policies."

It is also useful to remind ourselves that the heterogenization position comes close to what Aijaz Ahmad has pointed out as "endorsing the cultural claims of transnational capital itself," wherein most transnational capital corporations seem to have become the self-styled votaries of multiculturalism and diversity. Further, it is worthwhile to briefly note that the notion of culture used by many of the homogenization theorists mentioned earlier, although firmly viewed through a semiotic lens as embodied in signs (similar to the heterogenizers), had some benefits in that it also placed culture within its material contexts of capital and power especially, so that it is possible to argue that cultural products *in their use* do indeed effect a change of cultural identity. In other words, one cannot keep drinking Coca-Cola and not be drawn into the social relations of value (economics) and power (politics) that Coca-Cola represents.[24] It is less a question of meaning generation (what Coke means to the drinker or the group that drinks it) than a question of the social relations that Coke (its production, distribution, consumption, and representation) enters into, spawns, destroys, transforms, and dominates, and in that process *forces the drinkers of Coke* to live their lives within those relations and narrate their tales of living.

It is in this context that the alternatives offered by the sociologist Jan Nederveen Pieterse appear to be somewhat better than the two models reviewed earlier. Pieterse offers a vision of globalization as the "processes of hybridization" of forms and practices that organize social life and the world, where hybridization is "the ways in which forms become separated from existing practices and recombine with new forms in new practices." According to his vision, globalization structurally means the "increase in the available modes of organization."[25] Moving a step beyond Appadurai and Tomlinson, Pieterse connects identities to materiality by showing that cultural hybridization takes place when people avail themselves of multiple organizational options (including forms of production) to construct multiple and diversified forms of identity. Here culture itself is viewed as hybrid, but used in a self-reflexive manner that does not privilege a past when culture was not hybrid. Thus, for Pieterse, contemporary accelerated globalization means the hybridization of already hybrid cultures. Having provided such a caveat for the use of the term *hybridization*, Pieterse clarifies his understanding of culture with relation to both politics and economics by speaking of culture as "an arena of struggle" and developing it using Pierre Bourdieu's notions of cultural capital and the more important notion of the convertibility of different forms of capital.[26]

For our purposes here, it suffices to say that there exists a vast literature in anthropology wherein the concept of culture has been debated for over a century precisely around the notion of links between culture and utility, or the symbolic and the material.[27] Whereas the Tylorian notion of culture as an entire way of life broke away from the classical Arnoldian view of culture as an elite set of products of particular classes in society, the Geertzian notion of culture being a shared product of meanings (a web spun by us, within which we are suspended) helped to bring meaning to the core of culture. But the ones that I find most useful for grasping globalization are those that view culture as simultaneously contested, as structured and structuring dispositions, and as ordinary and material. While Pieterse's view of culture is obviously preferable to Clifford Geertz's view, it is the Mexican anthropologist Nestor Garcia-Canclini who provides a more succinct understanding of culture that clearly shows its material character. For Garcia-Canclini, culture is "the social production of phenomena that contribute, through symbolic representation or re-elaboration of material structures, to understand, reproduce or transform the social system."[28] I take the "phenomena" referred to in the quote to be the "struggles over production, distribution and consumption of meanings" engaged in by all individuals collectively. Although Appadurai's and Tomlinson's views of culture focus on these set of activities, their association of the *objects* of meaning production exclusively with identity formation fatally dissociates culture from its much broader set of objectives—to represent material (and I would add social) structures, including but not restricted to social relations, social organization, conflicts, classes, kinship, caste, gender, race, religion, political and legal subjectivities, social relations of production (that is, job descriptions), material forces such as means of production, and notions that acquire material force through economic organization such as value, utility, efficiency, and resources. Culture then may be seen as working through signs, but it is the "stuff" that makes us think of "economics" and "politics" as meaningful, and that enables the perception of utility and power. It accomplishes all this simultaneous to shaping what we call "identities."

As was seen in the last section, "identities" are usually linked to difference to speak of the cultural. In this regard, Pieterse addresses the issue of difference and diversity most clearly in his work on development when he says "when globalization and diversity are combined, as in 'glocalization,' globalization can be conceptualized as changing patterns of *diversification*" (my emphasis).[29] I think we should push this logic further to apply to globalization along the lines of Pierre Bourdieu, who takes the fundamental *differentiation* of society as his starting point. In fact, one may say that explaining the principles of differentiation is the goal of *all* his analysis. Thus, for Bourdieu, the task of social analysis would be to construct social space as a structure of differentiated positions according to the distribution of different forms of capital. He identifies three forms of capital: *economic* (related to a Marxist understanding of rights and powers over productive resources, their use, and products from their use), *cultural* (related to informational resources available chiefly through social networks such as educational institutions, family and kinship circles, and Weberian status groups), and *symbolic* (the form that both of the above forms of capital assume when they are perceived by people as distinctive, i.e., having value, prestige, legitimacy, authority). It is important to note that each of these forms of capital is *convertible* to the other forms. Social positions are thus distributed (in social and symbolic space) according to the volume and the structure of forms of capital. Needless to say, this is *uneven*—giving rise to class, gender, or ethnic/caste differences and misery. The next section will try to apply the notion of culture and differentiation to propose alternative constructions of representations of globalization.

*****

Let us consider a globalization effect. Many large American firms outsource part of their services to companies in India, including customer services and billing. As a result, there has been a growth of jobs in India over the last two to three years in what are known as call centers. These are the quintessential sites where we can see global practices, hybrid forms, and deterritorialized notions of culture being created. As a report on the workers in these call centers says,

> [t]heir training includes a smattering of U.S. history and geography, along with speech therapy [*sic*] so that they will sound "American." Some call centers are adorned with American flags to give a cultural feel to the place. Along the way, these employees are exposed to a way of life that can come into direct conflict with their conservative values and, sometimes, their sanity.[30]

We can discern here how the call centers are sites where "culture" may be said to represent the "economy" of business relationships, workspace organization, and work itself. "Ways of life" can come into conflict and get transformed or dominate. The report goes on to highlight various "situations" that face the employees. There is the instance of the young employee who, when he let his accent slip, had to reveal his actual location—Mumbai. As the story goes, to his horror the man on the line told him, "You guys blew up the WTC," to which despite his protestations that India had nothing to do with the event, the man hung up on him. There are other experiences that range from the absurd to the mildly humorous, but all of these experiences can be thought of as part of globalization.

We are now in a position to offer a constructive alternative or transformation to existing visions of globalization. In the homogenization-heterogenization debate, we saw that the homogenization or heterogenization referred to difference, but narrowly viewed only as cultural difference linked to identity. If one model viewed globalization as a process of homogenizing differences, the alternate (and better) model viewed globalization as homogenizing and heterogenizing simultaneously in disjunctive ways (Appadurai) and in ambiguous ways (Tomlinson). As Lechner and Boli put it, "[g]lobalization makes difference problematic while simultaneously accentuating difference."[31] Appadurai also captures this movement as "sameness and difference cannibalizing each other." But what none of these models attempts to explain are the reasons why this simultaneous movement occurs. Alternatively, we may raise the question about the conditions under which difference may become homogenized (due to it becoming threatening to hegemonic forces?) or difference may be promoted (due to its value or nonthreatening state to hegemonic forces?). The metaphor of disjuncture of spaces (political, economic, cultural) is similar to an older metaphor—uneven development (of flows in intensity or volume, direction, and speed). In fact, globalization (like capitalism and development, its close cousins—or synonyms, if we wish) needs unevenness. And a model of uneven or disjunctive globalization should generate a theory of differentiation.

As a very preliminary step toward this goal, I submit the following diagrammatic representation of globalization (see figure 9.2). In this model, we can speak of a *culture of globalization* that is inherently homogenizing, seeking to impose a degree of sameness in the quest for universalist hegemony. This tendency is not only a historical tendency of capital in search for markets and profits, but also a logical need of capital for increased commodification in order to promote market exchange. Abstract labor, in which particular differences get erased and equivalences get produced, is therefore necessary for the culture of globalization. On the other hand, there also exists a need to work with difference (borrowing from the heterogenizers and Pieterse) to an extent unknown of earlier, given the unevenness of capitalist development based on differences in use value *and* exchange value. This disposition of globalization that is inherently heterogenizing seeks not only to preserve difference but also to produce "new" differences. These differences may then become part of the construction of different identities, forms of organization, forms of power, and so on. We can speak thus of a *globalization of cultures* (in the plural)—a globalization as hybridization. Now, such a model becomes explanatory to whatever extent if we claim that the culture of globalization drives the globalization of cultures, which in turn supports or enables the culture of globalization to reproduce itself.

Figure 9.2
Model for Cultural Work Within Globalization

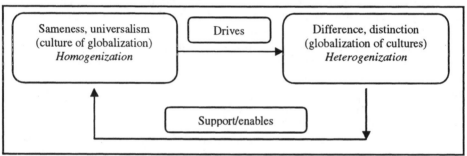

Source: Balmurli Natrajan, "Beyond Homogenization vs Heterogenization," in Hewa and Stapleton (eds.), Globalization, Philanthropy, and Civil Society, 2005.

As an additional level of understanding in such a model, I propose that the homogenization or heterogenization (or greater hybridization) of spaces operates only through the production of what I will call "distinctive differences" and "domesticated differences." From the call center example, we can see firstly that difference is sometimes emphasized and at other times erased. It is emphasized along what may be called the economic axis as the "value" of an Indian worker who has the comparative advantages of low wages, good English, computing skills, and perhaps even pliancy. Yet, the attempt is made to render the same difference indistinct in order to provide seamless service and retain market shares. But, from time to time, this "concealed" difference rears its head and either leads to a positive social interaction (one worker, for instance, got propositioned by a person on the line in the United States), or negative (the client in the example cited earlier threatened politically by the difference). We can say that globalizing firms can either make differences (ethnicities, nationalities, gender, race, religion, wages, skills, political orientation, sexual orientation, caste, etc.) matter in a context or not. Or, using Bourdieu's terminology, we can say that differences become "visible, perceptible, non-indifferent, socially *pertinent* difference if it is perceived by someone who is capable of *making the distinction.*"[32] I refer to the differences thus perceived as "distinctive differences."

Further, although "distinctive differences" produce value to the firm, they have to be "domesticated differences" in order for the orderly and efficient reproduction of capital to be possible. This will range from allowing the worker to display many aspects of his or her different identities to tightly controlling these signs of difference. The moment difference gets to be a threatening sign (such as veils during nationalistic or jingoistic times), cultural homogenization is put into high gear. Globalization cannot be said to love difference at all times and in all spaces. But it does value it in some spaces at some times. With regard to protests against globalization, building from this proposed model, we may observe that in many Third World spaces, globalization of cultures is seen to happen, and heterogenenization may be said to take place as well. However, this heterogeneity many times comes to be perceived as a threat because it changes locality drastically—economically and politically. Coke and Pepsi, for example, are not merely signs for consumption in India. They materialize and displace local producers of drinks, such as taking over land suitable for the farming of tomatoes for fruit juice, by placing political and economic pressures on the government to remove the land ceiling acts put in place to prevent concentration of wealth.

In summary, we may say that "domesticated differences" produce economic value when they are capable of being controlled, whereas "distinctive differences" produce symbolic value but could be viewed as threatening. Viewing difference in this manner, we are able to integrate an understanding of culture as a material reality that is constantly in need of reproduction, the forms of which depend on the economic and political realities. Globalization, then, does not need to be viewed in a disciplinary vision in which debates on cultural globalization grapple with issues of identity separated from interests and power. If difference is at the heart of identity, then such identities must always have been viewed as unstable and contingent upon the balance sheet of the twin tendencies—the culture of globalization and the globalization of cultures.

Endnotes

[1] Pierre Bourdieu's term *habitus* here could refer to the particular dispositions that everyone becomes habituated to over a period of time living within particular social structures and regularly (if not constantly) reproducing them in complex fashion; in this case, disciplines inculcate ways of thinking, valuing/evaluating, conceptualizing, arguing, and presenting/representing reality.

[2] Paraphrased from memory of a conversation with a student in the fall of 2002.

[3] The one exception that I have come across in this literature on globalization is the book edited by David Held and Anthony McGrew, *The Global Transformation Reader: An Introduction to the Globalization Debate,* Polity Press, Cambridge, UK, 2002.

[4] Michael Burawoy, "For a Sociological Marxism: The Complementary Convergence of Antonio Gramsci and Karl Polanyi," *Politics and Society* 31:2, 2003, pp.193–261. Burawoy attempts to weave these disparate thinkers together. The cultural dimension for most scholars in this disciplinary vision does not seem to be sociological enough in the sense that it refers more to dematerialized realms of ideas and beliefs that shape identities of collectives (as I will discuss throughout this paper). Therefore, we only have the state and the market represented in the political and economic globalization

debates and the realm of ideology/identity loosely represented in the cultural globalization debates. Tellingly, many globalization reader texts have additional separate sections (after the economic, political, and cultural sections) on human rights, environment, and gender—three key areas in which a notion of and the struggle to form "civil society" seems to be critically played out in a globalizing world. As Burawoy reminds us about Gramsci's contribution, the difference between advanced and backward capitalist nation-states is the development of a robust civil society and its absence or weakness.

5 The debate about the "age" of globalization is absolutely critical to fashioning our theories and politics. Given the varieties of historical and geographical positions on this issue, I tend to favor a position that does not work with a notion of different *national capitalisms* (such as Chinese, Indian, or Latin American versus some idealized advanced capitalism in Europe and North America). I also tend to favor a position that views the technological, legal, and sociological changes over the last half century as having produced a qualitatively different form of *dominant* capitalism (one that dictates the terms of doing business, governing a society, and relating to individuals in civil society). Such a dominant form of capitalism has been called post-Fordist capitalism, or lean production. Following Tony Smith, I consider such labels to be useful within limits, provided that they are viewed as capturing the most powerful tendencies of "leading sectors" of the economy, polity, and society that "are of most relevance to future historical development." See Tony Smith, *Technology and Capital in the Age of Lean Production: A Marxian Critique of the "New Economy,"* SUNY Press, Albany, NY, 2000, p. 2.

6 Held and McGrew (eds.), *The Global Transformations Reader*, p. 3.

7 Related to this is the fact that scholars and policy makers alike find it undesirable and unethical to show and ensure that globalization allows economic differences (rich/poor) or political differences (powerful/subaltern) to exist (witness the debates on whether globalization has increased or decreased inequality in the world). One can say with some certainty that not even the most pro-bourgeois or the most pro-elite set of scholars or policy analysts of globalization would openly claim that they wish to see economic and political differences exist. Everyone in this debate seems to desire the erasure of differences in wealth and power—and hence either critique globalization for not providing this or praise it for making strides towards this ideal (see the exchange between Robert Wade and Martin Wolf in Held and McGrew (eds.) *Global Transformation Reader*, pp. 440–7, as an example).

8 Frank Lechner and John Boli (eds.), *The Globalization Reader*, Blackwell Publishers, Malden, MA, 2000, p. 283, my emphasis.

9 H. Schiller, "Electronic Information Flows: New Basis for Global Domination?," in P. Drummond and R. Paterson (eds.) *Television in Transition*, BFI Publishing, London, 1985, pp. 11–20; C. J. Hamelink, *Cultural Autonomy in Global Communications*, Longmans, NY, 1983; Sean MacBride and Colleen Roach, The New International Informational Order, in Lechner Frank and John Boli (eds.) *The Globalization Reader*, Blackwell Publishers Malden, MA, 2000.

10 John Tomlinson, *Cultural Imperialism: A Critical Introduction*, Pinter Publishers London, 1991; John Tomlinson, *Globalization and Culture*, University of Chicago Press, Chicago, 1999; Arjun Appadurai, "Disjuncture and Difference in the Global Cultural Economy," in Frank Lechner and John Boli (eds.) *The Globalization Reader*,

Blackwell Publishers, Malden, MA, 2000; Arjun Appadurai, *Modernity at Large: Cultural Dimensions of Globalization*, University of Minnesota Press, Minneapolis, 1996; Jonathan Friedman, *Cultural Identity and Global Process*, Sage, London, 1994; Jan Nederveen Pieterse, *Development Theory: Deconstructions/Reconstructions*, Sage, London, 2001.

[11] Tomlinson, *Globalization and Culture*, p. 20.

[12] D. Howes (ed.), *Cross-Cultural Consumption: Global Markets, Local Realities*, Routledge, London, 1996; I. Ang, *Living Room Wars*, Routledge, London, 1996. Appadurai, *Modernity at Large*; Thomas Friedman, *Lexus and the Olive Tree*, Anchor Books, NY, 2000.

[13] Arjun Appadurai, "Disjuncture and Difference in the Global Cultural Economy," in Frank Lechner and John Boli (eds.) *The Globalization Reader*, Blackwell Publishers, Malden, MA, 2000, [originally published in 1990].

[14] Briefly, ethnoscape refers to flow of people; technoscape, to flow of technology; financescape, to flow of finance capital; mediascape, to flow of images; and ideoscape, to flow of ideas.

[15] Appadurai, "Disjuncture and Difference."

[16] Akhil Gupta and James Ferguson, *Culture, Power Place: Explorations in Critical Anthroplogy*, Duke University Press, Durham, 1997; James Clifford, *The Predicament of Culture*, Harvard University Press, Cambridge, MA, 1988.

[17] Appadurai, *Modernity at Large*, pp. 13, 15.

[18] Although there are other theorists who have used this term and related ones such as *delocalization, denationalization*, and *disembeddedness*, Tomlinson has in my opinion engaged most closely with "distilling" the concept of culture while working on the concept of deterritorialization.

[19] There is a song in a Hindi film called *Shree 420* that goes "My shoes are Japanese, these trousers are English, on my head is a red Russian cap, yet my heart is Indian." This may be a trite comparison to deterritorialization, but the ambiguous correlations between places, cultural products, and cultural identities is clear even in this song from the 1950s. See also Tomlinson, *Globalization and Culture*, pp. 115, 128.

[20] Ibid., p. 128.

[21] Ibid., pp. 18–19.

[22] In terms of Appadurai's scapes, I submit that cultural globalization (following his sense of the term *culture*) is restricted to ethnoscapes (ethnic and religious identity issues), ideoscapes, and mediascapes (issues related to imagined worlds).

[23] Available at: http://bss.sfsu.edu/fischer/IR%20305/Readings/global.htm.

[24] It is surprising that Appadurai's earlier work, *The Social Life of Things*, Cambridge University Press, Cambridge, UK, 1986, paid much more attention to this important detail about objects and their flows than his newer work on globalization.

[25] Jan Nederveen Pieterse, "Globalization as Hybridization," in Frank Lechner and John Boli (eds.) *The Globalization Reader*, Blackwell Publishers, Malden, MA, 2000, pp. 101, 103.

[26] Pieterse, *Development Theory*, p. 153.

[27] Key works would include Marshall Sahlins, *Culture and Practical Reason*, University of Chicago Press, Chicago, 1976; Pierre Bourdieu, *Outline of a Theory of Practice*, Cambridge University Press, Cambridge, UK, 1979. See also, William Roseberry, *Anthropologies and Histories: Essays in Culture, History and Political Economy*,

Rutgers University Press, New Brunswick, NJ, 1989; Sherry Ortner, "Theory in Anthropology since the Sixties," *Comparative Studies in Society and History,* 26, 1984, pp. 126–66.

[28] Nestor Garcia-Canclini, *Transforming Modernity*, University of Texas Press, Austin, 1993, p.10.

[29] Pieterse, *Development Theory*, p. 50.

[30] Available at: www.wired.com/news/business/0,1367,55799,00.htm.

[31] Lechner and Boli (eds.), *The Globalization Reader*. p. 320.

[32] Pierre Bourdieu, *Practical Reason*, Stanford University Press, Stanford, CA, 1998, p. 9.

Chapter 10

RISK, REFLEXIVE MODERNITY, AND THE UNBINDING OF POLITICS: AGRICULTURAL BIOTECHNOLOGY IN A GLOBALIZED WORLD

Michael D. Mehta

In his work on the "risk society" and "reflexive modernization," Ulrich Beck suggests that the influence of the nation-state in setting national priorities is weakening because of an *unbinding of politics*.[1] Due to the ascendancy of scientific rationality, the predominance of corporations, and the institutionalization of risk, Beck suggests that power is shifting away from the nation-state and accumulating in individuals, multinational corporations, industry associations, and other organizations that adopt strict legal and scientific discourses. The unbinding of politics represents a shift in the locus and timing of decision making whereby governmental policies and regulatory frameworks follow belatedly initiatives set in motion by agents of technological change. This shift in decision making to new sites and actors is a social reaction to the rise of a globalized risk society[2] and the growing interconnectedness of global processes, and can be examined by considering the case of agricultural biotechnology.

*****

In their introduction to Beck's *Risk Society*, Scott Lash and Brian Wynne describe three stages of modernity (pre-, simple, and reflexive). The shift from premodernity to simple modernity is described as resulting from the creation of industrial society and the emergence of classes, rapid wealth accumulation, and notable scientific achievements. The next shift, to reflexive modernity, coincided with a growing awareness that industrial society must deal with problems "resulting from techno-economic development itself." In other words, modernity becomes reflexive when it is a "theme and a problem for itself."[3] For Beck, reflexive modernity is a collective exercise in risk management. Instead of being obsessed solely with wealth accumulation, the risk society is oriented toward the social distribution of risk. When we become aware of new risks (e.g., bioterrorism, SARS, the West Nile virus), the risk society reacts with a reflex to minimize, redistribute and redefine the risk. In general, this reflex involves either an increased scientization of risk or, for Sheila Jasanoff,[4] a renewed interest in forging better relationships between traditional adversaries (e.g., government and civil society) to reduce conflict.

The risk society has several distinctive features worth examining briefly. First, modern-day risks are in many ways unique. Risks posed by global climate change, nuclear developments, and stratospheric ozone depletion are global in nature. Since many global-scale risks result from human activities, and elude our senses, the definition, quantification, and responses to such risks are dependent on complex scientific investigation, interpretation by the courts, and transmission by the media. Second, since risks and benefits are socially distributed, exposure is a function of sociostructural relations. In general, wealth provides greater opportunities for reducing exposure to hazards and their adverse consequences. Wealthier individuals can afford better medical care, air bags in their automobiles, and insurance. However, in the risk society, a "boomerang" effect exists. Efforts to reduce risk provide diminishing marginal returns, and some risks can be reduced to a certain point and then return with little warning. For example, to reduce the loss of crops associated with drought, farmers may choose to rely more on irrigation. By irrigating their crops, farmers may reduce their personal financial risk. However, long-term cycles of drought make this strategy more costly over time, and may reduce the quantity and quality of drinking water available for human consumption. Third, the concept of risk cannot be understood without a concept of benefit. Many technological advances create "winners" and "losers." By defining risk and benefit narrowly, powerful actors such as multinational corporations can facilitate an unbinding of politics by excluding ethical and social issues from formal consideration. Fourth, modern-day risks are complex and have several layers of uncertainty associated with them. As such, knowledge about risk, and the ability to use evidence or lack of evidence on risk for making decisions, becomes a key political tool. Failures to manage risk, and to facilitate public understanding of risk, demonstrate the centrality of this feature of the risk society. For example, concerns about new variant CJD (Creutzfeldt-Jakob disease, the human form of mad cow disease) increased dramatically in the UK when government scientists admitted being wrong about the possibility of this disease crossing the species barrier.[5] The risk society is a fickle form of modernity in which many individuals support science and technology, yet continue to question the motives and legitimacy of scientists, corporations, and governments when new risks emerge or when old risks are recast. Last, the risk society promotes subpolitical engagement by allowing civil society groups, and others, access to the unofficial political machinery of the corporate world, while distancing them from the machinery of government. Subpolitical activity includes lobbying, certain kinds of multi-stakeholder consultation, and other forms of engagement that barely touch the official political process.[6] Subpolitical activity has the potential to create new forms of governance, modify current understanding of the role of civil society, and promote an unbinding of politics by preempting government policy and weakening its base of legitimacy.

*****

The risk society is a metaphor for a society that has become obsessed with risk while remaining committed to industrial overproduction and the application of scientific rationality to maximize profit, reduce inefficiency, and exercise ever-increasing control over the processes and products of nature.[7] The risk society stimulates the unbinding of politics in the following manner. For Beck and other adherents of the risk society thesis, risk has become the key organizing principle of industrial society. As such, the risk society is bipolar and by its very nature hyperdialectical. By treating risk as a tradable commodity, or even as a futures market instrument, the Western world has decontextualized risk and bracketed off several of the nonmonetary and nonscientific dimensions associated with technologies that produce risk. This process of decontextualization connects squarely the assessment and management of risks to an innovation agenda in which the traditional role of the nation-state as guardian of the public good has been transformed into that of an enabler of technologically induced economic growth.

Many industrialized countries such as Canada and the United States are pursuing innovation agendas that place a heavy emphasis on scientific discovery as a driver of the knowledge-based economy. Investments in biotechnology, and now in nanotechnology and robotics, are being made in order to stimulate economic growth and to enhance international competitiveness. Additionally, commitment to these scientific areas of inquiry by government, industry, and universities has reproblematized several social, health, and environmental issues as being ultimately solvable by continuing support of the natural and physical sciences. Concurrent with this formal emphasis on science is a decline in trust in expertise, and for Beck, Anthony Giddens, and others[8] a weakening of the legitimacy of traditional political structures that must deal with risky technologies and the politics of knowledge associated with them. As a theoretical device, Beck's unbinding of politics demonstrates how quickly governance structures can change, and how other interests can gain ground. Alternatively, such an unbinding precipitates the growth of competing sources of knowledge and political participation, while fostering subpolitical social change and clearing fertile ground for globally coordinated civil society groups to manufacture new "political opportunity structures"[9] for mobilizing change and contributing to the discourse on public policy.

Since most governments have an interest in facilitating innovation and enabling technology, how can democratic societies minimize the inevitable social friction that emerges from this dynamic without being plagued by chronic change and instability?[10] What is the role of civil society and philanthropic organizations in responding to, or otherwise acting as intermediaries, in the risk society? This chapter will examine these questions by exploring a small set of civil society organizations and the role of the Rockefeller Foundation in developing Golden Rice technology.

*****

For Georg Hegel, the state was the highest form of reason, and was therefore seen as the ideal body for regulating human affairs.[11] For many, Hegel's political conception of the state and its relationship to the notion of citizenship has been disastrous due to the totalitarian implications that can be drawn.[12] More recent theorizing on the state tends to explore how it is being transformed by economic and social globalization, and by the growing influence of civil society. The traditional conception of the state, as guardian of the public good, is being questioned simultaneously by the economic elite and civil society organizations that appear to have a strong interest in shaping the contours of globalization. In this era of economic globalization, corporate interests lobby for rationalized world trade, less regulation, and the harmonization of standards. In short, economic globalization is about ensuring greater fluidity for traditional kinds of power while enshrining the dominance of Western business practices, market mechanisms, monetary policies, and conceptions of intellectual property. By contrast, civil society is responding to, and being fostered, by forces of social globalization. As B. Edwards and M. W. Foley suggest,[13] civil society is a useful heuristic for focusing attention on the nonmarket aspects of social reality. By creating "action spaces" within society, civil society organizations can put forward alternative viewpoints about how best to promote the public good,[14] and suggest other ways to build capital (e.g., social, human, institutional, and ecological). For Giddens,[15] social globalization is about transforming the political, technological, and cultural dimensions of everyday life into a "global cosmopolitan society" that functions within the electronic spaces carved out by the Internet. Due to social globalization, the influence of civil society appears to be increasing while institutions of the state find it progressively more difficult to govern. Many of the concerns expressed by people in the Western world have migrated beyond national boundaries, and have become entangled in risk issues.

A dominant theme in much of Beck's work is that risks escape the institutions of modern industrial society. To deal with this leakage, the state and other actors have embraced a philosophy of facilitating public involvement in environmental, and broader, decision making. However, there are several examples in the literature of how this approach has failed to create open and transparent decision making structures that are trusted by participants. For instance, in a case study on how Cumbrian sheep farmers interacted with the British government following the nuclear accident at Chernobyl, Brian Wynne[16] described the "private ambivalence" that he observed about the consultation process by farmers.

The emergence of the risk society, and the associated subpolitical opportunities it facilitates, is realigning corporate actors, civil society, and government. From the perspective of corporations, such realignment is desirable since it promises to weaken organized resistance to new technologies and helps to ensure that market and regulatory conditions are optimized. For civil society, this realignment may generate new opportunities; but it also creates positions that could be antithetical to core values and be the wellspring of renewed criticisms of being "special interest," and therefore illegitimate representatives of the public. From the perspective of government, this realignment is creating several fractures between elected officials and the bureaucracy, and raises doubts about science-based regulation and the interpretation of scientific uncertainty, and is stimulating debate about how best to address so-called nonregulatory issues (e.g., social, ethical). An examination of developments in agricultural biotechnology demonstrates how this realignment is being achieved, and the implications this raises for the state and other actors (e.g., philanthropic organizations).

In recent years, meetings of the World Trade Organization (WTO) have become the focal point of large-scale protests by so-called antiglobalization groups. A common argument of antiglobalization protesters is that multinational corporations are illegitimate because they are undemocratic, and that governments of the Western world have been "captured" by these economic interests. This problem of legitimacy in contemporary world politics has spawned various observations. David Held suggests that a "cosmopolitan democracy" is needed so that democratic control extends through local, national, and transnational contexts.[17] The need for thinking globally about these kinds of transcendent issues becomes clearer when the topics of food safety and security, and debates on agricultural policies, are raised.

Food technologies and their possible negative impacts (e.g., reduction of biodiversity, threat to traditional seed-saving practices, impact on human health, etc.) are now being interrogated within the public sphere. Peter Rosset[18] describes how the WTO protest in Seattle set the stage for a "new international food movement" by bringing together farmers from the developed and developing worlds, environmental activists, and others with an interest in social justice. Many of these actors have competed with each other historically, and yet have been galvanized most effectively by capitalizing on concerns arising from the introduction of modern biotechnology into crop production. This new alliance of actors points to a shift in how people perceive the role of science in agriculture and in food safety.

The literature on food adulteration is colorfully sprinkled with examples of how scientific techniques were developed for detecting such things as alum in bread and brick dust in cocoa. In the United States and elsewhere, these techniques developed in tandem with new regulatory approaches and the founding of institutions like the U.S. Food and Drug Administration. In short, science ensured that food was safe. However, early concerns about margarine, food irradiation, and microwave ovens, and now biotechnology, have transformed science from a "cultural hero to a villain."[19] This decline in trust in the science of food, or what C. Fischler[20] called "gastro-anomie," has been fueled by a diverse set of actors.

*****

Due largely to the popularization of the Internet in the mid-1990s, well-known activist organizations like Greenpeace International, A SEED (Action for Solidarity, Equality, Environment and Diversity), Friends of the Earth, and Via Campesina have been propelled into the global debate on agricultural biotechnology. The Internet allows organizations to communicate to the general and "converted" publics with relative ease and at low cost. The broad suite of network applications available through the Internet facilitates organizational needs around coordination and planning, and allows organizations to adopt a niche strategy that minimizes overlap on issues and campaigns, and assists in strategic fund-raising. Although many organizations such as Greenpeace Canada began moving in this direction prior to the Internet,[21] there is little doubt that the Internet, and its concomitant emergence with genetically modified foods onto the marketplace, has helped spawn a highly organized campaign of resistance against these foods. A question posed by Maria Margaronis on resistance to agricultural biotechnology will serve as a focus for the remainder of this section of the chapter: "How did a loose assemblage of European environmental activists, development charities, food retailers and supermarket shoppers stop a huge multinational industry, temporarily at least, in its tracks?"[22]

On a global basis, there are literally hundreds of civil society groups that focus, more or less, on issues related to agricultural biotechnology. An examination of the Web sites of Greenpeace International, A SEED Europe, Friends of the Earth, and Via Campesina was undertaken. These organizations are involved heavily in debates on agricultural biotechnology, and tend to have Web sites that are linked to frequently by a range of civil society groups, governments, and even industry actors.[23] A common underlying goal of these organizations is to expose and debunk arguments about the benefits of agricultural biotechnology. Greenpeace International takes a deliberately strong antibiotechnology position and uses a combination of rhetoric, emotionally potent images, and media-savvy protest strategies. For example, the front page of Greenpeace International's Web site (as of April 28, 2003) displayed a field of corn with question mark symbols superimposed over the ears. This particular campaign poses questions on the safety of genetically modified corn with a gene (Bt) that encodes for a protein with pesticidal properties. In an attempt to question the wisdom of investing in modern biotechnology, Greenpeace International states: "Monsanto, the company that gave us PCBs, Agent Orange, pesticides and beef growth hormones, is desperate to get us to plant their genetically engineered (GE) seeds, spray them with their herbicides and eat GE foods. Will they get away with it? Not according to a new study done by Innovest Strategic Value Advisors."[24] In short, this campaign is designed to alarm Monsanto investors by revealing the outcome of a Greenpeace-sponsored study on the corporation's environmental and management practices, and to raise questions on the specific benefits of GE crops to farmers and investors alike.

Another goal common to these organizations is to link the development and use of modern biotechnology to a set of broader social justice issues. For instance, A SEED Europe is an organization with a stated mission of preventing the exploitation of humans and the natural environment by being critical of patriarchal practices, colonialism, scientific reductionism, trade liberalization, and economic globalization. A SEED is a youth-oriented organization that was formed in 1992 following the United Nations Conference on Environment and Development in Rio de Janeiro. A SEED has hubs in Europe, Asia, North America, Africa, Latin America, and Japan. The European hub of A SEED has a campaign directed specifically against agricultural biotechnology. Known as "Ground Up," A SEED Europe states on its Web site: "Genetic engineering in agriculture is a key example of what a trade dominated political agenda means in practice: commercial interests over health and environmental concerns, corporate power over local communities. It is also about the desire to jump over species boundaries that have been in place since life first evolved on our planet billions of years ago and a wish to clone living beings."[25] Clearly, A SEED's biotechnology campaign is highly critical of corporate control over agriculture, and proposes a slippery-slope argument about how the exercise of power in this domain by corporate interests may ultimately lead to the genetic engineering of humans.

Many antibiotechnology organizations have an interest in empowering citizens to make changes in their consuming behavior by directing attention toward regulatory and food-handling issues. For example, Friends of the Earth have used the well-known StarLink corn case to illustrate why agricultural biotechnology is dangerous, requires better regulatory oversight, and needs mandatory labeling provisions for facilitating consumer choice and personal risk management. On its Web site, Friends of the Earth states:

> Past midnight on a summer's evening three years ago, Larry Bohlen walked out of a Safeway supermarket in Silver Spring totaling $66.32 worth of taco shells and other corn products. By the time Bohlen, director of health and environment programs at Friends of the Earth, and his allies in the environmental movement were done having the corn products tested for adulteration, they had forced American food and biotech companies into a recall costing hundreds of millions of dollars. . . . [These] problems have made large American food companies exceedingly nervous about biotechnology. More than half their products in the United States contain biotech ingredients, particularly lecithin or protein made from Roundup Ready soybeans,

and they live in fear that some contamination incident will provoke a U.S. consumer backlash.[26]

The quote from Friends of the Earth demonstrates how antibiotechnology organizations have taken into their own hands the task of testing food for what they perceive as "contaminants." Obviously, there is little trust in regulators to carry out these tasks in a timely or credible manner.

Last, the antibiotechnology organizations examined have a strong interest in promoting food sovereignty. For instance, Via Campesina connects food sovereignty with gender issues, human rights, agrarian reform, and biodiversity/biosafety issues. For Via Campesina, food sovereignty is a basic right that allows nations to define their own agricultural and food policies.[27] To achieve these goals, Via Campesina suggests (1) placing a priority on producing food for the domestic market that is healthy, of good quality, and is culturally appropriate; (2) providing payments to farmers that protect them from low-cost imports of food; (3) regulating production of the domestic market in order to avoid the creation of surpluses; (4) stopping the process of industrialization of production methods and promoting sustainable production through the family farm; and (5) abolishing all direct and indirect export aids. To help achieve these goals, Via Campesina has played a major role in the development of international networks, and has been involved in coordinating protests at various meetings of the WTO. Additionally, these campaigns, both implicitly and explicitly, provide critiques of agricultural biotechnology. Many of these critiques have been supported by other antibiotechnology organizations and by notable activists such as Vandana Shiva, David Suzuki, Brewster Kneen, and even Prince Charles.

The goals examined above illustrate the tremendous degree of overlap in the critiques of agricultural biotechnology put forward by key antibiotechnology organizations. By questioning the benefits (to producers and investors), the motivations of corporations involved in the sector, regulatory and consumer-oriented issues, and food sovereignty, these antibiotechnology organizations demonstrate how agricultural biotechnology generates new, or intensified, public sector–private sector boundary conflicts, and new debates about how best to serve the public good. Very few antibiotechnology campaigns deal with the scientific framing of issues (e.g., usually risk-based) that are promulgated by industry and enforced by governmental regulation. In fact, the issues raised by antibiotechnology organizations generally avoid these narrowly defined areas of concern (e.g., substantial equivalence, toxicity, and allergenicity), and concentrate on social and ethical issues.

*****

The emergence of modern biotechnology as a tool for producing crops with novel characteristics is the result of international collaborations between government, industry (chemical, seed, and life science sectors), university, and philanthropic actors. In Canada, the development of canola from rapeseed illustrates how University of Saskatchewan and Agriculture Canada researchers (a narrower set of actors than is in vogue currently) cooperated to develop a crop that is now the second most important in the prairie provinces (next to wheat).[28] The "Green Revolution" also spawned other kinds of agricultural research initiatives. For instance, the Consultative Group on International Agricultural Research (CGIAR) was formed in 1971 to promote applied and strategic research to improve the productivity of agriculture in the developing world. The stated mission of CGIAR is "to contribute to food security and poverty eradication in developing countries through research, partnerships, capacity building, and policy support, promoting sustainable agricultural development based on the environmentally sound management of natural resources."[29] CGIAR's research programs focus on poverty reduction, soil and water management, the protection of biodiversity through genebanking (also known as germplasm banking), and a commitment to using biotechnology in a sustainable fashion that is sensitive to ethical and safety issues. The role of philanthropic organizations like the Rockefeller Foundation is central to CGIAR's success. However, the development of so-called Golden Rice, and its framing by the biotechnology industry, may signal a shift in how philanthropic organizations may be thinking about their roles, and be another example of the unbinding of politics.

The Rockefeller Foundation was one of the original sixteen members of the CGIAR. However, its agricultural research activities date back to 1943 with the establishment of a food crops program in Mexico. With the Ford Foundation, the Rockefeller Foundation established the International Rice Research Institute (1959), the International Maize and Wheat Improvement Center (1963), the International Center for Tropical Agriculture (1967), and the International Institute for Tropical Agriculture (1967). However, Rockefeller is probably best known for its support of research on Golden Rice.[30] Invented by Ingo Protrykus and Peter Beyer, Golden Rice is a grain modified to express higher levels of beta-carotene and other carotenoids by inserting two genes from the daffodil plant and one from a bacterium into the japonica rice genome. Beta-carotene is a precursor for the synthesis of vitamin A, and is widely considered to be a necessary component of a healthy diet. Proponents of Golden Rice technology believe that making this product available to people in the developing world will help reduce vitamin A deficiency, and consequently lower mortality and the partial or total blindness that often accompanies this deficiency.

The creation of Golden Rice, and efforts to eventually make it freely available to the developing world, is a complex story. In short, the seventy or so pieces of technology that make Golden Rice viable were encumbered by patents held by the original inventors and by large biotechnology companies like AstraZeneca and Monsanto. In an uncharacteristic move, patent holders have agreed to make this technology available to the developing world at no charge, and to explore commercial opportunities for selling Golden Rice and other nutritionally enhanced products in the developed world. This is helping to make the mission of the Rockefeller Foundation a reality, but poses new challenges to its legitimacy.[31]

Since most of the products of agricultural biotechnology provide benefits primarily to producers and others in the supply chain (e.g., herbicide tolerance), several criticisms have been leveled at the industry. In short, opponents of agricultural biotechnology claim that this technology offers few benefits to consumers; exposes humans and the natural environment to unknown risks; concentrates corporate power even more fully; threatens traditional agriculture through patenting, experimental sterility technologies (e.g., Terminator), and use agreements; and poses a threat to the social cohesiveness of rural communities.[32] However, Golden Rice has become a foil against the claim that agricultural biotechnology represents the epitome of corporate greed in a globalizing world.

By supporting the development of Golden Rice technology, philanthropic organizations such as the Rockefeller Foundation have pushed research on biotechnology in a positive direction, and have improved generally the image of biotechnology. Simultaneously, Golden Rice has become a powerful propaganda tool for the biotechnology industry. According to Paul Brown, Syngenta made claims that every month of delay in marketing this technology to the developing world leads to fifty thousand more children going blind. Even former U.S. president Bill Clinton purportedly stated in 2000 that "if we could get more of this Golden Rice, which is a genetically modified strain of rice especially rich in vitamin A, out to the developing world, it could save 4,000 lives a day."[33] Clearly, there are many cheerleaders for this technology.

Critics of Golden Rice have also been highly vocal. In general, concerns have been raised on safety and environmental impacts, about the amount of Golden Rice that needs to be consumed in order to realize health benefits, the wisdom of pursuing this technology when lower-technology solutions are available (e.g., cultivation of yellow sweet potatoes and dark-green leafy vegetables), and the amount of inputs required in terms of irrigation, fertilizers, and herbicides for growing new hybrids. Vandana Shiva, the director of the Research Foundation for Science, Technology and Ecology, states that:

> Golden Rice is based on a false premise. The destruction of biodiversity by industrial agriculture is a primary cause of today's vitamin A deficiency across rural India, and it is only through rejuvenating biodiversity on our farms that we can solve problems of vitamin deficiency and malnutrition. In spite of all the hype about Golden Rice, it will not solve the vitamin A deficiency problems.[34]

These arguments about Golden Rice are making a dent. In response to Shiva's observation, Gordon Conway of the Rockefeller Foundation agreed that the "public relations uses of Golden Rice have gone too far," and that "[Rockefeller] does not consider Golden Rice to be the solution to the vitamin A deficiency problem."[35] In his own book, Conway suggests that biotechnology is needed to meet the needs of a growing global population, and that innovative public-private partnerships are required to prevent multinational corporations from monopolizing patents and consequently impairing the flow of benefits.[36]

The debate over Golden Rice has stimulated a different manifestation of the unbinding of politics. Antibiotechnology groups have traditionally expressed concerns that the social and ethical issues around biotechnology have been ignored in favor of scientific and economic considerations. However, Golden Rice poses a challenge to the moral authority of those who uniformly take an antibiotechnology stance, and may force such groups to rethink their positions. Philanthropic organizations such as Rockefeller risk losing credibility when research that they support becomes a propaganda tool for the biotechnology industry. By embracing the argument that some applications of agricultural biotechnology have humanitarian purposes, the agrochemical and pharmaceutical companies involved in this research and commercialization have shifted, perhaps somewhat unwittingly, toward a hybrid of civil society and philanthropic positions. These shifts represent an unbinding of politics, since most of the positioning around these debates touches minimally the official political machinery of the state. Additionally, although all products of agricultural biotechnology must go through a science-based assessment as part of the state's regulatory functions, technologies like Golden Rice are forcing a quasi-public debate on risk versus benefit on several subpolitical levels. This represents a challenge to regulating agricultural biotechnology in countries such as Canada and the United States where an approval system based on substantial equivalence only considers metabolic profiles for evidence of toxicity, allergenicity, and changes in nutritional composition of novel (modified) foods. Due to the support of the Rockefeller Foundation and others of Golden Rice, the unbinding of politics continues at a variable pace on a global level and has introduced nonregulatory issues into the equation.

Nonregulatory issues pose a significant challenge to the commercialization of genetically modified crops, as well as a growing problem for regulators. In other words, civil society and philanthropic organizations facilitate the unbinding of politics by exposing the inadequacy of science-based assessment, and by proposing novel kinds of issues and framing that allow, in theory, nonexpert citizen engagement in science and technology policy making and risk-versus-benefit analysis. At the same time, private sector interests are being forced to deal with the rising popularity of these traditionally nonregulatory issues, and are beginning to demonstrate an interest in engaging civil society in these debates. These new alignments are the result of an unbinding of politics, and are fueled by forces of economic and social globalization. To wit, economic globalization results in a weakening of nation-states and a strong impetus to ensure that scientifically defensible policies are put in place. For instance, many international agreements (e.g., Codex Alimentarius) require that only scientific reasons can be used to restrict entry of a food product from a trading partner.[37] Simultaneously, social globalization increases the reach and influence of civil society by forging new alliances, improving coordination and planning through the use of the Internet, and by amplifying a global undercurrent of concern about the social and ethical issues surrounding agricultural biotechnology. In closing, genetic modification is more than a sounding board for agricultural issues because it stimulates a materialization of the risk society and promotes an unbinding of politics.

Endnotes

[1] Ulrich Beck, "The Reinvention of Politics: Towards a Theory of Reflexive Modernization," in U. Beck, A. Giddens, S. Lash (eds.) *Reflexive Modernization: Politics, Tradition and Aesthetics in the Modern Social Order*, Polity Press, Cambridge, UK, 1994;   Ulrich Beck, *The Reinvention of Politics: Rethinking Modernity in the Global Social Order*, Polity Press, Cambridge, UK, 1997.

[2] Michael D. Mehta, "The Public in Re-licensing Nuclear Facilities in Canada: The 'Risk Society' in Action," *Electronic Journal of Sociology*, 3:1, 1997.

[3] Ulrich Beck, *Risk Society: Towards a New Modernity*, Sage. London, 1992, p.19; Beck, "The Reinvention of Politics." p. 8.

[4] Sheila Jasanoff, "Product, Process, or Programme: Three Cultures and the Regulation of Biotechnology," in M. Bauer (ed.) *Resistance to New Technology: Nuclear Power, Information Technology and Biotechnology*, Cambridge University Press, Cambridge, UK, 1995, pp. 311-31.

[5] D. Powell and W. Leiss, *Mad Cows and Mothers' Milk: The Perils of Poor Risk Communication*, McGill-Queen's University Press, Montreal, 1998.

[6] M. Aiken, "Reflexive Modernization and the Social Economy," *Studies in Social and Political Thought*, www.sussex.ac.uk/Units/SPT/journal/archive/issue2-1, 2000.

[7] Michael D. Mehta, "Risk and Decision-Making: A Theoretical Approach to Public Participation in Techno-Social Conflict Situations," *Technology in Society*, 20, 1998, pp. 87–98.

[8] See Beck, *Risk Society;* and Beck, *Reinvention of Politics*. Also refer to Anthony Giddens, *The Consequences of Modernity*, Stanford University Press, Stanford, CA, 1990; and Anthony Giddens, *Runaway World: How Globalization is Re-Shaping Our Lives*, Routledge, NY, 2000.

[9] P. K. Eisinger, "The Conditions of Protest Behavior in American Cities," *American Political Science Review*, 67, 1973, pp. 11–28; Sidney Tarrow, *Power in Movement: Social Movements and Contentious Politics*, Cambridge University Press, Cambridge, UK, 1998.

[10] A. Touraine, *Critique of Modernity*, Blackwell Publishers, Cambridge, UK, 1995.

[11] Georg W. Hegel, *The Philosophy of Right* (trans. T. M. Knox), Oxford University Press, Oxford, UK, [1821] 1967.

[12] S. Avineri, *Hegel's Theory of the Modern State*, Cambridge University Press, Cambridge, UK, 1972.

[13] B. Edwards and M. W. Foley, "Social Capital and Civil Society Beyond Putnam," *American Behavioral Scientist*, 42:1, 1998, pp. 124–39.

[14] A. Melucci, *Nomads of the Present*, Temple University Press, Philadelphia, 1989.

[15] Giddens, *Runaway World*.

[16] Brian Wynne, "Sheep Farming After Chernobyl: A Case Study in Communicating Scientific Information," *Environment*, 31:2, 1989, pp. 11-39.

[17] David Held, *Cosmopolitan Democracy and the Global Order*, Polity Press, Cambridge, UK, 1995.

[18] Peter Rosset, "A New Food Movement Comes of Age in Seattle," in K. Danaher and R. Burbach (eds.) *Globalize This! The Battle Against the World Trade Organization and Corporate Rule*, Common Courage Press, Monroe, ME, 2000, pp. 135–40. Also Rosset, "Towards a Political Economy of Opinion Formation on Genetically Modified Foods," *Medical Anthropology Quarterly*, 15:1, 2001.

[19] R. Fitzgerald and H. Campbell, "Food Scares and GM: Movement on the Nature/Culture Fault Line," *The Drawing Board: An Australian Review of Public Affairs*, University of Sydney, 2001: www.econ.usyd.edu.au/drawingboard.

[20] C. Fischler, "Gastronomie et gastro-anomie: Sagesse du corps et crise bioculturelle de l'alimentation moderne. *Communications*, 31: 1979, pp. 189–210.

[21] E. Ouellet, "Organizational Analysis and Environmental Sociology: The Case of Greenpeace Canada," in M. D. Mehta and E. Ouellet (eds.) *Environmental Sociology: Theory and Practice*, Captus Press, Toronto, 1995, pp. 321–37.

[22] Maria Margaronis, "The Politics of Food," *The Nation*, December 27, 1999: www.thenation.com/doc.mhtml?i=19991227&s=margaronis.

[23] Using Google, I examined the number of Web sites that link to these organizations directly. As of April 28, 2003, I was able to record the following link counts: www.greenpeace.org (11,200); www.aseed.net (844); www.foe.org (3,070); www.ns.rds.org.hn/via/ (294). Although these link counts represent external interest in the organization, and not just an interest in their biotechnology campaigns, the data provide evidence on the relative success of these organizations in building linkages. Such linkages are surrogate indicators of network density and perhaps of influence.

[24] "Monsanto: Heading for Disaster?" www.greenpeace.org/news.

[25] "Welcome to A SEED genetic engineering website," www.groundup.org/fabout.htm.

[26] "Quotable Quotes," www.foe.org.

[27] "Food Sovereignty and International Trade," www.ns.rds.org.hn.

[28] The first rapeseed variety, known as "Golden," was registered in 1954. For a history of canola, see P. Phillips and G. G. Khachatourians (eds.), *The Biotechnology Revolution in Global Agriculture: Invention, Innovation, and Investment in the Canola Sector,* Cabi Publishing, Wallingford, UK, 2001.

[29] "Who We Are," www.cgiar.org/who/index.

[30] Golden Rice research was supported also by the Swiss Federal Institute of Technology, the European Union under a community biotechnology program known as FAIR, and the Swiss Federal Office for Education and Science.

[31] John D. Rockefeller's original mandate was "to promote the well-being of mankind throughout the world," Rockefeller Archive Center, "The Charter (1910–1913)," in *Source Book for a History of the Rockefeller Foundation,* RF History, vol. 7, Rockefeller Foundation Archives, RAC, p. 6.

[32] Michael D. Mehta, "Agricultural Biotechnology and Social Cohesion: Is the Social Fabric of Rural Communities at Risk?" paper presented at the Canadian Weed Science Society Meeting, November 27, 2002. The proceedings of the conference are available at www.arts.usask.ca/policynut/mehta-cwss-proceedings.doc.

[33] Paul Brown, "GM Rice Promoters Have Gone Too Far," 2001, available at: www.biotech-info.net/too_far.html.

[34] Vandana Shiva, "World in a Grain of Rice," *The Ecologist* 2000. Shiva states that rice is more than just a foodstuff; it is an entire culture. And it's under threat," For more information, see www.theecologist.org/archive. November 22, 2000, article 167.

[35] Quoted in Brown, "GM Rice Promoters."

[36] Gordon Conway, *The Doubly Green Revolution,* Penguin Books, London, 1997.

[37] The Codex Alimentarius is administered jointly by the Food and Agriculture Organization (FAO) and World Health Organization (WHO). Codex's main goal is to "guide and promote the elaboration and establishment of definitions and requirements for foods to assist in their harmonization and in doing so to facilitate international trade." Codex recognizes provisions of the Sanitary and Phytosanitary (SPS) and the Technical Barriers to Trade (TBT) agreements. As such, it "acknowledges that governments have the right to take sanitary and phytosanitary measures necessary for the protection of human health. However, the SPS Agreement requires them to apply those measures only to the extent required to protect human health. It does not permit Member Governments to discriminate by applying different requirements to different countries where the same or similar conditions prevail, unless there is sufficient scientific justification for doing so." This is available at www.fao.org.

ABOUT THE AUTHORS

Helmut K. Anheier is the director of the Center for Civil Society at the School of Public Policy and Social Research, University of California, Los Angeles, and Centennial Professor in the Department of Social Policy at the London School of Economics. He is a founding board member of the International Society for Third-Sector Research and the founding editor of *Voluntas*, the international journal of research on nonprofit organizations. His recent publications include *Private Funds—Public Purpose* (Plenum, 1999) and *When Things Go Wrong–Organizational Failures and Breakdowns* (Sage, 1999).

Victoria Lyon Bestor is executive director of the North American Coordinating Council on Japanese Library Resources. She has coauthored several publications, including *Doing Fieldwork in Japan* (University of Hawaii Press, 2003), "The Philanthropic Roots of the Voluntary and Nonprofit Sector in Japan: The Rockefeller Legacy," in *The Voluntary and Nonprofit Sector in Japan: An Emerging Response to a Changing Society*, edited by Stephen B. Osborne (Routledge, 2003), and "Toward a Cultural Biography of Civil Society in Japan" in *Family and Social Policy in Japan: Anthropological Approaches*, edited by Roger Goodman (Cambridge University Press, 2002).

Kathy Brock is an associate professor and head of public policy and the third sector in the School of Policy Studies at Queen's University, Kingston, Ontario. Her most recent work includes *Delicate Dancers: Public Policy and the Nonprofit Sector* (McGill-Queen's University Press, 2003). She has served as the documentalist and occasional advisor to the federal government and voluntary sector, and has recently completed a survey of national leaders on globalization.

David Brook is a senior research associate at the Public Policy Forum in Ottawa, Ontario. In this capacity, he has organized and participated in numerous roundtables and panels on public policy issues including globalization, the environment, transportation, energy efficiency, and the implications of biometrics for citizenship and immigration. He recently completed a survey of national leaders on globalization.

Siobhan Daly is research manager of *Visions and Roles of Foundations in Europe* at the Centre for Civil Society, London School of Economics. Her recent publications include an annotated bibliography (with Helmut Anheier) of the Europeanization of social policy entitled *The European Union* (Observatory for the Development of Social Services in Europe, 2003), and "The Ladder of Abstraction: A Framework for the Systematic Classification of Democratic Regime Types," published in *Politics,* (May 2003). Her current research focuses on research methodology and the comparative analysis of foundations in Europe.

Janice Elliott is vice president of the Public Policy Forum in Ottawa, Ontario. She is an internationally recognized expert on citizen participation and consultation. She has organized various roundtables and completed numerous studies with the Forum on leading policy issues. She is actively engaged in advising policy makers on achieving a more open and inclusive policy process.

Peter Frumkin is associate professor of public policy at Harvard University. He is the author of *On Being Nonprofit* (Harvard University Press, 2002). His research interests include all aspects of philanthropy. Previously, he held positions as foundation program officer, nonprofit manager, and program evaluator in both nonprofit and public agencies.

Raymond Grew, Professor of History Emeritus, University of Michigan, and for many years editor of the journal *Comparative Studies in Society and History*, has received a number of awards for his work on the social and cultural history of modern France and Italy. He also writes on approaches to historical comparison and global history. His most recent book is an edited volume, *The Construction of Minorities*, (University of Michigan Press, 2001).

Gary R. Hess is Distinguished Research Professor of History at Bowling Green State University. A specialist in American foreign relations, Hess's research interests focus on U.S. political and cultural interests in South Asia. His publications include *Sam Higginbottom of Allahabad: Pioneer of Point Four to India* (University Press of Virginia, 1967) and *America Encounters India* (Johns Hopkins University Press, 1971). He is a four-time Fulbright scholar/lecturer in India.

Michael D. Mehta is an associate professor of sociology at the University of Saskatchewan. He is also director of the Sociology of Biotechnology Program and director of the Social Research Unit at the university. His research interests include risk perception and risk communication, environmental sociology, and the sociology of cyberspace.

Balmurli Natrajan is assistant professor of anthropology at Iowa State University. His research interests are globalization, development, artisans, community, technology, caste, and social theory. He has conducted field-based research in central India and United States and has recently begun a long-term study of the process of privatization in India and the discourses and practices of economic liberalization.

Lester M. Salamon is professor and director of the Center for Civil Society Studies of the Institute for Policy Studies at the Johns Hopkins University. He is a leading expert on alternative tools of government action and on the nonprofit sector in the United States and around the world. He has written or edited over a dozen books, and his articles have appeared recently in *Foreign Affairs, Social Service Review, the New York Times, Voluntas,* and numerous other publications.

Wolf Schäfer is professor of history and director of the Center for Global History at Stony Brook University. Having published on labor history, the history of science and technology, and new global history, he is currently completing a book of theoretical essays on global history.

The Editors

Soma Hewa is the principal investigator of a research program on philanthropy, civil society, and nonprofit activities based in Montreal (Châteauguay), Quebec. He taught sociology at Mount Royal College, Calgary, and the University of British Columbia, Vancouver. He has published widely in the sociology of health, philanthropy, and sociological theory. His major publications include *Colonialism, Tropical Disease and Imperial Medicine: Rockefeller Philanthropy in Sri Lanka* (University Press of America, 1995) and *Philanthropy and Cultural Context: Western Philanthropy in South, East, and Southeast Asia in the 20ᵗʰ Century* (University Press of America, 1997; co-edited with P. Hove).

Darwin H. Stapleton is the executive director of the Rockefeller Archive Center of the Rockefeller University, New York. He has published extensively in the history of science, technology, public health, philanthropy, and education. His most recent publications include *Dignity, Discourse and Destiny: The Life of Courtney C. Smith* (University of Delaware Press, 2004; coauthored with Donna H. Stapleton). He is a graduate of Swarthmore College and holds a doctorate in history from the University of Delaware.

SELECTED BIBLIOGRAPHY

The editors prepared the following list of readings on globalization, philanthropy, and civil society. Some items listed in the endnotes are not included here. For the archival sources quoted in the texts, readers should refer to the endnotes.

Akami, T., "The Rise and Fall of a 'Pacific Sense': Experiment of the Institute of Pacific Relations, 1925–1930," *Journal of Shibusawa Studies*, 7, October, 1994, pp. 2–37.

Albrow, M., *The Global Age: State and Society Beyond Modernity,* Stanford University Press, Stanford, CA, 1997.

Anderson, B., *Imagined Communities: Reflections on the Origin and Spread of Nationalism,* Verso, London, 1983.

Andrews, F. E., *Philanthropic Giving,* Russell Sage Foundation, NY, 1950.

Anheier, H. K., M. Glasius, and M. Kaldor (eds.), *Global Civil Society,* Oxford University Press, Oxford, 2001.

Anheier, H. K. and J. Kendall (eds.), *Third Sector Policy at the Crossroads: An International Nonprofit Analysis,* Routledge, London, 2001.

Anheier, H. K. and W. Seibel, *The Nonprofit Sector in Germany,* Manchester University Press, Manchester, UK, 2001.

Anheier, H. K. *When Things Go Wrong: Organisational Failures and Breakdowns*, Sage, London, 1999.

Anheier, H. K. and S. Toepler (eds.), *Private Funds—Public Purpose: Philanthropic Foundations in International Perspectives*, Plenum Publishers, NY, 1999.

Appadurai, A., *Modernity at Large: Cultural Dimensions of Globalization,* University of Minnesota Press, Minneapolis, 1996.

Archambault, E., *The Nonprofit Sector in France,* Manchester University Press, Manchester, UK, 1996.

Arnove, R. F., *Philanthropy and Cultural Imperialism,* Indiana University Press, Bloomington, 1982.

Arnove, R. F. (ed.), *Philanthropy and Cultural Imperialism: The Foundations at Home and Abroad,* G. K. Hall, Boston, MA, 1980.

Avineri, S., *Hegel's Theory of the Modern State,* Cambridge University Press, Cambridge, UK, 1972.

Azumi, K., "Voluntary Associations in Japan," in D. H. Smith (ed.) *Voluntary Action Research: The Nature of Voluntary Action Around the World*, Lexington Books, Lexington, MA, 1974, pp. 15–26.

Barbetta, G. P. (ed.), *The Nonprofit Sector in Italy*, Manchester University Press, Manchester, UK, 1997.

Barlow, M. and T. Clarke, *Global Showdown: How the New Activists are Fighting Global Corporate Rule*, Stoddart, Toronto, 2001.

Barraclough, G., "Universal History," in H. P. R. Finberg (ed.) *Approaches to History*, University of Toronto Press, Toronto, 1962.

Barraclough, G., "History in a Changing World," University of Oklahoma Press, Norman, 1955.

Barshay, A., "Capitalism and Civil Society in Postwar Japan: Perspectives from Intellectual history," in F. J. Schwartz and S. J. Pharr (eds.) *The State of Civil Society in Japan*, Cambridge University Press, London, 2003.

Baylis J. and S. Smith (eds.), *The Globalization of World Politics: An Introduction to International Relations*, Oxford University Press, Oxford, 1997.

Beck, U., *The Reinvention of Politics: Rethinking Modernity in the Global Social Order*, Polity Press, Cambridge, UK, 1997.

Beck, U., *Risk Society: Towards a New Modernity*, Sage, London, 1992.

Berliner, S. H., *A System of Scientific Medicine: Philanthropic Foundations in the Flexner Era*, Tavistock Publications, NY, 1985.

Berman, E. H., *The Influence of the Carnegie, Ford, and Rockefeller Foundations in American Foreign Policy: The Ideology of Philanthropy*, State University of New York Press, Albany, NY, 1983.

Bertelsmann Foundation, *Foundations in Europe: Society, Management and Law*, Directory of Social Change, London, 2001.

Bestor, V. L. and R. Maekawa, "The Philanthropic Roots of the Voluntary and Nonprofit Sector in Japan: The Rockefeller Legacy," in S. P. Osborne (ed.) *The Voluntary and Nonprofit Sector in Japan: An Emerging Response to a Changing Society*, Routledge, London, 2003.

Bestor, V. L., "Toward a Cultural Biography of Civil Society in Japan," in R. Goodman (ed.) *Family and Social Policy in Japan: Anthropological Approaches*, Cambridge University Press, London, 2002.

Bourdieu, P., *Outline of a Theory of Practice*, Cambridge University Press, Cambridge, UK, 1979.

Bourdieu, P., *Practical Reason*, Stanford University Press, Stanford, CA, 1998.

Braibante, R. J. D., "Neighborhood Associations in Japan and Their Democratic Potentialities," *Far Eastern Quarterly*, vol. 7, 1948, pp. 136–64.

Bratton, M., "Beyond the State: Civil Society and Associational Life in Africa," *World Politics*, vol. 41, 1989, pp. 407–30.

Bremner, R., *American Philanthropy*, University of Chicago Press, Chicago, 1988.

Brenner, N., "Beyond State-centrism? Space, Territoriality, and Geographical Scale in Globalization Studies," *Theory and Society*, vol. 28, 1999, pp. 39–78.

Brock, K. L., (ed.), *Delicate Dances: Public Policy and the Nonprofit Sector*, McGill-Queen's University Press, Montreal, 2003.

Brown, E. R., *Rockefeller Medicine Men*, University of California Press, Berkeley, CA, 1979.

Bu, L., "Cultural Understanding and World Peace: The Roles of Private Institutions in the Interwar Years," *Peace and Change*, 24: 2 (April), 1999, pp. 148–73.

Büchmann, G., *Geflügelte Worte*, Fischer Bücherei, Frankfurt Am Main, 1st edition 1864, Reprint, 1957.

Burawoy, M., "For a Sociological Marxism: The Complementary Convergence of Antonio Gramsci and Karl Polanyi," *Politics and Society*, vol. 31, 2003, pp. 193–261.

Buse K. and G. Walt, "Global Public–Private Partnerships: Part I–A New Development in Health?" *Bulletin of the World Health Organization*, 78:4, 2000, pp. 549–61.

Buse K. and G. Walt, "Global Public–Private Partnerships: Part II–What are the Health Issues for Global Governance?" *Bulletin of the World Health Organization*, 78:5, 2000, pp. 699–709.

Caldwell, J. and P. Caldwell, *Limiting Population and the Ford Foundation Contribution*, Pinter Publishers, London, 1986.

Cameron, D. and J. G. Stein (eds.), *Street Protests and Fantasy Parks: Globalisation, Culture and the State*, University of British Columbia Press, Vancouver, 2002.

Chase-Dunn, C., *Global Formation: Structures of the World-Economy*, Basil Blackwell, Cambridge, UK, 1989.

Chomsky, N., *Profit over People: Neoliberalism and the Global Order*, Seven Stories Press, NY, 1999.

Chomsky, N., *Class Warfare–Interviews with David Barsamian*, Pluto Press, London, 1996.

Clark, J., *Worlds Apart: Civil Society and the Battle for Ethical Globalization*, Kumarian Press, Bloomfield, CT, 2003.

Clark, R. P., *The Global Imperative: An Interpretive History of the Spread of Mankind*, Global History Series, (eds.) B. Mazlish, C. Gluck, and R. Grew, Westview Press, Boulder, CO, 1997.

Clifford, J., *The Predicament of Culture*, Harvard University Press, Cambridge, MA, 1988.

Clinton, B., "Globalization—America's Final Frontier," *The Independent Review*, London, January 31, 2000, p .4.

Cohen, J. L. and A. Arato, *Civil Society and Political Theory*, MIT Press, Cambridge, MA, 1997.

Colby, G. with C. Dennet, *Thy Will Be Done: The Conquest of the Amazon: Nelson Rockefeller and Evangelism in the Age of Oil*, Harper Collins, NY, 1995.

Coleman, J., *Foundations of Social Theory*, Harvard University Press, Cambridge, MA, 1990.

Conway, G., *The Doubly Green Revolution*, Penguin Books, London, 1997.

Cornia, G. A., *Liberalization, Globalization and Income Distribution*, WIDER Working Papers 157, Wider, Helsinki, 1999.

Correa C. M., *Intellectual Property Rights: the WTO and Developing Countries*, Zed Books and Third World Network, London, 2000.

Courchene, T. J., *A State of Minds: Toward a Human Capital Future for Canadians*, Institute for Research on Public Policy (IRPP), Montreal, 2000.

Cox, K. R. (ed.), *Spaces of Globalization: Reasserting the Power of the Local*, Guilford Press, NY, 1997.

Critchlow, D. T., "Implementing Family Planning Policy: Philanthropic Foundations and the Modern Welfare State," in D. T. Critchlow and C. H. Parker (eds.) *With Us*

Always: A History of Private Charity and Public Welfare, Rowman and Littlefield Publishers, New York, 1998, pp. 210–40.

Curti, M., *American Philanthropy Abroad: A History*, Rutgers University Press, New Brunswick, NJ, 1963.

Curtin, P., *Cross-cultural Trade in World History, Studies in Comparative World History*, Cambridge University Press, NY, 1984.

Dasgupta, P. and I. Serageldin (eds.), *Social Capital: A Multifaceted Perspective*, World Bank, Washington, DC, 1999.

Deakin, N., *In Search of Civil Society*, Palgrave, Basingstoke, UK, 2001.

Defourny, J. and P. Develtere, *The Social Economy: The Worldwide Making of a Third Sector*, Centre d'Economie Sociale, Liège, 1999.

Derber, C., *People Before Profit: The New Globalisation in an Age of Terror, Big Money and Economic Crisis*, St. Martin's Press, NY, 2002.

Derrida, J., *Specters of Marx*, (trans.) Peggy Kamuf, Routledge, NY, 1993.

Dowie, M., *American Foundations: An Investigative History*, MIT Press, Cambridge, MA, 2002.

Edwards, B. and M. W. Foley, "Social Capital and Civil Society Beyond Putnam," *American Behavioral Scientist*, vol. 42, 1998, pp. 124–39.

Edwards, B., M. W. Foley, and M. Diani, *Beyond Tocqueville: Civil Society and the Social Capital Debate in Comparative Perspective*, University Press of New England, Hanover, NH, 2001.

Edwards, M. and D. Hulme (eds.), *Beyond the Magic Bullet: NGO Performance and Accountability in the Post–Cold War World*, Macmillan, London, 1995.

Eisenstadt, S. N., *The Political Systems of Empires*, Free Press of Glencoe, London, 1963.

Eisinger, P. K., "The Conditions of Protest Behavior in American Cities," *American Political Science Review*, vol. 67, 1973, pp. 11–28.

Epstein, S., *The Buying of the American Mind*, Center for Public Integrity, Washington, DC, 1990.

Eto, S. (ed.), *Exhibition for Benefit Auction for Blanchette H. Rockefeller Fellowship Fund*, n.p., Tokyo, 1995.

European Commission, *The Commission and Non-Governmental Organisations: Building a Stronger Partnership*, Discussion Paper, European Commission, Brussels, 2000.

European Commission, *Promoting the Role of Voluntary Organisations and Foundations in Europe*, Office of Official Publications of the European Communities, Luxembourg, 1997.

Featherstone, M., S. Lash, and R. Robertson (eds.), *Global Modernities*, Sage, London, 1995.

Featherstone, M. (ed.), *Global Culture: Nationalism, Globalization and Modernity*, Sage, London, 1990.

Ferguson, N., *Empire: The Rise and Demise of the British World Order and the Lessons for Global Power*, Basic Books, NY, 2003.

Ferlie, E. (ed.), *The New Public Management in Action*, Oxford University Press, Oxford, UK, 1996.

Fidler, P. D., "The Globalization of Public Health: the first 100 years of International Health Diplomacy," *Special Theme—Globalization, Bulletin of the World Health Organization*, vol. 79, 2001, pp. 842–49.

Fischer, E., *The Passing of the European Age: A Study of the Transfer of Western Civilization and Its Renewal in Other Continents*, Harvard University Press, Cambridge, MA, 1943 (Revised edition 1948).

Fisher, J., *The Road from Rio: Sustainable Development and the Nongovernmental Movement in the Third World*, Praeger, Westport, CT, 1993.

Florini, A., *The Third Force: The Rise of Transnational Civil Society*, Washington, DC, and Tokyo: Carnegie Endowment for International Peace and Japan Center for International Exchange, 2000.

Ford Foundation, *The Ford Foundation, 1952–2002; Celebrating 50 Years of Partnership*, 11 vols., Ford Foundation, New Delhi, 2002.

Fosdick, R., *The Story of the Rockefeller Foundation*, Transaction Publishers, New Brunswick, NJ, 1989.

Fox, J., *PostModern Encounters: Chomsky and Globalization*, Icon Books, Duxford, UK, 2001.

Friedman, J., *Cultural Identity and Global Process*, Sage, London, 1994.

Friedman, T. L., *The Lexus and the Olive Tree: Understanding Globalization*, Anchor Books, NY, 2000.

Frumkin, P. and J. B. Imber (eds.), *In Search of the Nonprofit Sector*, Transaction Publishers, New Brunswick, NJ, 2003.

Frumkin, P., *On Being Nonprofit*, Harvard University Press, Cambridge, MA, 2002.

Fukuyama, F, *Trust: Social Virtues and the Creation of Prosperity*, Simon and Schuster, NY, 1995.

Fukuyama, F., *The End of History and The Last Man*, Free Press, NY, 1992.

Garcia-Canclini, N., *Transforming Modernity*, University of Texas Press, Austin, 1993.

Garon, S., *Molding Japanese Minds: The State in Everyday Life*, Princeton University Press, Princeton, NJ, 1997.

Geyer, M. and C. Bright., "World History in a Global Age," *The American Historical Review*, vol. 100, 1995, pp. 1034–60.

Giddens, A., *Runaway World: How Globalization is Re-Shaping Our Lives*, Routledge, NY, 2000.

Giddens, A., *The Third Way and Its Critics*, Polity Press, Cambridge, UK, 2000.

Giddens, A., *The Consequences of Modernity*, Stanford University Press, Stanford, CA, 1990.

Giddens, A., *The Third Way: The Renewal of Social Democracy*, Polity Press, Cambridge, UK, 1998.

Goldsmith, A. A., "The Rockefeller Foundation Indian Agricultural Program: Why It Worked," in S. Hewa and P. Hove (eds.) *Philanthropy and Cultural Context: Western Philanthropy in South, East and Southeast Asia in the Twentieth Century*, University Press of America, Lanham, MD, 1987, pp. 87–114.

Gordon, A. L., "Wealth Equals Wisdom? The Rockefeller and Ford Foundations in India," *Annals of the American Academy of Political and Social Science*, vol. 554, 1997, pp. 104–116.

Grew, R., Comparing *Modern Japan: Are There More Comparisons to Make*, Deutsches Institut für Japanstudien, Tokyo, 2002.

Grew, R., "Culture and Society," in J. A. Davis (ed.) *Italy in the Nineteenth Century*, Oxford University Press, Oxford, UK, 2000.

Grew, R., (ed.), *The Construction of Minorities*, University of Michigan Press, Ann Arbor, 2001.

Grew, R. (ed.), *Food in Global History*, Global History Series, Westview Press, Boulder, CO, 1999.

Gupta, A. and J. Ferguson, *Culture, Power, Place: Explorations in Critical Anthropology*, Duke University Press, Durham, NC, 1997.

Habermas, J., "Kant's Idea of Perpetual Peace, with the Benefit of Two Hundred Years' Hindsight," in J. Bohman and M. Lutz-Bachmann (eds.) *Perpetual Peace: Essays on Kant's Cosmopolitan Ideal*, MIT Press, Cambridge, MA, 1997, pp. 113–53.

Halecki, O., *The Limits and Divisions of European History*, Sheed and Ward, London, 1950.

Hall, A. J., "In Search of Civil Society," in J. A. Hall (ed.) *Civil Society: Theory, History Comparison*, Polity Press, Cambridge, UK, 1996, pp. 1–31.

Halman, L., *The European Values Study: A Third Wave, Source Book of the 1999/2000 European Values Study Surveys*, Tilburg University Press, Tilburg, 2001.

Hamelink, C. J., *Cultural Autonomy in Global Communications*, Longmans, NY, 1983.

Harkavy, O., *Curbing Population Growth: An Insider's Perspective on the Population Movement*, Plenum, NY, 1995.

Harr, J. E. and P. Johnson, *The Rockefeller Century*, Charles Scribner's Sons, NY, 1988.

Harr, J. E. and P. Johnson, *The Rockefeller Conscience: An American Family in Public and Private*, Charles Scribner's Sons, NY, 1991.

Hay, D., *Europe: The Emergence of an Idea*, Edinburgh University Press, Edinburgh, 1968.

Held, D. and A. McGrew, *Globalization and Anti-Globalization*, Polity Press, Cambridge, UK, 2002.

Held, D., A. McGrew, D., Goldblatt and J. Perraton, *Global Transformations: Politics, Economics and Culture*, Polity Press, Cambridge, UK, 1999.

Held, D., *Cosmopolitan Democracy and the Global Order*, Polity Press, Cambridge, UK, 1995.

Hess, G. R., "Waging the Cold War in the Third World: The Foundations and the Challenges of Development," in L. J. Friedman and M. D. McGarvie (eds.) *Charity, Philanthropy, and Civility in American History*, Cambridge University Press, NY, 2002, pp. 319–39.

Hess, G. R., *America Encounters India*, Johns Hopkins University Press, Baltimore, MD, 1971.

Hess, G. R., *Sam Higgenbottom of Allahabad: Pioneer of Point Four to India*, University Press of Virginia, Charlottesville, 1967.

Hewa, S., "Rockefeller Philanthropy and the Flexner Report on Medical Education in the United States," *International Journal of Sociology and Social Policy*, vol. 22, 2002, pp. 1–37.

Hewa, S., "The Protestant Personality and Higher Education: American Philanthropy Beyond the Progressive Era," *International Journal of Politics, Culture, and Society*, vol. 12, 1998, pp. 135–63.

Hewa, S., "The Protestant Ethic and Rockefeller Benevolence: The Religious Impulse in American Philanthropy," *Journal for the Theory of Social Behaviour*, vol. 27, 1997, pp. 419–52.

Hewa, S., *Colonialism, Tropical Disease, and Imperial Medicine: Rockefeller Philanthropy in Sri Lanka*, University Press of America, Lanham, MD, 1995.

Hewa, S. and P. Hove (eds.), *Philanthropy and Cultural Context: Western Philanthropy in South, East and Southeast Asia in the Twentieth Century*, University Press of America, Lanham, MD, 1997.

Hirschmann, A., *Exit, Voice, and Loyalty: Responses to Decline in Firms, Organizations and States*, Harvard University Press, Cambridge, MA, 1970.

Hirst, P. Q. and G. Thompson (eds.), *Globalization in Question: The International Economy and the Possibilities of Governance*, Polity Press, Malden, MA, 1999.

Hopkins, A. G. (ed.), *Globalization in World History*, Pimlico, London, 2002.

Horkheimer, M., *Eclipse of Reason*, Continuum, NY, 1992.

Howell, J. and J. Pearce, *Civil Society and Development: A Critical Exploration*, Lynne Rienner, Denver, CO, 2001.

Howes, D. (ed.), *Cross-Cultural Consumption: Global Markets, Local Realities*, Routledge, London, 1996.

Hulme, D. and M. Edwards, *NGOs, States, and Donors: Too Close for Comfort?* Macmillan, in association with Save the Children, London, 1997.

Hutton, W. and A. Giddens, *Global Capitalism*, New Press, NY, 2000.

Ilchman, W. F., "Philanthropy and Civil Society in Asia," in S. Hewa and P. Hove (eds.) *Philanthropy and Cultural Context: Western Philanthropy in South, East, and Southeast Asia in the Twentieth Century*, University Press of America, Lanham, MD, 1997, pp. 279–93.

Inglehart, R., *Culture Shift in Advanced Industrial Society*, Princeton University Press, NJ, 1990.

Iriye, A., *The Globalizing of America, 1913–1945*, Cambridge University Press, Cambridge, UK, 1993.

James, E., "The Non-profit Sector in Comparative Perspective," in W. W. Powell (ed.) *The Non-profit Sector: A Research Handbook*, Yale University Press, New Haven, CT, 1987.

Joseph, C. K., *Philanthropic Foundations in the Twentieth Century*, Greenwood Press, Westport, CT, 2000.

Kant, I., "Perpetual Peace," in Lewis White Beck (trans.) *On History*, The Library of Liberal Arts, NY, 1963, pp. 84–135.

Keck, M. and K. Sikkink, *Activists Beyond Borders: Advocacy Networks in International Politics*, Cornell University Press, Ithaca, NY, 1998.

Khagram, S., J. Riker and K. Sikkink (eds.), *Restructuring World Politics: Transnational Social Movements, Networks, and Norms*, University of Minnesota Press, Minneapolis, 2002.

King, A. D. (ed.), *Culture, Globalization and the World-System: Contemporary Conditions for the Representation of Identity*, University of Minnesota Press, Minneapolis, 1997.

Korten, D., *Getting to the Twenty-first Century: Voluntary Action and the Global Agenda*, Kumarian Press, Hartford, CT, 1990.

Kramer, R., *Voluntary Agencies in the Welfare State*, University of California Press, Berkeley, CA, 1981.

Lagemann, C. (ed.), *Philanthropic Foundation: New Scholarship, New Possibilities*, University of Indiana Press, Bloomington, 1999.

Lechner, F. and J. Boli (eds.), *The Globalization Reader*, Blackwell Publishers, Malden, MA, 2000.

Lee, K. and A. Zwi, "A Global Political Economy, Approach to Aids: Ideology, Interests and Implications," in K. Lee (ed.) *Health Impacts of Globalization,* Palgrave MacMillan, London, 2003, pp. 13–32.

Lele, U. and A. A. Goldsmith, "The Development of a National Agricultural Research Capacity: India's Experience with the Rockefeller Foundation and its Significance for Africa," *Economic Development and Cultural Change,* vol. 37, 1988, pp. 305–43.

Lewis, J. P. and N. T. Uphoff, *Strengthening the Poor: What Have We Learned?* Transaction Books, New Brunswick, NJ, 1988.

Lindberg, M. and J. P. Dobel, "The Challenges of Globalization for Northern International Relief and Development NGOs," *Nonprofit and Voluntary Sector Quarterly,* vol. 28, no. 4 supplement, 1999, pp. 4–24.

Lindenberg, M. and C. Bryant, *Going Global: Transforming Relief and Development NGOs,* Kumerian Press, Bloomfield, CT, 2001.

London, N. R., *Japanese Corporate Philanthropy,* Oxford University Press, NY, 1991

Maclachlan, P., "The Struggle for an Independent Consumer Society: Consumer Activism and the State's Response in Postwar Japan," in F. J. Schwartz and S. J. Pharr (eds.) *The State of Civil Society in Japan,* Cambridge University Press, London, 2003.

Maekawa, R., "The Allied Occupation, the Cold War, and American Philanthropy: The Rockefeller Foundation in Postwar Japan," in S. Hewa and P. Hove (eds.) *Philanthropy and Cultural Context: Western Philanthropy in South, East, and Southeast Asia in the Twentieth Century,* University Press of America, Lanham, MD, 1997, pp. 117–28.

Magat, R., "Organized Labor and Philanthropic Foundations: Partners or Strangers?" *Nonprofit and Voluntary Sector Quarterly,* 23:4 (Winter), 1994, pp. 353–70.

Maghroori, R. and B. Ramberg (eds.), *Globalism versus Realism: International Relations' Third Debate,* Westview Press, Boulder, CO, 1982.

Marcus, G. E. with P. D. Hall, *Lives in Trust: The Fortunes of Dynastic Families in Late Twentieth Century America,* Westview Press Boulder, CO, 1992.

Mathews, J., "Power Shift," *Foreign Affairs,* vol. 76, 1997, pp. 50–66.

Mazlish, B. and R. Buultjens (eds.), *Conceptualizing Global History,* Global History Series, Westview Press, Boulder, CO, 1993.

McCarthy, D. K., "From Government to Grassroots Reform: The Ford Foundation's Population Programs in South Asia 1959–1981," in S. Hewa and P. Hove (eds.) *Philanthropy and Cultural Context: Western Philanthropy in South, East, and Southeast Asia in the Twentieth Century,* University Press of America, Lanham, MD, 1997, pp. 129–56.

McCarthy, D. K., *Philanthropy and Culture: The International Foundation Perspective,* University of Pennsylvania Press, Philadelphia, 1984.

McLaughlin, K., S. P. Osborne and E. Ferlie (eds.), *New Public Management: Current Trends and Future Prospects,* Routledge, London, 2002.

McNeill, H. W., *The Rise of the West: A History of the Human Community,* University of Chicago Press, Chicago, 1963.

Meck, M. M. and K. Sikkink, *Activists Without Borders,* Cornell University Press, Ithaca, NY, 1998.

Mehta, M. D., "Risk and Decision-Making: A Theoretical Approach to Public Participation in Techno-Social Conflict Situations," *Technology in Society,* vol. 20, 1998, pp. 87–98.

Melucci, A., *Nomads of the Present,* Temple University Press, Philadelphia, 1989.

Mitchell, T. R. and R. Lowe, "To Sow Contentment: Philanthropy, Scientific Agriculture, and the Making of the New South, 1906–1920," *Journal of Social History* (Winter), 1990, pp. 317–40.

Moore Jr. B., *Social Origins of Dictatorship and Democracy: Lord and Peasant in the Making of the Modern World,* Beacon Press, Boston, MA, 1966.

Nakano, L., "Volunteering as a Lifestyle Choice: Negotiating Self-Identities in Japan," *Ethnology,* vol. 39, 2000, pp. 93–107.

Nielsen, W. A., *The Big Foundations,* Twentieth Century Fund Study, Columbia University Press, NY, 1972.

Ninkovich, F., "The Rockefeller Foundation, China, and Cultural Change," *The Journal of American History,* vol. 70, 1984, pp. 799–820.

Noda, P. (ed.), *Globalization, Governance, and Civil Society,* JCIE, Tokyo, 1998.

Organization for Economic Co-operation and Development (OECD), *Development Cooperation, 1999, Development Assistance Committee Report, OECD,* Paris, 2000.

O'Rourke, K. and J. Williamson, *Globalization and History,* MIT Press, Cambridge, MA, 1999.

Page, B. B., "The Rockefeller Foundation and Central Europe: Reconsideration," *Minerva,* 40:3, 2002, pp. 265–87.

Page, B. B., "First Steps: The Rockefeller Foundation in Early Czechoslovakia," *East European Quarterly,* 35:3 (September), 2001, pp. 259–308.

Parmar, I., "The Carnegie Corporation and the Mobilization of Opinion in the United States' Rise to Globalism, 1939–1945," *Minerva,* 37, 1999, pp. 355–78.

Perkins, J. H., *Geopolitics and the Green Revolution: Wheat, Genes, and the Cold War,* Oxford University Press, Oxford, UK, 1989.

Perkins, J. H., "The Rockefeller Foundation and the Green Revolution, 1941–1956," *Agriculture and Human Values,* 7 (Summer and Fall), 1990, pp. 6–18.

Perry, J. C., "Private Philanthropy and Foreign Affairs: The Case of John D. Rockefeller 3rd and Japan," *Asian Perspectives,* vol. 8:2, 1984, pp. 268–84.

Pieterse, N. J., *Development Theory: Deconstructions/Reconstructions,* Sage, London, 2001.

Powell, D. and W. Leiss, *Mad Cows and Mothers' Milk: The Perils of Poor Risk Communication,* McGill-Queen's University Press, Montreal, 1998.

Prewitt, K., "The Importance of Foundations in an Open Society," in Bertelsmann Foundation (ed.) *The Future of Foundations in an Open Society,* Bertelsmann Foundation Publishers, Gütersloh, Germany, 1999, pp. 17–29.

Prewitt, K., "Foundations as Mirrors of Public Culture," *American Behavioral Scientist,* vol. 42, 1999, pp. 987–97.

Putnam, R. D., *Bowling Alone: The Collapse and Revival of American Community,* Simon and Schuster, NY, 2000.

Putnam, R. (ed.), *Democracies in Flux,* Oxford University Press, Oxford, UK, 2002.

Rajaee, F., *Globalization on Trial: The Human Condition and the Information Civilization,* Kumarian Press, West Hartford, CT, 2000.

Report of the Commission on Global Governance, *Our Global Neighbourhood,* Oxford University Press, Oxford, UK, 1995.

Rhodes, R., *The Making of the Atomic Bomb*, Simon & Schuster, NY, 1986.

Richard, M., *The Ford Foundation at Work: Philanthropic Choices, Methods, and Styles*, Plenum, NY, 1979.

Robertson, R., *Globalization: Social Theory and Global Culture, Theory, Culture & Society*, Sage, Newbury Park, CA, 1992.

Rockefeller Archive Center, "The Charter (1910–1913)," *Source Book for A History of the Rockefeller Foundation*, RF-History, vol. 7, 1910, p. 6.

Rosen, G., *Western Economists and Eastern Societies; Agents of Change in South Asia*, Johns Hopkins University Press, Baltimore, MD, 1985.

Rosenberg, E. S., "Missions to the World: Philanthropy Abroad," in L. J. Friedman and M. D. McGarvie (eds.) *Charity, Philanthropy, and Civility in American History*, Cambridge University Press, NY, 2002, pp. 241–57.

Rosset, P., "Towards a Political Economy of Opinion Formation on Genetically Modified Foods," *Medical Anthropology Quarterly*, vol. 15, 2001, pp. 1.

Sahlins, M., *Culture and Practical Reason*, University of Chicago Press, Chicago, 1976.

Salamon, L. M., *The Tools of Government: A Guide to the New Governance*, Oxford University Press, NY, 2002.

Salamon, L. M., H. K. Anheier, R. List, S. Toepler, S. W. Sokolowski and Associates, *Global Civil Society: Dimensions of the Non-profit Sector*, Johns Hopkins University, Institute for Policy Studies, Center for Civil Society Studies, Baltimore, MD, 1999.

Salamon, L. M., *Partners in Public Service: Government-Nonprofit Relations in the Modern Welfare State*, Johns Hopkins University Press, Baltimore, MD, 1995.

Salamon, L. M., "The Rise of the Nonprofit Sector," *Foreign Affairs*, vol. 73, no. 4, 1994, pp. 111–24.

Salamon, L. M. and H. K. Anheier, *The Emerging Nonprofit Sector*, Manchester University Press, Manchester, UK, 1994.

Salamon, L. M., "Partners in Public Service: The Scope and Theory of Government-Nonprofit Relations," in W. Powell (ed.) *The Nonprofit Sector: A Research Handbook*, Yale University Press, New Haven, CT, 1987, pp. 99–117.

Salamon, L. M. and A. Abramson, *The Federal Budget and the Nonprofit Sector*, The Urban Institute Press, Washington, DC, 1982.

Schäfer, W., "The New Global History: Toward a Narrative for Pangaea Two," *Erwägen Wissen Ethik*, vol. 14, 2003, pp. 75–133.

Schäfer, W., "Global Civilization and Local Cultures: A Crude Look at the Whole," *International Sociology*, vol. 16, 2001, pp. 301–19.

Schäfer, W., "Stranded at the Crossroads of Dehumanization: John Desmond Bernal and Max Horkheimer," in S. Benhabib, W. Bonss and J. McCole (eds.) *On Max Horkheimer: New Perspectives*, MIT Press, Cambridge, MA, 1993, pp. 153–83.

Sealander, J., *Private Wealth and Public Life: Foundation Philanthropy and the Reshaping of American Social Policy from the Progressive Era to the New Deal*, Johns Hopkins University Press, Baltimore, MD, 1997.

Shapin, S., *The Scientific Revolution*, University of Chicago Press, Chicago, 1998.

Sharpless, J., "Population Science, Private Foundations, and Development Aid: The Transformation of Demographic Knowledge in the United States, 1945–1965," in F. Cooper and R. Packard (eds.) *International Development and the Social Sciences: Essays on the History and Politics of Knowledge*, University of California Press, Berkeley, CA, 1997, pp. 176–200.

Sirianni, C. and L. Friedland, *Civic Innovation in America: Community Empowerment, Public Policy, and the Movement for Civic Renewal,* University of California Press, Berkeley, CA, 2000.

Smith, J. A., "The Evolving American Foundation," in C. T. Clotfelter and T. Ehrlich (eds.) *Philanthropy and the Nonprofit Sector in a Changing America,* Indiana University Press, Bloomington, 1999, pp. 34–51.

Smith, J. and H. Johnston (eds.), *Globalization and Resistance: Transnational Dimensions of Social Movements,* Rowman and Littlefield, Lanham, MD, 2002.

Smith, M. R. and L. Marx (eds.), *Does Technology Drive History? The Dilemma of Technological Determinism,* MIT Press, Cambridge, MA, 1994.

Smith, T., *Technology and Capital in the Age of Lean Production: A Marxian Critique of the "New Economy,"* SUNY Press, Albany, NY, 2000.

Staples, S. E., *40 Years, A Learning Curve: The Ford Foundation Programs in India, 1952–1992,* Ford Foundation, NY, 1992.

Stapleton, D. H. and Donna H. Stapleton, *Dignity, Discourse and Destiny: The Life of Courtney C. Smith,* University of Delaware Press, Newark, DE, 2004.

Stapleton, D. H., "Joseph Willits and the Rockefeller's European Programme in the Social Sciences," *Minerva,* vol. 41, 2003, pp. 101–14.

Stapleton, D. H., "Internationalism and Nationalism: the Rockefeller Foundation, Public Health, and Malaria in Italy, 1923–1951," *Parassitologia,* vol. 42, 2000, pp. 127–34.

Stapleton, D. H., "The Past and Future of Research in the History of Science, Medicine and Technology at the Rockefeller Archive Center," *Manguinhos: Historia, Ciencias, Saude,* vol. 5, 1998–99, pp. 716–32.

Stapleton, D. H., "Archival Sources and the Study of American Philanthropy." *Nonprofit Management and Leadership* 5, Winter, 1994, pp. 221–4.

Starr, A., *Naming the Enemy: Anti-Corporate Movements Confront Globalization,* Zed Books, NY, 2000.

Stevens, C., *On the Margins in Japanese Society: Volunteer Work with the Urban Underclass,* Routledge, London, 1997.

Sutton, F. X., "The Foundations and Governments of Developing Countries," *Studies in Comparative International Development,* vol. 12, 1997, pp. 94–119.

Tarrow, S, "Making Social Science Work Across Space and Time: A Critical Reflection on Robert Putnam's Making Democracy Work," *American Political Science Review,* vol. 90, 1996, pp. 389–97.

Todd, E., *Après l'Empire,* Gallimard, Paris, 2002.

Tomlinson, J., *Globalization and Culture,* University of Chicago Press, Chicago, 1999.

Tomlinson, J., *Cultural Imperialism: A Critical Introduction,* Pinter Publishers, London, 1991.

Touraine, A., *Critique of Modernity,* Blackwell, Cambridge, UK, 1995.

Trescott, P. B., "American Philanthropy and the Development of Academic Economics in China before 1949," in S. Hewa and P. Hove (eds.) *Philanthropy and Cultural Context: Western Philanthropy in South, East, and Southeast Asia in the Twentieth Century,* University Press of America, Lanham, MD, 1997, pp. 157–81.

Union of International Organizations, *Yearbook of International Organizations: Guide to Civil Society Networks,* Union of International Organizations, Brussels, 2001.

Van Deth, J. W. and E. Scarbrough (eds.), *The Impact of Values,* Oxford University Press, Oxford, UK, 1995.

Waldemar, A. N., *The Big Foundations,* Columbia University Press, NY, 1972.

Walzer, M., "The Idea of Civil Society," *Dissent,* Spring, pp. 293–304, 1991.

Waters, M. (ed.), *Globalization,* Routledge, London, 2001.

White, L. Jr, *Machina Ex Deo: Essays in the Dynamism of Western Culture,* MIT Press, Cambridge, MA, 1968.

White, L. Jr, *Medieval Technology and Social Change,* Oxford University Press, Oxford, UK, 1962.

Wiarda, H. J. (ed.), *Non-Western Theories of Development: Regional Norms versus Global Trends,* Harcourt Brace, Orlando, 1999.

Yamamoto, T. (ed.), *The Nonprofit Sector in Japan,* University of Manchester Press, Manchester, UK, 1998.

Yamamoto, T., *Emerging Civil Society in the Asia Pacific Community,* Japan Center for International Exchange, JCIE, Tokyo, 1995.

Yamamoto, T. and T. Amenomori, *Japanese Private Philanthropy in an Interdependent World,* JCIE Papers, Tokyo, 1989.

Yamamoto, T., *Philanthropy in Japan,* Japan Center for International Exchange, Tokyo, 1978.

Zukin, S. and P. DiMaggio, *Structures of Capital: The Social Organization of the Economy,* Cambridge University Press, NY, 1990.

A

Accountability, 8, 107, 126, 158, 165
Africa
malaria, 55
sub-Sahra, 105
African
African American, 106
agricultural technology, 43, 197, 198, 201, 202
Agriculture Canada, 199
AIDS
vaccine, 105
Albrow, Martin, 47
Amato law, 120, 122
American Relief Administration, 100
Americanization, 57, 65, 180
Amnesty International, 118, 150
AMPO, 74, 79, 83, 93, 94
analysis, 8, 17–19, 24, 26, 65, 121, 123, 126–127, 132–133, 138, 142, 166, 172, 186, 202, 206
Anglo-Saxon pattern, 149
Anheier, Helmut K., 8, 17, 24, 117, 118, 132–135, 151–152, 157, 171, 205–206
Appadurai, Arjun, 23, 28–29, 181–187, 190–191
Arnove, Robert, 115
A SEED, 197
Asia, 4–5, 10, 27, 35, 40, 45, 51–52, 54–55, 58, 65, 70, 73, 75, 77–78, 80, 88, 90–91, 93, 101, 105, 137, 140, 142, 198
East Asia, 6
South Asia, 10, 27, 67, 70, 80, 142, 170, 206
Southeast Asia, 10, 11, 68, 88, 151
Association of Charitable Foundations, 127
Australia, 147–148, 162

B

Barbetta, G. P., 133, 152
Barlow, Maude, 167, 170, 173
Barraclough, Geoffrey, 34, 37, 39–42, 44–45, 47
Beard, Charles, 79
Beck, Ulrich, 193–196, 202–203
Beijing Conference, 149
Belgium, 100, 118, 121–123, 125, 132, 134
Bengal, 65
Bertelsmann Foundation, 118, 124, 133
Bestor, Victoria L., 7, 23, 56, 73, 91–92, 94–95, 205
bioterrorism, 193
Biro, Andras, 140
Blair, Tony, 139
Bosch Foundation, 118
Bourdieu, Pierre, 185–186, 188–189, 191–192
Brazil, 144, 181
British, 34, 37, 46, 52, 115, 127, 169–172, 196, 207
Brock, Kathy, 8, 17, 153, 170–171, 205
Buddhist, 81
bureaucratization, 110, 128
Bürgerstiftung, 125
Burma, 51

C

Calcutta, 65
Cameron Forbes Fund, 100
Canada, 8, 89, 92, 144, 153–154, 156–159,
    161–164, 167–170, 172–173, 195, 197,
    199, 202–203
provinces, 24, 155, 159, 161, 169–170, 172–
    173, 205–207
Canadian way, 162
Caritas, 124
Caritas Socialis Private Foundation, 124
Carnegie Corporation, 100–102, 104, 152
caste, 186, 188, 206
Castro Revolution, 140
Catholic Church, 45, 60, 140
CBCC, 86
CDU, 36
Ceylon (Sri Lanka), 51, 207
charity, 3, 9, 85, 108, 163
charitable giving, 81, 107, 110
child labor, 149
China, 23–24, 34, 36, 43, 51–54, 60, 67, 74–
    75, 78, 82, 92, 101, 190
Peking Union Medical College, 53
Chomsky, Noam, 11
Christianity, 4, 28
civil society, 73, 82, 88, 90–91, 95
civil society activity, 9, 147
civil society groups, 5–6, 8, 128, 194, 195,
    197
civil society organization, 5, 8, 110, 112,
    138–139, 140–141, 143–147, 149–150,
    154–162, 164–165–168, 173–174–195
global, 6, 25, 118–120, 129–131, 141, 148,
    150, 157
civil society activity
protests, 27
civilization, 3, 34, 36–38, 40, 42, 46, 48
CJD, 94, 194
classical liberal, 129
Coca-Cola, 180–181, 185 ˙
Cold War, 5, 7, 10, 18, 38–40, 51–53, 56–
    58, 66–67, 71, 73, 80, 87, 91, 100–101,
    118–119, 132, 151, 154
Columbia University, 46, 63, 66, 69–70, 80,
    91, 171
communications technologies, 119, 139–140
communism, 7, 51, 52, 53, 67, 77–78, 82–
    83, 102, 111, 125
Community Foundation network, 127
Community Foundation foundations
    Network, 127

Community Philanthropy Initiative, 128
Comparative, 138, 141, 171
Complementarity, 123
complex connectivity, 180, 182–183
conference, 3–4, 9, 19, 26, 44, 47, 60, 76,
    77, 92, 96, 154–155, 157, 204
conflicts, 5, 25, 178, 186, 199
Confucian, 81, 94
connectivity, 131, 183
Consultative Group on International
    Agricultural Research (CGIAR), 199
corporate philanthropy, 81, 84–86, 89–90,
    94, 163–164
cross-border, 102, 111, 119, 127
CSU, 36, 140
cultural gravity., 182
cultural homogeneity, 9, 180
cultural hybridization, 185
cultural superiority, 181
cultural transaction, 182
culture, 4, 9, 16–18, 22–23, 30, 36, 38, 45,
    48, 52, 59, 64, 66, 75–77, 80, 85–86, 117,
    119, 121, 125, 141, 146, 155, 157, 162–
    163, 172, 178–189, 191, 204
Curti, Merle, 114
Curtin, Philip, 29
Czech Republic, 120–121, 123, 125, 128,
    132, 134

D

Dallas, 162, 181
Daly, Siobhan, 8, 117, 132, 206
democracy, 81–82
democratic forms, 119
democratization, 82, 102, 111, 122, 155, 178
Denmark, 120–121, 123–124, 127, 132, 134
deterritorialized, 182, 187
development, 5, 6, 9, 22, 64, 101, 128, 140,
    159, 178, 200
Difference, 177, 182, 190–191
disjunctive, 180, 182, 187
Disneyfication, 181
distinctive difference, 180, 188–189
domesticated difference, 180, 188–189
domesticated differences, 188–189
Dulles, 73–80, 90–93
Durkheim, Emile, 16

E

Economics Club, 178

ECOWAS, 119
education, 4–5, 7, 53–57, 62, 64–65, 73, 75,
    86, 88, 101, 105, 108, 117, 119, 121, 130,
    134, 141, 145, 160, 163–164, 207
EFC, 127–128
Egypt, 115, 144, 152
Eisenhower, 61, 70, 83
empire
Roman, 35, 36, 44–45, 95
empowerment, 105–106, 124–125, 139–140,
    144, 146
Enlightenment, 38
Ensminger, Douglas, 55–57, 61–65, 67–68,
    70
Environment and Diversity, 197
environmental protection, 6, 119, 138, 146,
    149–150
Estonia, 120–121, 126, 132, 134
ethnic, 19, 138, 186, 191
Euro-American, 181
Eurocentrism, 35, 40
Europe, 4, 7–8, 25, 28, 30, 34–35, 36–38,
    40, 45–46, 51, 88, 100–101, 105, 117–
    118, 120–123, 127–128, 130–134, 137,
    140, 142, 144, 147–148, 190, 197–198,
    206
eastern, 111, 121–122, 125, 137, 140, 142,
    148, 162
European Commission, 134
European Foundations, 121, 123
European Union, 36, 38, 40, 111, 117, 119,
    126, 128, 132, 204, 206
western, 149
European Value Survey, 130
evolution, 25, 73, 77, 80–82, 90, 100–101,
    110, 149
external actors, 123, 140, 141

F

Fahs, Charles Burton, 77, 92
Filer Commission, 89, 95
foreign-funded, 125
Foundation Act, 122
foundations, 4–9, 85, 100, 155, 163, 168
American, 7–8, 23, 52, 89, 99–113
Foundations, 7–8, 23, 52, 89, 99–113, 119–
    120, 122–124
foundations in Europe, 8, 118, 120, 123, 206
France, 24, 39, 100, 121, 122, 129, 132, 133,
    134, 144, 148, 152, 206
Friedman, Jonathan, 10, 28, 114, 115, 154,
    169, 170, 181, 191

Friends of the Earth, 118, 197, 198, 199
Frumkin, Peter, 8, 23, 99, 114, 157, 206
Fukuyama, Francis, 115
fulltime, 57
Fund, 60
funding, 57, 60, 62–63, 65, 76, 85, 89, 95,
    99, 101–104, 107, 109, 112–113, 124–
    125, 128, 148, 161, 163, 166
abroad, 99

G

Garcia-Canclini, Nestor, 186, 192
gastro-anomie, 197, 203
GE, 198
GEB, 81
Geertzian, 186
gender, 15, 19, 21, 39, 129, 138, 159, 186,
    188, 190, 199
genetically engineered, 198
Geneva Research Center, 101
Germany, 24, 38, 39, 41, 45, 46, 118, 120–
    125, 127, 129, 132–134, 139, 171
Giddens, Anthony, 30, 134, 156, 158, 170,
    195–196, 202–203
global
era, 17–18
perspective, 7, 23, 35
perspectives, 7
present, 7, 33–35, 38–42
Global Age, 35, 42
global associational revolution, 137, 140,
    141
Global cultural, 182
global history, 7, 18–30, 33–35, 39–41, 43–
    44, 47–48, 206–207
global monoculture, 184
globalization, 3–9, 15–19, 23, 25–28, 30–31,
    34–35, 39–41, 44, 52, 66, 71, 100, 102,
    110–113, 115, 117–118, 126, 131–132,
    137–138, 140–141, 149–150, 153–170,
    172–173, 177–191, 195, 198, 202, 205–
    206
global, 3–9, 15–30, 33–36, 38–43, 45, 47–
    48, 76, 80, 85, 99, 101–102, 106, 109,
    111, 117–119, 129–131, 137, 140–141,
    148–150, 153–159, 161, 163–164, 168,
    170–172, 178–179, 181–182, 184, 187,
    191, 193–194, 196–197, 201–202,
    206–207
global governance, 5,–8, 16–17, 25, 35, 74,
    119, 120, 135, 138–139, 149–150, 155,
    158–159, 161, 167, 171, 178, 190, 199

glocalization, 186
GNP, 18, 64
Golden Arches, 180
Golden Rice technology, 195, 200
governance, 4, 6, 111, 119, 126, 130, 157–
    158, 160, 171–172, 177, 194–195
Gramsci, Antonio, 179, 189
grantmaking, 99–100, 102–105, 107, 109,
    112–113, 119–120, 123–124
Great Depression, 25
Greece, 34, 42, 120–122, 132, 134
Green Revolution, 9, 59, 65, 69–70, 199,
    204
Greenpeace, 43, 118, 130, 197, 203
Gulbenkian Foundation, 118

H

Hamburg, 125
Hamelink, C. J., 180, 190
Harvey, David, 185
health care, 86, 105–106, 117, 119, 121, 131
Helsinki Committee, 125
Helsinki Foundation, 125
Hess, Gary, 7, 23, 51, 66–67, 206
Heterogenization, 177
Hewa, Soma, 3, 10, 44, 68, 70, 207
Higginbottom, Sam, 54, 67, 206
Hiroshima, 82
historians, 18–23, 25–26, 33–35, 39, 41–42
historical, 4, 7, 9, 16–27, 33–47, 83, 92, 110,
    121, 130, 137, 144, 149, 177, 187, 190,
    206
history
global, 7, 18–27, 29–30, 33, 35, 39–41, 43–
    44, 48, 206–207
universal, 19, 34
world, 19–20, 29–30, 37, 44, 153
history of globalization, 7, 21
Hoffman, Paul, 51, 66
Homogenization, 177
Hoover, Edgar, 61, 69
Hove, Philo, 10, 68, 70
humanity, 3, 18
Hungary, 123–125, 128, 132, 134, 144
Hussein, Saddam, 40
hybridization, 182, 185, 188
hypernetwork, 143
Hypo-Kulturstiftung, 127
HYV, 7, 55, 58, 59, 65

I

identities, 36, 178, 181–182, 184–186, 188–
    189, 191
identity, 23, 39, 41, 79, 177–179, 181–187,
    189–191
IHB, 5
India, 7, 23, 51–71, 101, 108, 187, 189, 201,
    206
agriculture, 65
Allahabad Agricultural Institute, 54–55
Etawah Projects, 54
government, 52–55, 58, 60–65, 101
leaders, 52, 54, 56, 59–61, 63–64, 66–67
project, 55
projects, 54–56, 62
individualism, 129, 131, 141, 162
Indochina, 51
Indonesia, 51, 60
industrialized countries, 111, 119, 195
industry, 4, 23, 199
INGOs, 118, 129, 130
Innovation, 107, 124, 134, 204
Innovest Strategic Value Advisors, 198
Institut Curie, 121
Institut Pasteur, 121
Institute of Pacific Relations, 5, 10, 76–77,
    78, 92, 101
International House of Japan, 75–76, 79–80,
    88–89, 91, 93, 95
International Maize and Wheat
    Improvement Center, 200
international organization, 6, 63, 111, 128,
    129, 134, 139, 141, 150
international organizations, 6, 184, 196, 203
International Philanthropy Project, 89
Internet, 5, 23, 26, 110–111, 119, 132, 138,
    157, 160–161, 196–197, 202
IPR, 5, 10, 76–79, 92–93, 101
Iraq, 37, 39–41, 45–46, 51, 53, 76–78, 80,
    82–84, 87–88, 94, 101, 157
Ireland, 120–121, 123, 128, 132, 134
Israel, 132, 144, 147
Italy, 25, 118, 120–123, 125, 128, 132–34,
    144, 148, 152, 206

J

Japan, 10, 73–74, 76, 78, 80, 87–88, 90
Japan Council, 78–79
Japanese League of Nations Association, 78
JCIE, 86, 88–91, 94–96, 152

Johns Hopkins Comparative Comparative
  Nonprofit Sector Project, 138, 141, 171
Jospin, Lionel, 139

K

Kellogg Foundation, 100, 102, 104
King Baudouin, 118, 125
Kobe, 86
Korea, 60, 63, 101
Korean War, 75, 78, 82, 92
Kyoto, 43, 75, 76, 79
Kyoto Protocol, 6–7, 15, 19, 39, 65, 83–84,
  102, 105, 119, 125, 129, 130, 134, 138,
  139, 146, 149–150, 184, 195–198, 201,
  206

L

Lash, Scott, 27–28, 30, 193, 202
Latin America, 52, 65, 68, 101–102, 105,
  140, 142, 148, 190, 198
Liechtenstein, 120, 121, 132
local
communities, 4–5, 106, 155, 164, 198
cultures, 9, 42, 165
issues, 6, 130, 157
Locke, John, 81

M

MacArthur, Douglas, 79, 102, 130
MacBride, Sean, 180, 190
Malaysia, 24
Marshall Plan, 52, 86–87, 100–101, 105,
  118
Marx, Karl, 16
Mayer, Albert, 54, 67
Mazlish, Bruce, 26, 29, 30, 154
McDonaldization, 181
Mehta, Michael, 9, 17, 193, 202–204, 206
Meiji Civil Code, 85
Meiji era, 78, 81, 84–85, 93–95
mercy-giving, 4, 5, 18, 22, 24
Middle East, 36, 111, 115, 142, 163
middle way, 129, 139
Minamata, 83, 84
minimalist, 119, 131
Minobe, 83, 84, 94
Mission, 73, 79, 91
missionaries, 4, 5, 18, 22, 24
MIT, 53

modernization theory, 77
Möller, A. P., 126
Monsanto, 198, 200, 203
multilateral, 141, 155, 161
multinational, 8, 17, 42, 65, 85, 141, 150,
  159, 165, 171, 193–194, 196–197, 201

N

Nagasaki, 82
National Survey of Giving, 157, 172
Nationalist, 82
nationalized, 120
NATO, 36, 40
Natrajan, Balmurli, 9, 23, 158, 177, 206
neoliberal, 129–131, 139–140, 154, 156,
  159, 166
neoliberalism, 16, 141
neo-Tocquevillian, 129
Netherlands, 118, 121, 132, 134, 144
New Delhi, 27, 54, 55, 57, 61–62, 66–67,
  70–71
New England Belgian Relief Fund, 30, 100,
  134
New Global History, 33–34, 44–44
New Policy Agenda, 119
New public management, 131
NGOs, 5, 118, 140–141, 149, 153, 155, 158
non-Euro-American, 181
Nordic pattern, 149
Norway, 117, 121, 132, 144
NPO Law, 87, 89, 95

O

Occupation, 74, 78, 81–82, 90–93
Occupationaires, 82
OECD, 118–119, 128
OECD countries, 118
Oil Shock, 84
Open Society, 102, 104, 122, 133
Oppenheimer, Robert, 80
organized philanthropy, 5
Oxfam, 118, 130

P

Pakistan, 51, 66–67
Pan-European, 118
Peace Mission, 73, 78–79, 90–91
Pepsi, 189
Pfoten Foundation, 128

philanthropic foundations, 6, 10, 53, 55–56, 58, 60–61, 62–63, 66–68, 71, 77, 95, 101–104, 107, 110, 114, 118, 121–122, 124, 127–128, 133, 163, 170–171, 200–201, 204
Carnegie Corporation, 100, 104
Ford Foundation, 7, 10, 51, 53, 55–58, 61–64, 66–71, 100–101, 104, 106, 200
Gates Foundation, 102, 110
Kellogg Foundation, 100, 102
Rockefeller Foundation, 5, 9, 10, 23, 51, 53, 55–57, 60–61, 64–65, 68–70, 76–77, 80–81, 92, 100–101, 110, 114, 195, 200–202, 204
philanthropy, 5
American foundations, 6, 99
benevolence, 120, 157
pluralism, 109–110, 123, 125, 131
redistribution, 108–110, 123–124, 127, 168
Philippines, 51, 58, 60, 181
Pieterse, Nederveen, 181–182, 185–186, 188, 191–192
pluralism, 109–110, 123, 125, 131
Poland, 120–121, 123–125, 132, 134
Polanyi, Karl, 29, 179, 189
Polanyi, Michael, 16
policy makers, 8, 83
population
research, 60–63, 69
Portugal, 34, 36, 118, 121–132
post-materialist, 119
post-nation-state, 129
professional organizations, 143
professionalization, 86, 95, 156
progress, 18, 37–38, 43, 51–52, 59–60, 66, 83, 108, 141, 172
progressive era, 5

Q

quasi-public, 120, 123, 201
Quebec City, 155

R

race, 129, 186, 188
Reagan, Ronald, 139, 151
Redistribution, 108, 109, 123
reflexive modernization, 193
Rekart, Josephine, 156, 158, 170, 171
Republic, 67, 82, 128
revenue, 85, 147–148, 151

revenue sources, 147
risk society, 9, 193–196, 202
Roach, Colleen, 180, 190
Rockefeller
John D. Rockefeller 3rd, 73, 75–80, 88–93, 95
John D. Rockefeller Sr., 3, 9, 54, 59–60, 73–74, 76, 87, 91–93, 151, 204
philanthropy, 75, 80–81, 88, 90–91
Rockefeller Archive Center, 3, 9–10, 68, 92, 204, 207
Roma, 125
Rome, 35–36, 42, 45
Roosevelt, Eleanor, 80
Rosset, Peter, 197, 203
Rusk, Dean, 52

S

Salamon, Lester, 8, 11, 17, 21, 115, 132–134, 137, 150–152, 157, 171, 207
SARS, 111, 193
Save the Children, 118
Schäfer, Wolf, 7, 19, 28–29, 33, 44, 46–47, 154, 207
Schiller, H., 180, 190
Schröder, Gerhard, 139
Schumpeter, Joseph, 16
Seattle, 16, 30, 155, 184, 197, 203
sector leaders, 167–168
sexual orientation, 129, 188
Shiva, Vandana, 199, 201, 204
Smith, Adam, 16
social capital, 112, 117, 129–130, 139, 167
Social capital scenario, 131
social entrepreneurs, 117, 140
social origins approach, 149
social services, 108, 119, 121, 146, 157
society, 7, 8, 183
sociological, 120, 189–190, 207
Spain, 36, 118, 121–132, 134, 144
Sri Lanka, 51, 207
Stapleton, Darwin, 3, 44, 68, 207
Stapleton, Donna, 207
structural adjustment, 139
Substitution, 123
Suzuki, David, 199
Sweden, 118, 120–124, 126, 132, 134, 144, 152

T

Taiwan, 34, 60, 63, 87
Tanzania, 144
technological, 9, 17, 28, 81, 86, 111–120,
   169, 190, 193–194, 196
telecommunication, 119
Thatcher, Margaret, 139
The corporate scenario, 131
The mellow weakness scenario, 131
the New Middle Mass, 84
third sector, 117, 126, 141, 148, 205
Third Way, 134, 139, 170
Third World, 10, 44, 53, 57, 63, 65, 67, 70,
   189
trajectory, 17, 36, 179
transnational, 5, 15, 22, 25, 111–112, 117–
   119, 121, 129–132, 134, 141, 149, 154,
   166, 185, 196
transnational actors, 111, 118, 121
transnational philanthropy, 118
transparency, 126, 127
Tropical Agriculture, 200
Truman, Harry S., 51, 66, 74
Turkey, 45, 120, 122
two-sector model, 141

U

UN, 5–6, 39, 63, 101–102, 149–152, 171,
   198
underdevelopment, 64
United Kingdom, 42, 120–123, 129, 132–
   134, 139, 144, 171
United States
agencies, 55, 101
foreign policy, 4, 16, 38–40, 42, 44, 46, 51–
   54, 59–60, 62, 66, 69, 74–79, 83, 85–
   86, 88–89, 91–95, 99–101, 106–109,
   113, 119, 121–122, 129, 132–134, 139,
   144, 147– 148, 154, 158, 163–164,
   169, 171, 173, 188, 195, 197–198, 202,
   206–207
universalism, 141
University of Saskatchewan, 199, 206

V

Via Campesina, 197, 199
vision, 5, 8, 18–19, 29, 52, 55, 63, 80, 88,
   110, 127, 131, 177–179, 181–183, 185,
   189

Volkswagen Foundation, 118

W

Wallerstein, Immanuel, 20
Wal-Martization, 181
war, 5, 7, 25, 34, 36, 38, 52, 60, 74, 78–79,
   81–83, 85, 92–93, 100–101, 122, 154
welfare states, 117, 128
well-being, 5
West Nile virus, 193
western
capitalism, 9, 15, 18, 20, 34, 37, 44, 153,
   165, 172, 179–180, 187, 190
democracy, 5–9, 52, 79, 81–82, 88, 101,
   111, 115, 119, 139–140, 148, 158, 167,
   172, 178, 196
imperialism, 18, 21, 23, 34, 44, 79, 106,
   161, 180, 183
western European pattern, 149
WHO, 5, 10, 204
Wilson, Woodrow, 52, 66
worker rights, 149
World Bank, 6, 63, 111, 128–129, 134, 139,
   141, 150
world citizenship, 141
World Wide Web, 157, 160, 170
WTO, 6, 184, 196, 197, 199, 203
Wynne, Brian, 193, 196, 203

Y

Yamamoto, Tadashi, 88, 94–95, 157–158,
   171–172
Yearbook of International Organizations,
   149, 152